Everyday
PRESSURE
COOKER
RECIPES

HB
HINKLER
BOOKS

Author: John Blackett-Smith
Typesetter: MPS Limited
Designer: Imagine Graphic Design Pty Ltd
Prepress: Graphic Print Group

 Published in 2010 by Hinkler Books Pty Ltd
45–55 Fairchild Street
Heatherton VIC 3202 Australia
www.hinklerbooks.com

ISBN: 978 1 7418 5609 5
Printed and bound in China

Contents

Introduction 5

Pressure Cooking: Quick, Easy, Rich in Flavours and Variety 6

Some Things to Know About Pressure Cookers......................................8

Using an Electric Pressure Cooker 10

Cleanliness Helps Prevent Foodborne Illness 11

Meat, Poultry, Game and Egg Timing Charts......................................13

Beans – Speed Soaking 19

Basic Guidelines for Pressure Steaming Vegetables 20

Frequently Asked Questions...24

Recipes..29

    Soups and Stocks..29

    Sauces 79

    Beef and Veal 82

    Pork..131

    Poultry 155

    Lamb 189

Seafood 192

Pasta and Rice 199

Vegetables 219

Desserts, Cakes and Breads 257

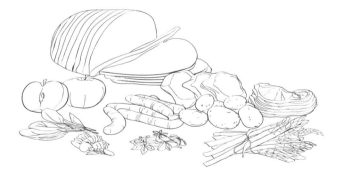

Introduction

Pressure Cooking: Quick, Easy, Rich in Flavours and Variety

Nearly everyone has a story about the pressure cooker that 'blew up', often spraying stew, rhubarb or spinach over kitchen walls, ceilings and even the cook! Perhaps this explains why the very few pressure cookers owned in the Western world are hidden in dark corners of kitchen cupboards and never brought out to prepare tasty, fast and nutritious meals.

In countries such as Australia, Britain and the USA, it seems the popular belief is that pressure cookers are only good for pea soup, beef casseroles using the cheapest cuts of meat and stewed fruit. Nothing could be further from the truth. Even regular users of pressure cookers seldom realise they have the ability to prepare a wide variety of enticing dishes, ranging from soups and entrees through to delicate or robust main courses to sweets and even cakes.

Like many other kitchen appliances, technology has seen the humble pressure cooker of the post-wartime era develop into a flexible, more efficient, easily controlled food-preparation appliance that can rapidly become as indispensable as the toaster, electric frypan and blender.

First-generation pressure cookers regulate the internal pressure with a heavy weight placed over an escape valve. When the pressure inside the pot exceeds 106 kilopascals (kPa), equal to 15 lb per square inch (psi), the weight can no longer hold in the steam and begins to rock, allowing the steam to hiss out around the sides of the valve.

Second-generation cookers have a spring-loaded mechanism instead of a weight. Some have indicator rods that pop up to indicate the level of pressure; others send steam hissing gently out a side-release escape valve.

All of the cookers today have multiple backup mechanisms. It is a very rare occurrence that there is any problem with a vent and, when used correctly, no second-generation pressure cooker 'explodes'.

Both kinds of cookers provide a steady pressure. At 106 kPa (15 psi), the temperature inside the pot will climb to 120°C (250°F), and food will cook in about a third of the time.

The downside (isn't there always a downside?!) is that cooking time tolerances with a pressure cooker are narrower and, frequently, ingredient quantities vary from those used to achieve the same results with conventional cooking methods.

This book sets out to assist both the novice and the experienced user. The novice will find much information about the 'basics' of pressure cooking, while the experienced user will find whole new variations of recipes and uses for their old friend.

This book is laid out in logical sections, beginning with general information on pressure cooking followed by some specifics for those who own an electric pressure cooker. Food-handling procedures and kitchen hygiene are briefly covered, then we're down to the real nitty-gritty, with very detailed charts providing information on cooking times for every imaginable cut of meat followed by some pointers for cooking dried beans and a chart of cooking times and liquid quantities for both frozen and fresh vegetables. Finally, there is a 'Frequently Asked Questions' section designed to answer the questions I am asked most often when cooks find things aren't working as intended. The recipes themselves are grouped into meal courses, with each recipe recommending the ideal size of pressure cooker to use and the number of adult serves provided.

It is my hope that your pressure cooker, and this book, will become indispensable.

Some Things to Know About Pressure Cookers

What Model to Buy

First-generation cookers (the kind with the weights that jiggle) still work just fine. However, I believe you should invest in a stainless steel 6 L (6 quart), or larger, second-generation cooker, preferably with a pressure gauge. There are now many different brands on the market from simple pots with just a pressure valve and safety valve through to fully featured electric, automatic models. Most of the better brands come from Europe, although their manufacturers have strong representation in most other Western countries. Second-generation pressure cookers are better designed and manufactured and, therefore, do a better job of maintaining constant pressure, ensuring more success with the critical timing needed for many recipes. Some even have variable pressure settings, which can come in handy.

India is a country where pressure cookers are usually found wherever there is a reliable source of heat. In Western countries, Indian markets offer a great variety of cookers, some with lids that lock underneath a lip on the pot, obviating the need for a rubber gasket. If you purchase one of these models, it is vital that the metal-to-metal surfaces are kept scrupulously clean to avoid leakage.

Pressure cookers generally come with a booklet of instructions, tips, techniques and some basic recipes. But, as always, there are some additional things to consider.

Natural Release vs Quick Release

The cooker must return to normal atmospheric pressure before it is safe or (given the many safety mechanisms) even possible to open. All pressure cooker recipes call for one of two methods. All recipes in this book clearly state which pressure release method to use.

Natural release means just turning off the heat and letting the pressure cooker sit on the hotplate. The food will keep cooking as the internal temperature of the pot drops from 120 to 100°C (250 to 212°F), at which time it is possible to open the pot. Indeed, the food will still continue to cook even after the lid has been removed, albeit more slowly. This process can take up to 15 minutes; you will note throughout this book that we have recommended it for tough cuts of beef, grains and beans, which all emerge more tender.

Quick release means you bring the pressure down fast. The most efficient method is to put the pressure cooker under cold running water, which will drop the pressure in a matter of seconds. With second-generation cookers, you can open a quick-release valve that will send out a lengthy hiss of steam.

A Word of Warning

Even at normal boiling point (approximately 100°C/212°F), your pressure cooker generates a substantial amount of steam. This steam has the ability to inflict severe burns after only a couple of seconds exposure. Always open the lid away from you, or any other person standing nearby. This can be difficult with those pressure cookers where the lid fits inside the bowl. I've found the easiest way to overcome this is to drape a tea towel over the side of the lid nearest you.

Measuring and Regulating Pressure

Always bring the cooker to pressure over high heat unless indicated otherwise. When your pressure gauge rises to the required pressure (or your weight begins jiggling), begin timing the recipe. Lower the heat immediately to high or medium-high (or medium, depending on your cooker) to maintain even pressure.

Watch the Liquids

When adjusting favourite recipes, you should reduce the amount of liquid, since little of it escapes. Different models lose varying amounts of steam, and until you have a feel for your cooker, you may suffer through a watery stew or two.

Watch the Flavouring Ingredients

Pressure cookers are so efficient at forcing flavours into meat fibres that it can become a bit overpowering. As with liquids, it is often better to reduce the amount of strong flavourings by an eighth and noting the flavours that result before increasing quantities.

You Don't Have to Submerge Foods

Your pressure cooker is a steamer rather than a pot. For example, artichokes will be just fine with 2.5 to 5 cm (1 to 2 in) of water, while pot roast will braise properly with a little liquid and a few juicy vegetables. Remember, it's the steam and the pressure that cooks the food in a pressure cooker.

A Few Don'ts

There is no need to marinate meats. Pressure cookers do a wonderful job of pushing aromatic flavours into meat.

There are two schools of thought about browning meats before cooking. Many cooks don't brown meats, because the crustiness doesn't survive the pressure cooking. However, I believe that the flavour of browning meat informs the final sauce.

There is no need to pre-sauté vegetables for soups or stews. Just chop your onions and garlic right into the pressure cooker.

Using an Electric Pressure Cooker

Most electric pressure cookers have a very high or BROWN setting. Use this setting to do any cooking required before bringing up the pressure.

Program the cooker for HIGH PRESSURE.

If the recipe calls for natural pressure release, reduce cooking time by approximately 2 minutes to adjust for the longer time it takes for the electric cooker to release its pressure. Some manuals offer extensive instructions, while others don't even mention it. Two minutes is a good 'rule of thumb'.

If the recipes in this book call for quick releasing the pressure by setting the cooker under cold running water, ignore this instruction. Instead, subtract 4 minutes from cooking time and allow the pressure to come down naturally for 4 minutes, then press the quick-release button in very short spurts ensuring that the steam blows away from you and anyone else nearby. During this process, if any liquid is ejected from the valve, wait another 30 seconds before continuing to release the pressure.

Use the BROWN setting to do any final cooking after the pressure is released.

Cleanliness Helps Prevent Foodborne Illness

Food that is mishandled can lead to foodborne illness. While most Western countries have safe food supplies, preventing foodborne illness remains a major public health challenge. There are four critical food safety principles:

Clean	Wash hands and surfaces often
Separate	Don't cross-contaminate
Cook	Cook to proper temperatures
Chill	Refrigerate promptly

Cleanliness is a major factor in preventing foodborne illness. Even with food safety inspection and monitoring at many commercial and government facilities, the consumer's role is to make sure food is handled safely after it is purchased. Everything that touches food should be clean. Following are steps we can take to help prevent foodborne illness by safely handling food in the home:

Always wash hands with hot, soapy water:
• before handling food
• after handling food
• after using the bathroom
• after changing a nappy (diaper)
• after tending to a sick person
• after blowing your nose, coughing or sneezing
• after handling pets.

If your hands have any kind of skin abrasion or infection, always use clean disposable gloves. Wash hands (gloved or not) with hot, soapy water.

Thoroughly wash all surfaces that come in contact with raw meat, poultry, fish, and eggs with hot, soapy water before moving on to the next step in food preparation. Consider using paper towels to clean kitchen surfaces. If you use dishcloths, wash them often in the hot cycle of your washing machine or put a thoroughly wet cloth in your microwave, on high, for 60 seconds. Keep other surfaces, such as sinks, tapware and benchtops, clean by washing with hot, soapy water.

To keep cutting boards clean, wash them in hot, soapy water after each use; then rinse and air or pat dry with fresh paper towels. Cutting boards can be sanitised with a solution of one teaspoon liquid chlorine bleach per litre (quart) of water. Flood the surface with the bleach solution and allow it to stand for several minutes; then rinse and air or pat dry with fresh paper towels.

Nonporous acrylic, plastic, glass and solid wood boards can be washed in a dishwasher (laminated boards may crack and split). Even plastic boards wear out over time. Once cutting boards become excessively worn or develop hard-to-clean grooves, replace them.

Don't use the same platter and utensils that held the raw product to serve the cooked product. Any bacteria present in the raw meat or juices can contaminate the safely cooked product. Serve cooked products on clean plates, using clean utensils and clean hands.

When using a food thermometer, it is important to wash the probe after each use with hot, soapy water before reinserting it into a food.

Keep the refrigerator clean by wiping up spills immediately. Clean surfaces thoroughly with hot, soapy water and rinse. Once a week, make it a habit to throw out perishable foods that should no longer be eaten.

Keep pets, household cleaners and other chemicals away from food and surfaces used for food.

When picnicking or cooking outdoors, take plenty of clean utensils. Pack clean, dry, and wet and soapy cloths for cleaning surfaces and hands.

Because bacteria is everywhere, cleanliness is a major factor in preventing foodborne illness. By keeping everything clean that comes in contact with food, consumers can be assured they are helping to do their part to reduce the risks of illness.

Meat, Poultry, Game and Egg Timing Charts

Timing Chart for Cooking Beef

Type of beef	Brown	Liquid minimum	Cooking time (in minutes)	Release
Brisket, corned; 8–10 cm (3–4 in) thick	No	Cover completely	55–60	Natural
Brisket, fresh; 8–10 cm (3–4 in) thick	Yes	500 mL (2 cups)	55–60	Natural
Ground or minced, crumbled or patties	Yes	250 mL (1 cup)	6	Natural
Heart; 1.5–2 kg (3–4 lb)	No	Cover completely	50–75	Natural
Kidney, sliced; 0.5 kg (1 lb)	No	Cover completely	8–10	Natural
Liver, sliced; 1–1.5 kg (2–3 lb)	No	250 mL (1 cup)	5	Natural
Neck bones	Yes	Cover completely	45	Natural
Oxtails	Yes	Cover completely	40–45	Natural
Pot roast, round, blade, chuck or rump; 1.5–2 kg (3–4 lb)	Yes	500 mL (2 cups)	35–45	Natural
Rolled or rib roast; 1.5–2 kg(3–4 lb)	Yes	500 mL (2 cups)	35–45	Natural
Round, chuck, blade or rump; 5–8 cm (2–3 in) thick	Yes	310 mL (1¼ cups)	20–25	Natural
Short ribs	Yes	310 mL (1¼ cups)	20–25	Natural
Steak, cubed; 1.5–2 kg (3–4 lb)	Yes	250 mL (1 cup)	6	Natural
Steak, flank; 1.5–2 kg (3–4 lb)	Yes	250 mL (1 cup)	35	Natural
Steak, tri-tip, sirloin, triangle; 8–10 cm (3–4 in) thick	Yes	250 mL (1 cup)	8–12	Natural
Stew meat; 2.5 cm (1 in) cubes	Yes	625 mL (2½ cups)	15–20	Natural
Tongue, fresh or smoked; 1–1.5 kg (2–3 lb)	No	Cover completely	75–100	Natural

Timing Chart for Cooking Chicken

Type of chicken	Brown	Liquid minimum	Cooking time (in minutes)	Release
Boned breasts or thighs, frozen	Yes	250 mL (1 cup)	7–10	Natural
Boned pieces, cut up; 1–1.5 kg (2–3 lb)	Yes	250 mL (1 cup)	4	Quick or cold water
Boned strips; 1–1.5 kg (2–3 lb)	Yes	250 mL (1 cup)	5–6	Quick or cold water
Breasts with bone	Yes	250 mL (1 cup)	10–12	Natural
Cornish hen, 2 whole	Yes	250 mL (1 cup)	8–10	Natural
Ground or minced; 1–1.5 kg (2–3 lb)	Yes	250 mL (1 cup)	2–3	Quick or cold water
Legs or thighs	Yes	250 mL (1 cup)	5–7	Quick or cold water
Livers	No	250 mL (1 cup)	2	Quick or cold water
Parts containing bone	Yes	250 mL (1 cup)	9–11	Natural
Stewing; 2–2.5 kg (4–5 lb)		Cover completely	30–40	Natural
Whole, roasted; 1.5–2 kg (3–4 lb)	Yes	500 mL (2 cups)	25	Natural

Timing Chart for Cooking Pheasant

Type of pheasant	Brown	Liquid minimum	Cooking time (in minutes)	Release
Whole bird	Yes	310 mL (1¼ cup)	15–20	Natural

Timing Chart for Cooking Pigeon

Type of pigeon	Brown	Liquid minimum	Cooking time (in minutes)	Release
Squab, halved	Yes	375 mL (1½ cup)	25–30	Natural

Timing Chart for Cooking Duck

Type of duck	Brown	Liquid minimum	Cooking time (in minutes)	Release
Pieces; 1–1.5 kg (2–3 lb)	Yes	250 mL (1 cup)	8–10	Natural

Timing Chart for Cooking Eggs

Type of egg	Brown	Liquid minimum	Cooking time (in minutes)	Release
Hard cooked	No	Cover completely; must use a rack	5	Cold water
Stirred or poached	Yes	125 mL ($^1/_2$ cup); in ramekins; must use a rack	2	Cold water

Timing Chart for Cooking Ham

Type of ham	Brown	Liquid minimum	Cooking time (in minutes)	Release
Hocks, smoked	No	Cover completely	40–50	Natural
Picnic or shoulder, uncooked; 1.5–2.5 kg (3–5 lb)	No	625 mL ($2^1/_2$ cups)	45–60	Natural
Shank or butt, fully cooked; 1.5–2.5 kg (3–5 lb)	No	625 mL ($2^1/_2$ cups)	35–45	Natural
Shank or butt, not fully cooked; 1.5–2.5 kg (3–5 lb)	No	625–170 mL ($2^1/_2$–3 cups)	45–60	Natural
Slice, fully cooked; 1.25 cm ($^1/_2$ in) thick	No	190 mL ($^3/_4$ cup)	5–6	Natural
Slice, fully cooked; 2.5 cm (1 in) thick	No	190 mL ($^3/_4$ cup)	9–12	Natural
Slice, fully cooked; 5 cm (2 in) thick	No	250 mL (1 cup)	12–20	Natural

Timing Chart for Cooking Lamb

Type of lamb	Brown	Liquid minimum	Cooking time (in minutes)	Release
Breast; 1 kg (2 lb)	Yes	500 mL (2 cups)	35	Natural
Chops; 1.25 cm (1/2 in) thick	Yes	250 mL (1 cup)	5	Quick or cold water
Chops; 6 mm (1/4 in) thick	Yes	250 mL (1 cup)	4	Quick or cold water
Leg; 1.5 kg (3 lb)	Yes	500 mL (2 cups)	20	Natural
Mutton; 2–3 kg (4–6 lb)	Yes	625 mL (2 1/2 cup)	45	Natural
Shoulder; 1.5–3 kg (3–6 lb)	Yes	750 mL (3 cups)	25	Natural
Shanks	Yes	500 mL (2 cups)	20	Quick or cold water
Steak; 1.25 cm (1/2 in) thick	Yes	190 mL (3/4 cup)	9	Quick or cold water
Stew meat; 2.5 cm (1 in) thick	Yes	250 mL (1 cup)	20	Natural

Timing Chart for Cooking Turkey

Type of turkey	Brown	Liquid minimum	Cooking time (in minutes)	Release
Breast, boned (rolled); 0.5–1 kg (1–2 lb)	Yes	375 mL (1 1/2 cups)	15–20	Natural
Breast, whole or half containing bone; 1–1.5 kg (2–3 lb)	Yes	375 mL (1 1/2 cups)	20–30	Natural
Legs; 2–4	Yes	375 mL (1 1/2 cups)	15–20	Natural
Parts, thawed; 0.5–1 kg (1–2 lb)	No	250 mL (1 cup)	5	Natural
Whole; 2.5–3 kg (5–6 lb)	Yes	500 mL (2 cups)	40	Natural

Timing Chart for Cooking Pork

Type of pork	Brown	Liquid minimum	Cooking time (in minutes)	Release
Chops; 2.5 cm (1 in) or more thick, or stuffed	Yes	250 mL (1 cup)	12	Natural
Chops; less than 2.5 cm (1 in) thick	Yes	250 mL (1 cup)	8	Natural
Loin; 1.5–2 kg (3–4 lb)	Yes	625 mL (2$^1/_2$ cup)	50–60	Natural
Pigs feet; 2 pieces	No	Cover completely	30–45	Natural
Ribs, spareribs; 1–1.5 kg (2–3 lb)	No	250 mL (1 cup)	15	Natural
Ribs, baby back ribs; 1–1.5 kg (2–3 lb)	No	250 mL (1 cup)	15	Natural
Ribs, country-style ribs; 1–1.5 kg (2–3 lb)	No	250 mL (1 cup)	20	Natural
Roast, any cut; 1.5–2 kg (3–4 lb)	Yes	500 mL (2 cups)	45–55	Natural
Sausage, Italian, Polish, Kielbasa	Yes; steam on a rack	250 mL (1 cup)	10	Quick or cold water
Shanks; 2 pieces	Yes	500 mL (2 cups)	35–40	Natural
Shoulder; 1.5–2 kg (3–4 lb)	Yes	500 mL (2 cups)	35–45	Natural
Smoked neck bones; 1.5–2 kg (3–4 lb)	No	Cover completely	45–55	Natural

Timing Chart for Cooking Rabbit

Type of rabbit	Brown	Liquid minimum	Cooking time (in minutes)	Release
Whole	Yes	250 mL (1 cup)	12–15	Natural

Timing Chart for Cooking Veal

Type of veal	Brown	Liquid minimum	Cooking time (in minutes)	Release
Chops or steak; less than 2.5 cm (1 in) thick	Yes	250 mL (1 cup)	5	Natural
Leg; 1.5–2 kg (3–4 lb)	Yes	625 mL (2$^1/_2$ cups)	50–60	Natural

Timing Chart for Cooking Venison

Type of venison	Brown	Liquid minimum	Cooking time (in minutes)	Release
Roast, any cut; 8–10 cm (3–4 in) thick	Yes	500 mL (2 cups)	30–40	Natural

The liquid amounts indicated are based on the average used by today's modern pressure cookers with a spring valve pressure release system. The amounts can vary depending on the type of pressure cooker and the length of cooking time. When using a jiggle-top model, plan on doubling the amount of liquid used. Check your owner's manual for the manufacturer's recommendation; generally the minimum amounts recommended for jiggle-top models is 250 mL (1 cup), and 125 mL ($^1/_2$ cup) for the valve type pressure cookers, which is sufficient for approximately 15 minutes of cooking time. To determine the amount of liquid used by your pressure cooker, do a test drive. Pressure cookers will lose more water in cooking time over 15 minutes, or if the heat is not lowered correctly once it comes to pressure.

When using cuts of meat over 4 cm (1$^1/_2$ in) thick always use a meat thermometer to check the temperature for doneness. Find out more by looking at the temperature charts in your manual.

Beans – Speed Soaking

If you haven't soaked the beans in advance, use this 20 minute speed soak technique. Use 750 mL (3 cups) of water for the first cup of dried beans and 500 mL (2 cups) of water per additional cup of beans. Place the beans and water in the cooker. (Owners of jiggle-top cookers should add 20 mL/1 Tbsp of oil per 250 mL/1 cup of dried beans.) Lock the lid in place and, over high heat, bring to high pressure.

For small beans (such as navy or azuki), turn off the heat as soon as high pressure is reached and allow the pressure to come down naturally for 10 minutes. Release any remaining pressure with a quick-release method.

For medium beans (such as red kidney or pinto), cook for 1 minute under high pressure. Turn off the heat and allow the pressure to come down naturally (10 to 15 minutes).

For very large beans (such as chickpeas or Black Valentine), cook for 2 to 3 minutes under high pressure. Turn off the heat and allow the pressure to come down naturally (10 to 15 minutes).

To determine if beans are thoroughly soaked, remove a few beans from the pot with a slotted spoon. Slice the beans in half with a sharp paring knife. If there is an opaque spot in the centre, the beans require more soaking. You can do one of three things:
1. Return to high pressure for another 1 to 2 minutes and again let the pressure come down naturally.
2. If time permits, replace (but do not lock) the lid and let the beans soak until the insides of the beans are all one colour.
3. Rinse and drain the beans. Proceed with preparing the dish, using your judgement to increase the cooking time by 1 to 5 minutes under high pressure. Alternatively, use the cooking time indicated and be prepared to do some stovetop simmering as needed. The latter is a safer way to go, but may take more time.

ALWAYS discard the bean soaking liquid and use fresh water or stock as directed in the recipe.

Basic Guidelines for Pressure Steaming Vegetables

1. Trim and prepare the vegetables as directed in the charts on pages 21–23. Vegetables with the same cooking times may be steamed together.
2. Pour in the minimum amount of liquid required by your cooker's manufacturer.
3. Set the rack or basket in place. If your cooker comes with a steaming basket rather than a rack, it is easier to fill it with the vegetables and lower it in after the water begins to boil.
4. Bring the liquid to boil.
5. Unless otherwise stated in the manual, distribute the vegetables evenly on the rack or in the steaming basket. Remember not to fill cooker over two-thirds full.
6. Lock the lid in place, set the timer and cook according to time indicated in Frozen Vegetable and Fresh Vegetable charts.
7. Always use a quick-release method after cooking vegetables, which are quite delicate and can easily be overcooked.

Notes

- The conventional way to pressure cook plain fresh vegetables is to set them on a rack above the water and steam them. Certain vegetables – sliced carrots or baby okra, for example – take so well to steam heat that they emerge from the cooker with enhanced flavour.
- For variety, try steaming vegetables over an aromatic broth, which not only contributes subtle flavour, but fills the kitchen with an irresistible fragrance.
- For preparing a large quantity of longer-cooking vegetables, like beetroot (beet) or whole button squash, the efficiency of the pressure cooker can't be beaten.
- Pressure steaming is also a great way to set time records for cooking quartered potatoes, pumpkin and turnips that are to be mashed or pureed.
- I don't recommend the pressure cooker for all steaming tasks. Whole potatoes or parsnips become soggy on the outside by the time their insides are cooked; the same is true of large globe artichokes and Brussels sprouts.
- I seriously question the value of pressure steaming quick-cooking vegetables such as asparagus or fresh young corn when the savings in time is negligible and the danger of overcooking is enormous.

Timing Chart for Cooking Frozen Vegetables

Vegetables	Liquid minimum	Cooking time (in minutes)
Asparagus	190 mL ($^3/_4$ cup)	2
Beans, green or wax	190 mL ($^3/_4$ cup)	2–3
Beans, lima	190 mL ($^3/_4$ cup)	$2^1/_2$–4
Broccoli	190 mL ($^3/_4$ cup)	2–3
Brussels sprouts	190 mL ($^3/_4$ cup)	$2^1/_2$
Cauliflower	190 mL ($^3/_4$ cup)	2
Corn on the cob	190 mL ($^3/_4$ cup)	2
Corn, whole kernel	190 mL ($^3/_4$ cup)	2
Mixed vegetables	190 mL ($^3/_4$ cup)	2
Peas	190 mL ($^3/_4$ cup)	1
Peas and carrots	190 mL ($^3/_4$ cup)	2
Spinach	190 mL ($^3/_4$ cup)	1

Timing Chart for Cooking Fresh Vegetables

Vegetables	Liquid minimum	Cooking time (in minutes)
Artichoke	310 mL (1^1/$_4$ cups)	15
Asparagus	190 mL (^{3}/$_4$ cup)	2–2^1/$_2$
Beans, green or wax	190 mL (^{3}/$_4$ cup)	2–3
Beans, lima, fresh	190 mL (^{3}/$_4$ cup)	2
Beetroots (beets), small, whole	250 mL (1 cup)	12
Beetroots (beets), large, whole	375 mL (1^1/$_2$ cups)	18
Broccoli	190 mL (^{3}/$_4$ cup)	2–2^1/$_2$
Brussels sprouts	250 mL (1 cup)	5
Cabbage, shredded	250 mL (1 cup)	2–3
Cabbage, wedges	250 mL (1 cup)	5–8
Cabbage, red, shredded	250 mL (1 cup)	5
Carrots, sliced	125 mL (^{1}/$_2$ cup)	2^1/$_2$
Carrots, small, whole	125 mL (^{1}/$_2$ cup)	2^1/$_2$
Cauliflower, florets	190 mL (^{3}/$_4$ cup)	2–3
Cauliflower, whole	310 mL (1^1/$_4$ cups)	6–8
Celery	190 mL (^{3}/$_4$ cup)	3–5
Corn on the cob	310 mL (1^1/$_4$ cups)	5
Corn, whole kernel	190 mL (^{3}/$_4$ cup)	3
Eggplant (aubergine)	190 mL (^{3}/$_4$ cup)	3
Kale or collard greens	190 mL (^{3}/$_4$ cup)	4–6
Okra	190 mL (^{3}/$_4$ cup)	3
Onion, medium, whole	250 mL (1 cup)	7–10
Onion, sliced	190 mL (^{3}/$_4$ cup)	3
Parsnip, sliced	190 mL (^{3}/$_4$ cup)	2
Parsnip, halved	250 mL (1 cup)	2
Peas	190 mL (^{3}/$_4$ cup)	2–3
Potato, sliced	310 mL (1^1/$_4$ cups)	2^1/$_2$
Potato, medium, halved	500 mL (2 cups)	8
Potato, medium, whole	500 mL (2 cups)	12–15

Timing Chart for Cooking Fresh Vegetables (continued)

Vegetables	Liquid minimum	Cooking time (in minutes)
Pumpkin (squash)	250 mL (1 cup)	8–10
Sauerkraut	190 mL ($^3/_4$ cup)	12
Spinach, silverbeet (Swiss chard) and other leafy green vegetables	190 mL ($^3/_4$ cup)	1
Squash, acorn or dumpling	250 mL (1 cup)	6–7
Squash, hubbard	250 mL (1 cup)	8–10
Swede (rutabaga)	250 mL (1 cup)	5
Sweet potato (yam)	375 mL (1$^1/_2$ cups)	6
Sweet potato (yam), halved	375 mL (1$^1/_2$ cups)	8–10
Turnip	250 mL (1 cup)	5
Zucchini (courgette, summer squash)	250 mL (1 cup)	2–3

Frequently Asked Questions

Is pressure cooking safe?
The pressure cooker has several systems that guarantee safety.

Safe closing system (depending on models)
• The pressure cooker is equipped with a safety system that prevents any rise in pressure if the lid is not completely or properly closed. If the lid is incorrectly positioned, the safety system will prevent the locking indicator pin from rising and consequently pressure from building up.

Safe opening system (depending on models)
• If the pressure cooker is under pressure, the locking indicator pin is raised and prevents it from being opened. To allow the pin to drop, it is necessary to evacuate the pressure and only then is it possible to open the pressure cooker. Check the locking indicator pin or pressure indicator (depending on models) position. It must be in low position to be opened.

Safety with excess pressure during cooking
• Should the steam outlet become blocked, the excess pressure safety systems will come into operation.

What should I do if one of the safety systems is activated?
• Turn off the heat and let the pressure cooker cool down.
• Check the locking indicator pin or pressure indicator (depending on models), the pressure regulator valve and its seat (steam outlet).

My pressure cooker will not come to pressure.
Failure to develop pressure may be caused by any one or more of the following:
• This is normal for the first few minutes while the fluid contents are heated to boiling point.
• The lid is not correctly closed. Refer to your instruction booklet.
• The gasket is not installed properly. Some models require the gasket to be lined up with a peg under the lid. Insert peg in the hole in the gasket. Some require the gasket to be inserted and secured under small triangle-shaped wires.
• You do not have enough liquid in the pot. Usually, approximately 250 mL (1 cup) of liquid is required. Consult your recipe for more information.
• The regulating valve is not placed correctly on the pipe or the regulator is not in position 1 or 2 (depending on models). Refer to your instruction booklet.
• The heat is too low. Always use high heat to bring the pressure cooker up to pressure. Once you get a strong flow of steam, lower the heat source to establish an even flow and start timing from this point. All recipes require the heat source to be lowered once pressure has been reached.
• The locking indicator is stuck. This is a locking indicator pin or pressure indicator (depending on models) that rises when pressure builds inside.

What should I do if steam escapes from around the lid?
Check:
- The lid is properly closed. Some models have clamps that close when you press the top knob (Clipso styles). Others have a twist motion (SAFE II, Sensor II). Line up the arrows on the lid with the arrow on the handles (the lid handle will stick out to the right if handles are pointing towards you), then grip and squeeze both handles causing the top lid handles to 'click' over the pan handle.
- The gasket is correctly positioned inside the lid. If your gasket has a small hole, be sure to line it up and insert it over the peg under the lid.
- The gasket is not dirty. If it is, clean it.
- The gasket is in good condition. Replace it after one year's use.
- The lid is damaged or dented. Replace it.
- The pot is not out of shape and hasn't been damaged. Replace it.
- The lid, safety valve and pressure regulator valve are all clean.
- The rim of the pan is in good condition.

The lid on my pressure cooker is stuck.
- Before opening your pressure cooker, be sure you have released all the steam and that the locking indicator pin is down. Tap it. If you are sure the steam has escaped, it may stay up from moisture or food particles.
- If you are sure all steam has been released, shake the cooker and see if the locking indicator pin or pressure indicator (depending on models) goes down. If it does not, run the cooker under cold water and try opening it again.
- An air pocket could have formed. Take pot to sink using pot holder mitts. With the lid in a closed, locked position, turn it upside down and back to straight up. This could undo the air pocket. Try to open again.

It is impossible to close the lid or the lid is too stiff to close.
- Check the locking indicator pin is correctly positioned. Remove and replace it, if necessary.
- On certain models (Sensor II, Safe II, Visio, Delicio), check the position of the lock (under handle). Hold the lid with the handle pointing to you. If it is in the forward position (2 cm/$^3/_4$ in spring showing), hold the lid horizontally, push the triangle-shaped lever in towards the lock and push on the lock until it is back in position (towards handle).
- If the lid is stiff to close, wipe a little cooking oil around the rim of the lid and pan.

Steam and/or food escapes from the pressure regulator valve, locking indicator or safety device.
- The pressure cooker is overfull.
- The heat is too high.
- The pressure regulator valve, locking indicator pin or safety device are blocked due to inadequate maintenance, preventing normal operation.

My food is not cooked or it is overcooked.
Check:
- The cooking time. Remember to start timing when pressure is reached and you have lowered the heat to produce an even controlled steam release.

- Whether the source of heat is turned up enough after reaching the working pressure. Not enough heat will cause the pressure to drop.
- The proper positioning of the pressure regulator valve.
- The quantity of liquid.
- Overcooking can result with an electric stove. You cannot lower the heat as fast as a gas stove. Use another preheated burner once pressure is reached and you need to lower the temperature. Example: if using a high temperature on an electric coil stove, set another burner to medium high for the transition.

I recently purchased my first pressure cooker – do you have any suggestions?
- Refer to the 'using for the first time' instructions. It is very important to bring water up to pressure, release it and then wash your pressure cooker before you use it. Follow a structured pressure cooker recipe for the first time you prepare a meal. Perhaps one that is similar to your own pot roast or stew. Make a note of the time you save!
- Try a simple recipe from the recipe book included with your pressure cooker.

What kind of food can I prepare in my pressure cooker?
- Practically everything! You can prepare soups, cook meat, fish and vegetables, and also create delicious desserts. For more recipe ideas, apart from this book, please refer to your pressure cooker recipe book.
- Precooking meats for the grill (broiler) is possible as well. Sausages and spareribs can be precooked and then grilled with your favourite sauce. For example, to cook sausages (6–8 dinner sausage links): wash, put into steam basket, add 250 mL (1 cup) of water, close the lid, bring to pressure, cook under pressure for 10 minutes, remove and grill for another 7 to 10 minutes. They will melt in your mouth.
- You can also cook the same barbecue favourites, like chicken, ribs and sausage dishes, right in the pressure cooker with sauce.
- Vegetables are ideal. Because pressure cooking keeps the flavours in food, and little water is necessary for cooking, vegetables retain much more flavour as they are not washed out by boiling in water.
- Vegetables that take a very long time to cook the conventional way, such as turnips, can be ready to mash in 10 to 12 minutes (depending on large cut or small) and cooked in 250–500 mL (1–2 cups) of water.
- Desserts and fresh apple sauce are other popular favourites.

What else can I do with my pressure cooker?
- You can use the pot as a huge saucepan. For this particular purpose, some manufacturers sell glass lids with their pressure cookers.
- Steam baskets are also available for use with pressure cookers so that they can be used on stovetops like a stock pot.

On which heat sources can I use my pressure cooker?
- Refer to your instruction booklet for heat sources suitability.
- Use a burner with a flame diameter equal to or less than the diameter of the base of your pressure cooker.

How much liquid is required for pressure cooking?
- Always use at least 250 mL (1 cup) of liquid, depending on recipe.
- Do not fill pressure cooker more than two-thirds with food and liquid.

When do I start timing my recipes?
- Cooking begins when the pressure regulator valve allows a steady release of steam, making a regular hissing noise. At this point, turn the heat down to maintain an even hiss and start calculating the recipe cooking time.

How do I release the steam when cooking is finished?
- Use the quick-release method. Put the cooking regulator valve to the steam release position (on some models).
- Place the pressure cooker under cold running water. When the pressure cooker is under pressure, take care when moving it. Use pot holders.

The actual cooking times are much shorter than stated in my recipe book. Why?
- You may not have lowered the heat when the pressure regulator valve started, allowing steam to escape at a constant rate, making a regular hissing noise. Note, since an electric stove may not cool down when turned to a lower temperature, have another burner ready and preheated at a lower temperature so that you can transfer your pot when it reaches full pressure.
- You may not have released steam at the end of cooking time. If you leave the pressure cooker release steam alone without any decompression, food continues to cook as long as the cooker is under pressure.
- When cooking time has lapsed, you need to turn the heat down and release the steam.
- Cooking times depend on quantities, size of food and personal taste. For example, a 1 kg (2 lb) whole chuck roast will take a little longer than the same meat cut up for a stew.

Why does overcooking by just one minute make such a difference?
- Pressure cooking is much quicker than conventional cooking. It requires some adjustment to become familiar with this method of cooking, but the benefits are huge when you consider the reduced cooking times and the healthier meals that result.
- If you find the texture too soft or overcooked, reduce the cooking time by 2 to 3 minutes the next time you prepare the recipe. If the food is undercooked, add 1 to 2 minutes to the cooking time.

At which moment after cooking can I open my pressure cooker?
- The pressure cooker can be opened when the internal pressure has been reduced (when the locking indicator pin or pressure indicator, depending on models, has gone down completely).
- To hasten the cooling process, use the quick-release method by placing the cooker under cold running water. This does not apply to electric cookers.

How can I adapt my recipes from conventional cooking to pressure cooking?

- Pressure-cooking times can be up to three times faster than conventional cooking. Read the recipes in the recipe/instruction book that came with your cooker. Once you understand the principles, you can apply them to all recipes. Be sure to include at least 250–500 mL (1–2 cups) of liquid.
- Write down all the ingredients for your favourite conventionally cooked recipes. Check the time chart for suggested cooking times. Remember that texture is a personal preference. If a firmer texture is desired, lower the cooking time by a few minutes.

Can I store food in my pressure cooker?

- Do not leave food in the pressure cooker before and after cooking. Pour your preparation into a food storage container and place it in the fridge.

Can I do steam cooking with my pressure cooker?

- You can use the pressure cooker to steam cook. It is a high-quality method of cooking vegetables, as it preserves vitamins, nutrients and flavour.

For steam cooking:
- Use no more than 500 mL (2 cups) of liquid.
- Use the steam basket; put it on the rack or suspend it from the rivets on the pan (depending on models).
- Close and lock lid (set dial to 1 if using dial-style pressure cooker), bring to pressure and then start timing. Note: vegetables cook fast!

What is the best way to clean my pressure cooker?

- For all components, warm soapy water is sufficient for proper cleaning.
- The stainless steel pot can be put in the dishwasher. If it is stainless steel, it can also be scoured. Do not scour if the interior is non-stick.
- The gasket, pressure regulator valve and safety devices should be cleaned and checked separately after each use to make sure the pressure cooker will operate safely during its next use.

What is the best way to clean my pressure cooker if it has darkened?

- For aluminium models, repeat 'using for the first time' operations with a $1/4$ cup of lemon juice added to the water.
- For stainless steel models, clean the pan with a scouring pad.

When should I replace the gasket?

- The gasket should be replaced every year. If the pressure cooker does not reach pressure and there is steam escaping around the lid, please check that the gasket is fitted correctly. This is also an indication that the gasket may need replacing. Store gasket within position on lid to retain its round shape.

How do I store my pressure cooker?

- Turn the lid upside down on the pot. Keep cleaned gasket in position on lid to retain its round shape.

Soups
and
Stocks

Watusi Peanut Soup

- **40 mL (2 Tbsp) cooking oil**
- **500 g (1 lb) boned beef chuck or pork sirloin roast, cut in 2.5 cm (1 in) pieces**
- **1 cup onion, sliced**
- **½ cup green capsicum (pepper), chopped**
- **½ tsp red capsicum (pepper), crushed**
- **420 g (14.5 oz) can Italian-style Roma tomatoes, or whole tomatoes, diced**
- **125 mL (½ cup) beef stock (broth)**
- **¼ cup peanut butter**
- **salt and black pepper to taste**
- **2 cups hot cooked rice or hot cooked noodles**
- **chopped peanuts for garnish**

Pressure Cooker

4–6 L (4–6 quart)

Serves 4

In pressure cooker heat half the oil over medium heat. Cook meat, half at a time, until brown on all sides. Add more oil if needed. Remove meat and set aside. Drain off fat. Return all the meat to cooker and add onion, green capsicum (pepper), red capsicum (pepper), undrained tomatoes and beef stock (broth).

Lock the lid in place and over high heat bring to high pressure. Adjust heat to maintain high pressure and cook for 12 minutes. Let the pressure drop naturally. Remove the lid, tilting it away from you to allow any excess steam to escape.

Add peanut butter to cooker and stir to mix. Season with salt and pepper to taste. Sprinkle with peanuts. Serve with rice or noodles.

Leek, Potato and Butternut Pumpkin Soup

- 2 Tbsp butter
- 40 mL (2 Tbsp) olive oil
- 1 medium onion, peeled and chopped
- 2 ribs celery, sliced
- 2 leeks, white portion only, sliced
- 5 large garlic cloves, peeled and minced
- 1 Tbsp brown sugar, firmly packed
- 2 Tbsp fresh thyme leaves, minced
- 1 Tbsp fresh sage leaves, minced
- 1 bay leaf
- 1 kg (2 lb) butternut pumpkin (squash), peeled and cut in 2.5 cm (1 in) cubes

- 500 g (1 lb) thin-skinned white potatoes, cut in 2.5 cm (1 in) cubes
- 1 L (4 cups) vegetable or chicken stock (broth)
- ½ tsp nutmeg, freshly grated
- salt to taste
- ½ tsp ground white pepper
- 170 mL (⅔ cup) buttermilk
- fresh chives or parsley, minced, for garnish

Pressure Cooker

5 L (5 quart)

Serves 6–8

In pressure cooker heat butter and olive oil over medium-high heat. Add onion, celery, leeks and garlic. Stir to mix. Add brown sugar, thyme and sage. Stir to mix. Add bay leaf, pumpkin, potatoes and 750 mL (3 cups) of stock (broth).

Lock the lid in place and over high heat bring to high pressure. Adjust heat to maintain high pressure and cook for 12 minutes. Let the pressure drop naturally. Remove the lid, tilting it away from you to allow any excess steam to escape.

Discard bay leaf and add nutmeg, salt and pepper. Puree mixture in a food processor, blender or mill. Return pureed soup to a large saucepan and add remaining stock (broth) and buttermilk. Mix well and heat without boiling. Serve in bowls and sprinkle with chives or parsley.

Bean and Barley Soup with Mushrooms

- **250 g (½ lb) dried lima beans**
- **¼ cup pearl barley**
- **2 large onions, peeled and chopped**
- **2 stalks celery, chopped**
- **1 carrot, peeled and chopped**

- **2 Tbsp chopped fresh parsley**
- **2 L (8 cups) vegetable stock (broth)**
- **250 g (½ lb) fresh mushrooms, sliced**
- **salt to taste**
- **freshly ground black pepper to taste**

Pressure Cooker

5 L (5 quart)

Serves 8

Wash, sort and soak beans.

In pressure cooker combine soaked, drained beans, barley, onion, celery, carrot, parsley and stock (broth).

Lock the lid in place and over high heat bring to medium pressure. Adjust heat to maintain medium pressure and cook for 25 minutes. Reduce the pressure with a quick-release method. Remove the lid, tilting it away from you to allow any excess steam to escape.

Add mushrooms, salt and pepper. Close lid and let stand for 10 minutes. Adjust seasoning and serve.

Hungarian Beef Goulash Soup

- 40 mL (2 Tbsp) cooking oil
- 500 g (1 lb) beef chuck roast, cut in bite-size pieces
- 2 cups potatoes, peeled and cut in 1.25 cm (½ in) cubes
- ¾ cup onion, chopped
- 2 cloves garlic, minced
- 1 Tbsp fresh thyme, snipped, or 1 tsp dried thyme, crushed
- 500 mL (2 cups) beef stock (broth)
- 250 mL (1 cup) Napoletana sauce
- 40 mL (2 Tbsp) red wine vinegar
- 10 mL (2 tsp) Worcestershire Sauce
- 250 mL (1 cup) water
- ¼ cup plain (all-purpose) flour
- 2 Tbsp sweet paprika
- 125 mL (½ cup) water
- ¾ cup frozen peas, loose
- ¼ cup fresh parsley, snipped
- salt to taste
- freshly ground black pepper to taste

Pressure Cooker

4–6 L (4–6 quart)

Serves 4

In pressure cooker heat half of the oil over medium heat. Cook meat, half at a time, until brown on all sides. Add more oil, if needed. Remove the meat and set aside. Drain off fat.

Return all the meat to cooker and add potatoes, onion, garlic, thyme, beef stock (broth), Napoletana sauce, vinegar, Worcestershire Sauce and 250 mL (1 cup) water.

Lock the lid in place and over high heat bring to high pressure. Adjust heat to maintain high pressure and cook for 10 minutes. Let the pressure drop naturally or use the quick-release method. Remove the lid, tilting it away from you to allow any excess steam to escape.

Meanwhile, in a small mixing bowl stir together flour, paprika and 125 mL (½ cup) water. Add peas and parsley to cooker. Slowly add flour mixture to cooker. Cook and stir until thickened and bubbly. Season with salt and black pepper to taste. Cook and stir for 1 minute more. Serve.

Winton Beef Soup

- **500 g (1 lb) stewing beef, fat removed and cut in bite-size pieces**
- **¼ cup plain (all-purpose) flour**
- **60 mL (3 Tbsp) oil**
- **¾ cup onion, chopped**
- **250 mL (1 cup) tomato juice mixed with some stewed tomatoes**
- **1 tsp salt**
- **⅛ tsp pepper**
- **½ tsp garlic powder**
- **1 cup potatoes, chopped**
- **1 cup carrots, chopped**
- **½ cup celery, sliced**
- **½ tsp salt**
- **250 mL (1 cup) water**
- **5 mL (1 tsp) Worcestershire Sauce**

Pressure Cooker

4 L (4 quart)

Serves 4

Dredge cut meat in flour and brown in oil in pressure cooker. Add onion, tomato juice/stewed tomato blend, 1 tsp salt, pepper and garlic powder. Stir.

Lock the lid in place and over high heat bring to high pressure. Adjust heat to maintain high pressure and cook 15 minutes. Let the pressure drop using the quick-release method. Remove the lid, tilting it away from you to allow any excess steam to escape.

Add potatoes, carrots, celery, ½ tsp salt, Worcestershire Sauce and water. Replace lid and, again, bring to high pressure. Adjust heat to maintain high pressure and cook 15 minutes. Thicken if required and serve.

Gramma's Beefy Vegetable Soup

- **20 mL (1 Tbsp) olive oil**
- **750 g (1½ lb) lean beef, cut in 2.5 cm (1 in) cubes**
- **1 large onion, coarsely chopped**
- **2 large carrots, sliced into discs**
- **1 cup celery, sliced**
- **2 large turnips, cut in 2.5 cm (1 in) cubes**
- **500 g (16 oz) can tomatoes**
- **2 cloves garlic, minced**
- **2 tsp salt**
- **½ tsp coarse ground black pepper**
- **½ cup fresh parsley, snipped**
- **2 tsp dried basil**
- **1 tsp ground cumin**
- **2 L (4 cups) beef stock (broth)**
- **500 g (16 oz) can sliced green beans, drained**
- **1 cup frozen corn kernels**
- **1 cup elbow macaroni**
- **crackers or bread and butter to serve**

Pressure Cooker

8 L (8 quart)

Serves 8

Heat pressure cooker, add olive oil and brown beef well. Add everything except turnips, green beans, corn and macaroni.

Lock the lid in place and over high heat bring to high pressure. Adjust heat to maintain high pressure and cook for 15 minutes. Let the pressure drop naturally. Remove the lid, tilting it away from you to allow any excess steam to escape and bring to boil.

Add remaining ingredients. Keep at steady boil until macaroni is cooked, about 6 to 8 minutes. Serve in soup bowls with crackers or thick slices of warmed bread and lots of butter.

Shanghai Black Bean Soup

- **40 mL (2 Tbsp) olive oil**
- **1 Tbsp cumin seeds**
- **2 cloves garlic, minced**
- **2 large onions, coarsely chopped**
- **4 stalks celery, cut in chunks**
- **1 large green capsicum (pepper), diced**
- **1.5 L (6 cups) water**
- **1 smoked ham hock or pig's knuckle, optional**
- **3 large carrots, peeled and cut in chunks**
- **2 bay leaves**
- **1 tsp ground coriander**
- **1 tsp dried thyme**
- **1½ cups dried black beans, picked over and rinsed**
- **⅓ cup coarse bulgur wheat, optional**
- **1 cup minced fresh coriander (cilantro) or parsley, tightly packed**
- **1 tsp salt or to taste**
- **125 mL (½ cup) dry sherry, optional**

Pressure Cooker

6–8 L (6–8 quart)

Serves 8

In pressure cooker heat oil and add the cumin seeds, stirring constantly for 5 seconds. Add the garlic and onions and sauté until the onions are soft, about 3 minutes. Add the remaining ingredients except the fresh coriander (cilantro), salt and sherry.

Lock the lid in place and over high heat bring to high pressure. Adjust heat to maintain high pressure and cook for 35 minutes. Let the pressure drop naturally or use the quick-release method. Remove the lid, tilting it away from you to allow any excess steam to escape.

Remove the bay leaves and ham hock (if using). Stir in the ground coriander, salt and the sherry (if desired) while the soup is simmering. Adjust the seasonings and serve.

Tips and Techniques

A smoked ham hock or pig's knuckle gives this soup an appealing smoky flavour, but the vegetarian version is equally delicious. The bulgur wheat acts as a thickener; alternatively, you can puree about a cupful of the cooked beans and stir them into the soup if it is too thin.

Black-eyed Pea and Sausage Soup

- 250 g (½ lb) bacon, cut in 1.25 cm (½ in) pieces
- 1 large red onion, minced
- 2 cloves garlic, chopped
- 500 mL (2 cups) dried black-eyed peas, soaked overnight and rinsed
- 1.5 L (6 cups) chicken stock (broth)
- ¼ cup tomato paste
- 2 tsp dried oregano
- 1 bay leaf
- 1 tsp coarse sea salt or granulated salt
- 1 tsp crushed red chilli pepper flakes
- 3 Tbsp brown sugar
- 250 g (½ lb) Polish sausage or smoked turkey sausage, cut in bite-size pieces
- ⅓ cup green capsicum (pepper), chopped
- ⅓ cup parsley, coarsely chopped for garnish

Pressure Cooker

6–8 L (6–8 quart)

Serves 6–8

In pressure cooker sauté bacon until crisp. Add red onion and garlic and cook until onion becomes translucent, about 3 minutes. Add black-eyed peas to bacon mixture and stir well. Add stock (broth), tomato paste, oregano, bay leaf, salt, red chilli pepper flakes and brown sugar. Stir until thoroughly mixed.

Lock the lid in place and over high heat bring to high pressure. Adjust heat to maintain high pressure and cook for 5 minutes. Let the pressure drop naturally. Remove the lid, tilting it away from you to allow any excess steam to escape.

Add sausage and green capsicum (pepper). Bring to boil and cook, uncovered, for 3 minutes, stirring occasionally to prevent soup catching. Discard bay leaf. Serve garnished with parsley.

Vegetarian Broccoli Corn Chowder

- **40 mL (2 Tbsp) butter or oil**
- **2 medium leeks, white part only, thinly sliced**
- **1 medium onion, coarsely chopped**
- **2 large potatoes, peeled and cut in 1.25 cm (½ in) cubes**
- **2 stalks broccoli (stalks from 2 heads only), peeled and chopped**
- **1 cup fresh or frozen corn kernels**
- **1.25 L (5 cups) vegetable stock (broth)**
- **½ tsp salt or to taste**
- **¼ cup fresh parsley, finely chopped**
- **½ cup milk, or for a creamier consistency use half pouring cream and half milk**

Pressure Cooker

6 L (6 quart)

Serves 6

In pressure cooker melt butter and sauté the leeks and onions, stirring frequently, until the onion is lightly browned, about 4 minutes. Stir in the potatoes, broccoli, corn, stock (broth), salt and half the parsley.

Lock the lid in place and over high heat bring to high pressure. Adjust heat to maintain high pressure and cook for 3 minutes. Let the pressure drop using the quick-release method. Remove the lid, tilting it away from you to allow any excess steam to escape.

Stir in the remaining parsley and milk. Adjust seasonings before serving.

Borscht

- 5 mL (1 tsp) oil
- 2 cups onion, coarsely chopped, or leeks, thinly sliced
- 875 mL (3½ cups) vegetable or chicken stock (broth)
- 500 g (1 lb) beetroot (beets), trimmed, scrubbed and cut in 1.25 cm (½ in) chunks
- 250 g (½ lb) thin-skinned white potatoes, cut in 2.5 cm (1 in) cubes
- 500 g (1 lb) cabbage, cored and thinly shredded
- 2 Tbsp tomato paste
- 2 large bay leaves
- 2 tsp dried dill seeds or dried dill leaves (dill weed)
- salt to taste
- freshly ground black pepper to taste
- 60 mL (3 Tbsp) freshly squeezed lemon juice
- 1 cucumber, diced
- non-fat plain yoghurt for garnish
- ½ cup fresh dill, minced, for garnish

Pressure Cooker
6–8 L (6–8 quart)

Serves 8

In pressure cooker heat oil and cook onions over medium heat for about a minute. Add stock (broth), beetroot (beets), potatoes, cabbage, tomato paste, bay leaves and dill seeds. Bring the mixture to the boil.

Lock the lid in place and over high heat bring to high pressure. Adjust heat to maintain high pressure and cook for 10 minutes. Let the pressure drop using the quick-release method. Remove the lid, tilting it away from you to allow any excess steam to escape.

Test the beetroot (beet) is cooked and replace the lid (but do not put under pressure) until it is tender. (Beetroot will vary depending on size and age.) Remove bay leaves. Add salt and pepper to taste.

Puree the soup with a hand-held blender or blend in batches in a food processor or blender.

Garnish with the cucumber, yoghurt and fresh dill. Serve hot or chilled.

Tips and Techniques
Cut the beetroot (beet) smaller than the potatoes as it is a more dense vegetable and takes longer to cook. You can choose to peel or not peel either vegetable. Just be sure to scrub them well to remove dirt.

Butternut Pumpkin Bisque

- **20 mL (1 Tbsp) olive oil**
- **2 large onions, peeled and chopped into large pieces**
- **1.25 L (48 oz) chicken stock (broth)**
- **1.5 kg (3 lb) butternut pumpkin (squash), peeled, seeded and cut in 2.5 cm (1 in) chunks**
- **3 large red delicious apples, peeled and cut in 2.5 cm (1 in) pieces**
- **¾ cup long grain rice**
- **1½ tsp ground cumin**
- **2 tsp ground ginger**
- **560 mL (1 pint) milk, or for a creamier consistency use half pouring cream and half milk**
- **salt to taste**

Pressure Cooker
6–8 L (6–8 quart)

Serves 8

In pressure cooker sauté onions in olive oil for approximately 3 minutes, or until they begin to soften, but not brown. Add remaining ingredients, except milk (or half cream/half milk) and salt.

Lock the lid in place and over high heat bring to high pressure. Adjust heat to maintain high pressure and cook for 10 minutes. Let the pressure drop naturally or use the quick-release method. Remove the lid, tilting it away from you to allow any excess steam to escape and let cool slightly.

Place ingredients into blender or food processor, along with milk and salt, if desired. Puree until smooth. Serve medium hot.

Cabbage Sweet and Sour Soup with Caraway

- 2 Tbsp butter or oil
- 1 cup onion, coarsely chopped
- 1 Tbsp caraway seeds
- 2 bay leaves
- 500 mL (2 cups) apple cider
- 500 mL (2 cups) vegetable stock (broth)
- 500 mL (2 cups) cold water
- 40 mL (2 Tbsp) cider vinegar
- 2 Tbsp tomato paste

- 840 g (28 oz) can diced tomatoes with juice
- $\frac{2}{3}$ cup raw white rice
- 1 medium head cabbage, cored and shredded
- 1 tsp salt or to taste
- freshly ground black pepper to taste
- wholegrain bread, for serving

Pressure Cooker

6–8 L (6–8 quart)

Serves 8–10

In pressure cooker heat butter. Sauté the onions and caraway seeds until the onions are soft, about 3 minutes. Add the remaining ingredients and stir to combine.

Lock the lid in place and over high heat bring to high pressure. Adjust heat to maintain high pressure and cook for 5 minutes. Let the pressure drop using the quick-release method. Remove the lid, tilting it away from you to allow any excess steam to escape.

Discard the bay leaves. Adjust seasonings and serve with a hearty wholegrain bread.

Cajun Black Bean and Sausage Gumbo

- 2 cups dried black beans
- 1.75 L (7 cups) water
- 125 mL (½ cup) vegetable oil
- ½ cup plain (all-purpose) flour
- 1 kg (2 lb) spicy Italian sausage, casings removed and meat crumbled
- 6 cloves garlic, minced
- 4 onions, chopped
- 4 stalks celery, chopped
- 1 red capsicum (pepper), chopped
- 2 tsp dried thyme
- 1 L (4 cups) chicken stock (broth)
- 60 mL (3 Tbsp) Worcestershire Sauce
- ½ cup green onions (shallots, scallions), chopped
- ½ cup parsley, minced
- salt and pepper to taste
- 3 cups cooked white rice
- ½ cup tomato, seeded and chopped

Pressure Cooker

6–8 L (6–8 quart)

Serves 8

Soak beans overnight in water to cover or cook in pressure cooker according to instructions for speed soak.

In pressure cooker combine beans and new water. Lock the lid in place and over high heat bring to full pressure. Adjust heat to medium-low to maintain even pressure and cook for 10 minutes. Remove from heat and let pressure drop naturally. Drain beans and set aside.

Wipe cooker clean and heat oil over medium-low heat, sprinkle in flour and cook, stirring constantly until the roux turns the colour of peanut butter, about 12 minutes. (Be careful, this mixture gets very hot and burns easily.) Reduce heat to low.

Stir in sausage, garlic, onions, celery, red capsicum (pepper) and thyme. Cook, stirring, for about 10 minutes or until vegetables are very tender. Stir in beans, stock and Worcestershire Sauce.

Lock the lid in place and over high heat bring to high pressure. Adjust heat to medium-low to maintain even pressure and cook for 8 minutes. Remove from heat and let pressure drop naturally.

Stir in green onions (shallots, scallions) and parsley; season to taste with salt and pepper. Using a large spoon place a big mound of rice in the centre of each soup plate. Ladle gumbo around the rice. Garnish with chopped tomato.

Les Halles Five Onion Soup

- **40 mL (2 Tbsp) olive oil**
- **1 large white onion, sliced**
- **1 medium red onion, sliced**
- **1 medium brown onion, sliced**
- **1 large or 2 small green onions (shallots, scallions), sliced**
- **250 g (8 oz) leek, trimmed to white and light green parts, sliced and rinsed well**
- **2 cloves garlic, minced**
- **2 Tbsp sugar**
- **20 mL (1 Tbsp) balsamic vinegar**
- **1 tsp dried thyme**
- **900 mL (3½ cups) beef stock (broth)**
- **6 garlic cheese croutons (see page 45)**
- **6 slices French bread**
- **6 Tbsp gruyere cheese, shredded**
- **2 cloves garlic, minced**
- **1 Tbsp parmesan cheese, freshly grated**

Pressure Cooker

6 L (6 quart)

Serves 4–6

Preheat pressure cooker over medium heat and swirl in the oil. Add the onions, green onions (shallots, scallions), leek and garlic. Cook, stirring occasionally, until the onions have wilted, about 10 minutes. Add the sugar and balsamic vinegar. Cook, stirring occasionally, until the onions are well caramelised, about 20 minutes. Add the thyme and stock (broth).

Lock the lid in place and over high heat bring to high pressure. Adjust heat to maintain high pressure and cook for 10 minutes. Remove from heat and let pressure drop naturally.

Serve about 1 cup per person, ladled over a garlic cheese crouton (see page 45).

Garlic Cheese Croutons
Preheat griller (broiler). Toast the French bread on one side in griller. Turn the slices over and scatter 1 Tbsp of the gruyere cheese on each slice. Sprinkle garlic and parmesan cheese on top of each slice and return to griller until gruyere has melted.

Tips and Techniques
If you want to use one variety of onions to simplify the recipe, use about 1 kg (2 lb) of sliced brown onions instead.

Chucky's Carrot Soup

- **3 large carrots, cut in 1.25 cm (½ in) pieces**
- **1 large potato, peeled and cut in 2.5 cm (1 in) pieces**
- **1 medium onion, chopped**
- **1½ tsp ground cumin**

- **1 bay leaf**
- **⅛ tsp pepper**
- **¼ tsp salt**
- **1.2 L (4½ cups) chicken stock (broth)**
- **120 mL (6 Tbsp) yoghurt or thickened cream**

Pressure Cooker

6 L (6 quart)

Serves 6

Put all ingredients except yoghurt in pressure cooker.

Lock the lid in place and over high heat bring to high pressure. Adjust heat to maintain high pressure and cook for 4 minutes. Let the pressure drop naturally. Remove the lid, tilting it away from you to allow any excess steam to escape.

Discard bay leaf. Mix the soup smooth in a blender or mash it through a sieve. Return soup to cooker and reheat. Serve hot. Garnish each individual serving with a tablespoon of yoghurt or thickened cream.

Tips and Techniques

To cook smaller quantities, reduce all ingredients proportionally.

Quick 'n' Easy Chicken Soup

- **750 g (1½ lb) chicken pieces**
- **1 tsp salt**
- **1 stalk celery, chopped**
- **1 carrot, diced**
- **1 small onion, diced**
- **1 L (4 cups) water**

Pressure Cooker

4 L (4 quart)

Serves 4

Place all ingredients in pressure cooker.

Lock the lid in place and over high heat bring to high pressure. Adjust heat to maintain high pressure and cook for 15 minutes. Let the pressure drop naturally. Remove the lid, tilting it away from you to allow any excess steam to escape.

Remove chicken and allow to cool. Remove meat from bones and return to cooker. Heat through.

Southern Chicken and Sausage Gumbo

- 125 mL (½ cup) oil (peanut or canola)
- ½ cup plain (all-purpose) flour
- 2 large onions, diced
- 3 stalks celery, finely chopped
- ½ green capsicum (pepper), chopped
- 2 links Italian sausage, sliced
- 3 cups boned chicken, cut into bite-size pieces (see below)
- 4 L (4 quart) chicken stock (broth)
- garlic to taste, chopped
- 1 bunch parsley, chopped
- 1 cup green onions (shallots, scallions) including leaves, chopped
- salt to taste

Pressure Cooker
8 L (8 quart)

Serves 8

Make a roux by cooking equal amounts of flour and oil. Cook over a medium-high heat, stirring the roux for a few minutes to combine. Turn the heat down very low until roux bubbles very slowly. It will look like the bubbles rising from a pancake before you flip it. Cooking time varies, but 30–45 minutes would be normal.

When the roux is a dark, rich brown, add onions, celery, capsicum (pepper) and garlic. Sauté until softened. Add the sliced sausage, cooking until sausage is lightly browned. Add chicken and stock (broth). Stir well to mix and ensure that any roux sticking to the bottom of the pressure cooker is loosened.

Lock the lid in place and bring to high pressure over high heat. Adjust heat to maintain high pressure and cook for 20 minutes. Let the pressure drop naturally. Remove the lid, tilting it away from you to allow any excess steam to escape.

Replace pressure cooker on medium heat and stir in parsley and green onions (shallots, scallions). Salt to taste. Simmer for 5 minutes to allow seasonings to blend. By the end, the sauce should be rich, dark and thick. If not, simmer gently until desired consistency is reached. Serve with rice.

Tips and Techniques
To prepare boned chicken, boil cleaned and cut-up chicken in lightly salted water with peeled carrot, two stalks celery and one small whole onion. Cool and debone, discarding skin and bones. Cut into bite-size pieces.

There are no real rules with gumbo other than the roux and the 'trinity' of celery, onions and green capsicum (pepper). As a variation, prawn and crab or duck and smoked chicken sausage or prawns and hard-boiled eggs are well worth trying.

For a thicker gumbo, add 1 cup of chopped okra when you add the celery, onions and green capsicum (pepper).

Chicken Noodle Soup

- 60 mL (¼ cup) olive oil
- 1 small onion, minced
- 2 cups noodles, broken into pieces
- 1.25 L (5 cups) chicken stock (broth)
- 1 chicken breast, skin removed
- 40 mL (2 Tbsp) fresh lemon juice
- 1 cup celery, chopped
- ¼ cup parsley, chopped
- 1 tsp coarse salt
- ¼ tsp white pepper
- 1 bay leaf
- 1 tsp dried tarragon
- fresh parsley, chopped, to serve

Pressure Cooker

4 L (4 quart)

Serves 6

In pressure cooker, heat oil. Add onion and sauté in hot oil for 2 minutes. Add noodles and cook, stirring often, for 1 minute. Add stock (broth), chicken, lemon juice, celery, parsley, salt, pepper, bay leaf and tarragon.

Lock the lid in place and over high heat bring to high pressure. Adjust heat to maintain high pressure and cook for 10 minutes. Let the pressure drop naturally. Remove the lid, tilting it away from you to allow any excess steam to escape.

Remove chicken from soup. Remove chicken from bones, cut in bite-size cubes and add to soup, discarding bones. Serve hot, garnishing individual servings with chopped parsley.

Tips and Techniques

A variety of noodles are available. The vermicelli noodle is delicious in this soup.

Chicken Soup with Rice

- **1.5 L (6 cups) chicken stock (broth)**
- **1 chicken breast, cut in bite-size pieces**
- **3 carrots, peeled and thinly sliced**
- **5 stalks celery, trimmed and thinly sliced**
- **2 large leeks, light green and white parts only, trimmed, washed well and thinly sliced**
- **½ cup uncooked rice**

Pressure Cooker

4 L (4 quart)

Serves 6

Add all ingredients to pressure cooker.

Lock the lid in place and over high heat bring to high pressure. Adjust the heat to maintain high pressure and cook for 10 minutes. Let the pressure drop using the quick-release method. Remove the lid, tilting it away from you to allow any excess steam to escape.

Serve immediately.

Cuban Black Bean Soup

- **500 g (1 lb) dried black beans**
- **2.5 L (10 cups) water**
- **1 small green capsicum (pepper)**
- **1 medium onion**
- **125 mL (½ cup) olive oil**
- **1 large onion**
- **1 large green capsicum (pepper)**
- **4 cloves garlic**
- **4 tsp salt**
- **½ tsp pepper**
- **1 tsp oregano**
- **1 bay leaf**
- **2 Tbsp sugar**
- **40 mL (2 Tbsp) vinegar**
- **white rice, cooked, optional**

Pressure Cooker

6–8 L (6–8 quart)

Serves 8

Wash the beans and pick over to remove any small stones. Allow them to soak overnight in the water, with the small green capsicum (pepper) and medium onion.

Dice the large onion and large green capsicum (pepper), and mince the garlic. Sauté onion, capsicum (pepper) and garlic in a frying pan until soft. Take approximately 1 cup of the beans and mash in the frying pan with onion, capsicum (pepper) and garlic.

Pour frying pan mixture into pressure cooker. Lock the lid in place and over high heat bring to high pressure. Adjust heat to maintain high pressure and cook for 45 minutes. Let the pressure drop naturally. Remove the lid, tilting it away from you to allow any excess steam to escape.

Add remaining ingredients and let them simmer uncovered for about 1 hour or until they have reached the consistency that you like. Remove the bay leaf.

Enjoy a bowlful on its own or serve over white rice as a side dish.

Fennel and Scallop Bisque

- 2 small fennel bulbs
- 1 medium onion, thinly sliced
- 1 medium red potato, thinly sliced
- 1 stalk celery, strings removed and thinly sliced
- 1 large clove garlic, minced
- 3 Tbsp unsalted butter
- 125 g (¼ lb) sea scallops (roe removed)

- 250 mL (1 cup) fish stock or clam juice
- 250 mL (1 cup) water
- 125 mL (¼ cup) dry white wine
- salt and pepper to taste
- nutmeg, freshly ground
- 60 mL (¼ cup) whipping cream, optional

Pressure Cooker
4 L (4 quart)

Serves 2

Trim the long stalks from the fennel down to the bulb. Peel the outside of the bulb, remove the core and cut the bulb into thin slices.

Melt the butter in pressure cooker. Add the fennel, onion, potato, celery and garlic and cook over medium-high heat, stirring often, until soft, about 7 minutes.

Rinse and drain the scallops. Add the scallops, fish stock or clam juice, water and wine to pressure cooker. Lock the lid in place and over high heat bring to high pressure. Adjust heat to maintain high pressure and cook for 10 minutes. Let the pressure drop using the quick-release method. Remove the lid, tilting it away from you to allow any excess steam to escape.

Puree with a hand-held blender or food processor. Add salt, pepper and nutmeg to taste. If a richer soup is desired, add whipping cream.

Tips and Techniques
This soup can be prepared the day before. Reheat gently, without letting soup come to the boil.

For a soup with more heat, add some hot pepper sauce to taste when pureeing.

Five Bean Soup

- ½ cup black turtle beans
- ½ cup navy beans
- ½ cup red kidney beans
- ½ cup green split peas
- ½ cup pinto beans
- 4 slices bacon, cut in 1.25 cm (½ in) pieces
- 1 onion, diced in 1.25 cm (½ in) pieces
- 2 stalks celery, diced in 1.25 cm (½ in) pieces
- 2 large carrots, diced in 1.25 cm (½ in) pieces
- 1 tsp dried thyme
- 3 potatoes, cut in 1.25 cm (½ in) cubes
- 1 L (1 quart) chicken stock (broth)
- 500 mL (2 cups) warm water
- 15 g (½ oz) dried mushrooms, rehydrated in warm water
- salt and pepper to taste
- 1–2 Tbsp fresh parsley, chopped

Pressure Cooker

6–8 L (6–8 quart)

Serves 4

Soak all the beans in cold water, overnight. Drain and discard soaking liquid.

In pressure cooker, cook the bacon until crisp and all the fat has rendered out. Remove the crispy bacon pieces with a slotted spoon and set aside. Drain away all but 20 mL (1 Tbsp) of the bacon fat.

Add the onion, celery, carrots and dried thyme to pressure cooker and continue to cook until the vegetables become tender, about 3 minutes. Add the beans and potatoes and stir to combine well. Add the chicken stock (broth).

Strain the dried mushrooms, reserving the liquid, and add them to the cooker as well. Add the mushroom liquid carefully, making sure not to pour out any of the sediment that might have accumulated on the bottom of the bowl.

Lock the lid in place. Over high heat bring to high pressure. Adjust heat to maintain high pressure and cook for 20 minutes. Let the pressure drop naturally or use the quick-release method. Remove the lid, tilting it away from you to allow any excess steam to escape.

Season to taste with salt and pepper. Return the bacon to the pot and stir in the fresh parsley. Serve.

Tips and Techniques
It is worth noting that there are many types of dried beans, most of which can be used in this recipe.

Tangy Gingered Pumpkin and Apple Soup

- **1.25 kg (2½ lb) Japanese or butternut pumpkin (squash)**
- **2½ Tbsp butter**
- **1 large red onion, coarsely chopped**
- **750 mL (3 cups) vegetable stock (broth)**
- **500 g (1 lb) sweet apple, peeled, cored and sliced**
- **salt to taste**
- **40 mL (2 Tbsp) rice vinegar**
- **2 Tbsp fresh ginger, minced**
- **2 Tbsp fresh coriander (cilantro), chopped**
- **pepper to taste**
- **dollop cream, plain yoghurt or crème fraiche, optional**

Pressure Cooker

6 L (6 quart)

Serves 6

Peel and seed pumpkin (squash) and cut in 5 cm (2 in) chunks.

In pressure cooker, melt butter over medium-high heat. Add pumpkin and cook until it begins to caramelise on the bottom. Stir and cook a bit longer until pumpkin is nicely coloured. Stir in onion. Cook for 2 minutes, stirring occasionally. Stir in stock (broth), carefully scraping up all browned bits off the bottom of the pan. Add remaining ingredients.

Lock the lid in place. Over high heat bring to high pressure. Adjust heat to maintain high pressure and cook for 12 minutes. Let the pressure drop using the quick-release method. Remove the lid, tilting it away from you to allow any excess steam to escape.

The pumpkin (squash) should be very tender. If not, return to heat and simmer until cooked. Correct seasoning.

Puree in batches in a blender or food processor, or in the cooker using a hand-held blender. Sprinkle additional coriander (cilantro) on top for garnish and serve.

Tips and Techniques
Cream can be added for richness or serve with a dollop of plain yoghurt or crème fraiche.

Green Bean and Ham Soup

- 4 cups fresh green beans, cut in 2.5 cm (1 in) pieces
- 3 cups potatoes, peeled and cut in 2.5 cm (1 in) cubes
- 2 cups cooked ham, cubed
- 1 cup onion, chopped
- 1 L (4 cups) water

- 20 mL (1 Tbsp) oil
- ¼ cup plain (all-purpose) flour
- 1 Tbsp fresh dill, snipped, or 1 tsp dried dill, crushed
- ¼ tsp salt
- ¼ tsp black pepper
- 250 mL (1 cup) milk or light cream

Pressure Cooker

4–6 L (4–6 quart)

Serves 6

In pressure cooker, combine green beans, potatoes, ham, onion, water and oil.

Lock the lid in place. Over high heat bring to high pressure. Adjust heat to maintain high pressure and cook for 3 minutes. Let the pressure drop using the quick-release method. Remove the lid, tilting it away from you to allow any excess steam to escape.

Stir together flour, dill, salt, pepper and milk or light cream until smooth.

Add to cooker. Cook over medium heat until thickened and bubbly. Stir for 1 minute more, then serve.

Amarillo Chicken Soup Served Over Mexican Rice

Soup

- 60 mL (3 Tbsp) olive oil
- 2 chicken breast halves, boned, skinned and cubed
- 1 cup onion, coarsely chopped
- ¼ cup carrots, peeled and thickly sliced
- 1 cup celery, coarsely chopped
- 2 cloves garlic, minced
- 2 jalapeño peppers, seeded, membranes removed and finely chopped, optional
- 2 L (8 cups) chicken stock (broth)
- 2 large potatoes, cut in large chunks
- 1 tsp ground cumin
- ¼ tsp dried thyme
- 1 bay leaf
- 1 Tbsp salt (if using bought stock (broth), taste after pressuring and adjust salt then)
- 3 ears corn, each cut in 3 pieces
- ¾ cup salsa, to garnish
- 6 slices avocado, to garnish

Rice

- 20 mL (1 Tbsp) olive oil
- ¼ cup onion, chopped
- ¼ cup celery, chopped
- ¼ cup carrots, chopped
- 1 cup fresh tomatoes, chopped
- ⅛ tsp cayenne pepper, or more to taste
- 1 Tbsp sweet paprika
- 1½ cups rice
- 750 mL (3 cups) chicken stock (broth)
- ½ tsp salt, or adjust seasonings after pressuring

Pressure Cooker

6–8 L (6–8 quart)

Serves 6

58

Soup

Place oil in hot pressure cooker. Sauté cubed chicken until lightly browned on all sides. Add onion, carrots, celery and garlic. Continue to sauté until vegetables are crisp-tender. Add the rest of ingredients to cooker.

Lock the lid in place. Over high heat bring to high pressure. Adjust heat to maintain high pressure and cook for 10 minutes. Let the pressure drop naturally or use the quick-release method. Remove the lid, tilting it away from you to allow any excess steam to escape.

Rice

Place oil into hot pressure cooker. Sauté all raw vegetables until crisp-tender, about 3 minutes, constantly stirring. Add remaining ingredients.

Place lid on pressure cooker and lock down. Bring up to full pressure. Reduce heat until you have a gentle rocking and continue cooking for 10 minutes from this point. Bring pressure down naturally or quick release by putting cooker in sink and running cold water over top.

Place half a cup or more rice in large shallow soup bowl. Ladle 1¹/₂ cups of soup over rice.

Final Assembly

Garnish with 2 Tbsp of salsa and a slice of avocado.

Tomato and Roasted Capsicum Soup

- **125 mL (½ cup) water**
- **1.5 kg (3 lb) large tomatoes, cored and cut in chunks**
- **2 large red capsicums (peppers), roasted, seeded and cut in eighths**
- **1 cup onion, coarsely chopped**
- **2 tsp garlic, minced**
- **2 large bay leaves**
- **¼ tsp saffron threads (optional but highly recommended)**
- **salt to taste**
- **⅓ cup fresh basil, minced, or fresh dill, minced**

Pressure Cooker

8 L (8 quart)

Serves 8

Bring the water and tomatoes to the boil in pressure cooker as you prepare and add the capsicums (peppers), onions, garlic, bay leaves, saffron (if using) and salt.

Lock the lid in place. Over high heat bring to high pressure. Adjust heat to maintain high pressure and cook for 3 minutes. Let the pressure drop using the quick-release method. Remove the lid, tilting it away from you to allow any excess steam to escape.

Puree the soup in three or four batches in a food mill, food processor or blender. Return to the cooker to reheat before serving. Garnish with basil or dill.

Savoury Meatball Soup

- 250 g (½ lb) lean hamburger mince
- ½ cup cooked rice
- 1 Tbsp salt (for meatballs)
- ¼ tsp pepper (for meatballs)
- ¼ tsp oregano (for meatballs)
- 1 egg white
- 3 large carrots, sliced
- 3 stalks celery, sliced
- 1 medium onion, diced
- 2 cloves garlic, crushed
- ½ small head green cabbage

- 1 small zucchini (courgette) sliced
- 420 g (14 oz) can diced tomatoes
- ½ cup frozen corn
- 1 Tbsp salt
- ¼ tsp pepper
- ¼ tsp ground cumin
- ¼ tsp oregano
- 4 sprigs fresh coriander (cilantro)
- 1.5 L (6 cups) water
- corn tortillas, warmed

Pressure Cooker

6 L (6 quart)

Serves 4

Combine hamburger mince, rice, salt, pepper and oregano. Add egg white and hand mix well.

Place water in pressure cooker and bring to boil. By hand, shape meat mixture into balls, dropping gently into the boiling water. Add carrots, celery, onion, garlic, green cabbage, zucchini, tomatoes and corn. Mix in salt, pepper, cumin, oregano and coriander (cilantro). Stir gently.

Lock the lid in place and over high heat bring to high pressure. Adjust heat to maintain high pressure and cook for 15 minutes. Use the quick-release method or cold water to drop the pressure quickly. Remove the lid, tilting it away from you to allow any excess steam to escape.

Serve with warm corn tortillas.

Minestrone

- ¾ cup dried navy beans, picked over and rinsed
- 40 mL (2 Tbsp) olive oil
- 2 cloves garlic, finely minced
- 1 large onion, coarsely chopped
- 3 large carrots, cut in thick slices
- 1 medium leek, thinly sliced
- 3 stalks celery, cut in 2.5 cm (1 in) slices
- 1 cup tightly packed fresh basil, minced, or Italian (flat-leaf) parsley, divided
- 1 tsp dried thyme or dried oregano
- 400 g (14 oz) can Italian Roma tomatoes with juice
- 750 mL (3 cups) cold water
- 750 mL (3 cups) vegetable stock (broth)
- 2 cups green beans, trimmed and cut in thirds
- ½ cup orzo, tubettini or other small Italian pasta
- 250 mL (1 cup) boiling water, optional
- 2 large zucchini (courgette), cut in 1.25 cm (½ in) slices
- 3 cups cabbage, shredded and cored
- 1 tsp salt
- freshly ground black pepper to taste
- parmesan or romano cheese, grated

Pressure Cooker
8 L (8 quart)

Serves 8–10

Soak the navy beans overnight or use the pressure cooker speed soak method (see Beans – Speed Soaking, page 19). Rinse, drain and set aside.

Heat the olive oil in pressure cooker and sauté the garlic and onion until the onion becomes translucent, about 3 minutes. Add carrots, leek, celery, half the basil (or Italian parsley), thyme, reserved navy beans, Roma tomatoes with their juice, water and stock (broth).

Lock the lid in place. Over high heat bring to high pressure. Adjust heat to maintain high pressure and cook 20 minutes. Let the pressure drop naturally or use the quick-release method. Remove the lid, tilting it away from you to allow any excess steam to escape.

Add the green beans and orzo and cook uncovered over medium heat for 5 minutes, stirring frequently so that the soup doesn't catch. If the soup becomes too thick, add boiling water as required. Add zucchini (courgette), cabbage, remaining basil (or Italian parsley), and salt and pepper to taste. Cook until the zucchini (courgette) and green beans are crisp-tender, about 3 to 5 additional minutes.

Serve in bowls, garnished with parmesan or romano cheese.

Tips and Techniques
In Italy, minestrone often contains one secret ingredient: a tablespoon of sugar (added with the cold water) to enhance all of the flavours.

New England Fish Chowder

- **40 mL (2 Tbsp) butter or oil**
- **1 large onion, finely chopped**
- **3 stalks celery, finely chopped**
- **1 cup carrot, finely chopped**
- **500 g (1 lb) potatoes, peeled and cut in 1.25 cm (½ in) cubes**
- **1 lb (500 g) firm-fleshed white fish fillets (like cod), cut in 4 cm (1½ in) chunks**
- **500 mL (2 cups) fish stock or clam juice**
- **250 mL (1 cup) cold water**

- **1 bay leaf**
- **½ tsp dried thyme**
- **250 mL (1 cup) milk**
- **1 cup fresh or frozen corn kernels, thawed**
- **½ cup parsley, finely chopped**
- **salt to taste**
- **white or black pepper to taste**
- **butter, cut in pats, for garnish**
- **milk, pouring cream or heavy cream to taste**

Pressure Cooker

6 L (6 quart)

Serves 4

Heat the butter or oil in pressure cooker. Sauté the onions until soft, about 2 to 3 minutes. Toss in the celery, carrot and potatoes, and sauté for an additional minute. Add the fish chunks, stock or clam juice (watch for sputtering oil), water, bay leaf and thyme.

Lock the lid in place. Over high heat bring to high pressure. Adjust the heat to maintain high pressure and cook for 4 minutes. Let the pressure drop using the quick-release method. Remove the lid, tilting it away from you to allow any excess steam to escape.

Remove the bay leaf and stir in the milk, corn, parsley, and salt and pepper to taste. Simmer until the corn is cooked and the chowder is hot.

Transfer to a serving tureen or individual bowls and top with additional butter, if desired. Make it as rich as you like by stirring in either milk, pouring cream or heavy cream at the end.

Pinto Bean and Pepper Soup

- 1½ cups dried pinto beans, soaked overnight or speed soaked (can also use canned equivalent)
- 20 mL (1 Tbsp) safflower oil
- 1 tsp cumin seeds
- 1 tsp garlic, finely minced
- 2 cups onions, coarsely chopped
- 1 large red capsicum (pepper), seeded and diced
- 1½ cups corn kernels
- 1½ tsp dried oregano
- 1 dried chipotle (smoked jalapeño) pepper, stemmed, seeded and snipped into bits, or 1–2 jalapeño peppers, or generous pinch crushed red chilli pepper flakes
- 1 L (4 cups) boiling water
- 2 Tbsp tomato paste
- ½ cup fresh coriander (cilantro) or parsley, minced
- 20–40 mL (1–2 Tbsp) freshly squeezed lime juice
- salt and freshly ground pepper
- 1 ripe or firm avocado, cut in 1.25 cm (½ in) pieces

Pressure Cooker

6 L (6 quart)

Serves 6

Drain and rinse beans; set aside.

Heat oil in pressure cooker. Sizzle cumin seeds over medium heat just until they begin to pop, about 5 to 10 seconds. Add the garlic and cook, stirring constantly, until garlic turns light brown. Immediately add the onion and red capsicum (pepper) and cook, stirring frequently, for 1 minute. Add the reserved beans, corn kernels, oregano, chipotle (smoked jalapeño) and water.

Lock the lid in place. Over high heat bring to high pressure. Adjust heat to maintain high pressure and cook for 8 minutes. Let the pressure drop naturally or use the quick-release method. Remove the lid, tilting it away from you to allow any excess steam to escape. Simmer beans until done if they aren't quite cooked.

With a slotted spoon, transfer a generous cupful of beans to a food processor (or puree all of soup) and puree with tomato paste. Stir back into soup. Add the coriander, lime juice, salt and pepper. Gently stir in avocado just before serving.

Irish Potato Soup

- **4 potatoes, diced**
- **1 onion, finely chopped**
- **3 stalks celery, finely sliced**
- **1 tsp salt**
- **⅛ tsp white pepper**

- **1 L (4 cups) water**
- **2 Tbsp plain (all-purpose) flour**
- **250 mL (1 cup) skim milk**
- **250 mL (2 Tbsp) margarine or butter**

Pressure Cooker

6 L (6 quart)

Serves 6

Place potatoes, onion, celery, salt, white pepper and water in pressure cooker.

Lock the lid in place. Over high heat bring to high pressure. Adjust heat to maintain high pressure and cook for 5 minutes. Let the pressure drop naturally. Remove the lid, tilting it away from you to allow any excess steam to escape.

Moisten flour with part of milk. Beat until smooth and stir in remaining milk. Stir mixture and margarine or butter into soup and simmer, uncovered, to thicken. Serve.

Creamy Potato Soup with Onions and Cheddar

- **40 mL (2 Tbsp) butter or oil**
- **1 clove garlic, finely minced**
- **4 stalks celery, thinly sliced**
- **3 scallions (green onions, shallots), thinly sliced**
- **300 g (10 oz) small pickling onions, peeled**
- **1 kg (2 lb) potatoes, scrubbed, halved and cut in 6 mm (¼ in) slices**

- **1.5 L (6 cups) beef, chicken or vegetable stock (broth)**
- **½ cup fresh parsley, finely minced**
- **½ cup milk, optional**
- **1 cup sharp cheddar cheese, grated**
- **salt and white pepper to taste**

Pressure Cooker
6–8 L (6–8 quart)

Serves 6

Heat the butter or oil in pressure cooker. Sauté the garlic, celery and scallions (green onions, shallots) for 1 or 2 minutes. Stir in the onions and potatoes, tossing to coat with the butter. Add the stock (broth) and half the parsley.

Lock the lid in place. Over high heat bring to high pressure. Adjust heat to maintain high pressure and cook for 5 minutes. Let the pressure drop naturally or use the quick-release method. Remove the lid, tilting it away from you to allow any excess steam to escape.

Add the remaining parsley and milk (if using). Over low heat, gradually stir in the grated cheese, simmering until the cheese is melted and the soup is hot. Add salt and pepper to taste before serving.

Tips and Techniques
Thin-skinned potato varieties, such as Sebago, russet, Nicola and new potatoes, can be used without peeling. During pressure cooking, their skins become very tender and impart a fuller flavour to the soup.

Chicken, Vegetable and Saffron Soup

- **625 g (1¼ lb) chicken pieces, skinned**
- **2 stalks celery, cut in chunks**
- **1 cup onion, coarsely chopped**
- **1 medium carrot, cut in 8 cm (3 in) chunks**
- **4 cloves garlic, halved**
- **2 sprigs fresh parsley**
- **4 cloves**
- **¾ tsp salt**
- **¾ tsp dried thyme, crushed**
- **¼ tsp black pepper**
- **1 L (4 cups) water**
- **⅛ tsp saffron threads or ¼ tsp turmeric**
- **¼ tsp crushed red chilli pepper flakes, optional**
- **1 cup frozen peas**
- **1 cup cooked wild or regular rice**
- **⅓ cup tomato, seeded and chopped**
- **2 medium green onions (shallots, scallions), thinly sliced**

Pressure Cooker

4–6 L (4–6 quart)

Serves 4

In pressure cooker place chicken pieces, celery, onion, carrot, garlic, parsley, cloves, salt, thyme, black pepper and water.

Lock lid in place. Over high heat bring to high pressure. Adjust heat to maintain high pressure and cook for 8 minutes. Let the pressure drop using the quick-release method. Remove the lid, tilting it away from you to allow any excess steam to escape.

Remove chicken. Pour stock through a large sieve or colander lined with two layers of cheesecloth. Discard vegetables and return strained stock to cooker.

Add saffron or turmeric and crushed red chilli pepper flakes, if desired. Bring to boil. Add peas. Reduce heat to low. Cover loosely (do not lock lid) and cook for about 5 minutes until peas are tender.

Meanwhile, remove meat from bones and cut in bite-size pieces. Discard bones. Stir chicken, rice, tomato and green onions (shallots, scallions) into soup and heat through. Serve.

Traditional Scotch Broth

- 1.25 kg (2½ lb) lamb neck, cut in large bite-size pieces and trimmed of excess fat
- 2 L (8 cups) cold water
- ¾ tsp salt or to taste
- ½ cup pearl barley, picked over and rinsed
- ½ cup split peas, picked over and rinsed

- 2 medium leeks, white part only, thinly sliced
- 1 large onion, coarsely chopped
- 2 large carrots, scrubbed or peeled, each cut in 3–4 chunks
- 2 stalks celery, finely chopped
- 2 bay leaves
- 4 sprigs fresh parsley

Pressure Cooker
6–8 L (6–8 quart)

Serves 8

Rinse the lamb neck under cold water and place it in the bottom of pressure cooker. Add the water and slowly bring to the boil. Skim off any white scum that forms on the surface. Add the salt and skim again. Add the remaining ingredients.

Lock lid in place. Over high heat bring to high pressure. Adjust heat to maintain high pressure and cook for 20 minutes. Let the pressure drop naturally or use the quick-release method. Remove the lid, tilting it away from you to allow any excess steam to escape.

Remove the bay leaves and parsley. Add additional salt if desired and serve.

Tips and Techniques
In Scotland, some versions traditionally add chunks of swede (rutabaga) and chopped cabbage at the time the remaining ingredients are added.

If you prepare this soup a day in advance, you can remove the fat that congeals on the surface before reheating and serving.

Split Pea with Ham Soup

- **500 g (1 lb) dried split peas**
- **2 L (8 cups) water**
- **1 small ham bone**
- **1 medium onion, diced**
- **2 large carrots, diced**
- **2 stalks celery, diced**
- **1½ tsp dried thyme**
- **salt to taste**
- **sherry, optional**

Pressure Cooker

6–8 L (6–8 quart)

Serves 6–8

Fill pressure cooker with water and other ingredients, except sherry. Make sure the pot is no more than half full.

Lock lid in place. Over high heat bring to high pressure. Adjust heat to maintain high pressure and cook for 30 minutes. Let the pressure drop naturally. Remove the lid, tilting it away from you to allow any excess steam to escape.

If using a ham bone, remove and pull all meat off and add to soup. Adjust salt to suit your taste. Serve with a splash of sherry if you wish.

Tips and Techniques

You can also use bacon bones instead of the ham bone. Beware of small bits of bone that may break off during cooking.

For a 'creamier' soup, puree with a hand-held blender after removing ham bone, then add meat off the bone.

Beef Stock

- **10 mL (2 tsp) cooking oil**
- **1.5 kg (3 lb) meaty beef soup bones**
- **3 medium carrots, cut in 2.5 cm (1 in) pieces**
- **3 stalks celery, cut in 2.5 cm (1 in) pieces**
- **2 bay leaves**
- **1⅓ cups onion, sliced**
- **¾ tsp salt**
- **7 whole black peppercorns**
- **2 L (8 cups) water**

Pressure Cooker

8 L (8 quart)

Makes approximately 2 L (6³/₄ cups)

In pressure cooker heat 1 Tbsp of the cooking oil over medium heat. Cook soup bones, half at a time, until brown on all sides. Add more oil, if needed.

Remove the meat from bones and set aside. Drain off fat. Add all ingredients.

Lock lid in place. Over high heat bring to high pressure. Adjust heat to maintain high pressure and for pressure regulator to rock gently; cook for 45 minutes. Let the pressure drop naturally. Remove the lid, tilting it away from you to allow any excess steam to escape.

Pour stock through a large sieve or colander lined with two layers of cheesecloth. Discard bones, vegetables and seasonings. If desired, reserve and freeze meat for another use.

Clarifying Stock

Combine stock, 60 mL (¹/₄ cup) cold water and an egg white after reducing the pressure. Bring to boil, then remove from heat and let stand for 5 minutes before straining through a colander lined with cheesecloth as directed above. If time permits, chill stock first, then you can easily skim off fat layer.

Tips and Techniques

Store stock in covered containers in the refrigerator up to 3 days or in freezer up to 3 months.

This recipe was tested in an 8 L (8 quart) pressure cooker. If using a 4 L (4 quart) pressure cooker, halve the ingredients.

Use this stock as a base for your favourite soup or stew, or any recipe requiring beef broth.

Poultry Stock

- 1.25 kg (2½ lb) stewing chicken or turkey carcass, cut in 6 pieces
- 2 stalks celery, cut in 3–4 chunks
- 2 large carrots, cut in 3–4 chunks
- 1 parsnip, cut in 3–4 chunks, optional
- 1 large onion, coarsely chopped
- 3–4 leeks, green part only, optional
- 4 dried mushrooms, optional
- ¼ tsp whole black peppercorns
- 1 tsp salt or to taste
- 5 sprigs fresh parsley
- 1 bay leaf
- 3 L (3 quart) cold water

Pressure Cooker

6–8 L (6–8 quart)

Makes approximately 2.5 L (2¹/₂ quart)

Place all ingredients in pressure cooker.

Lock lid in place. Over high heat bring to high pressure. Adjust heat to maintain high pressure and cook for 30 minutes. Let the pressure drop naturally. Remove the lid, tilting it away from you to allow any excess steam to escape.

Allow the stock to cool slightly. Strain into a large storage container. Cover and refrigerate overnight. Remove the congealed fat from the top before using or freezing.

Tips and Techniques
Adding parsnips gives the stock a subtle, haunting sweetness. Dried mushrooms darken the stock considerably, and the green part of leeks add interesting and wonderful tastes.

This stock can be refrigerated for 5 days or frozen for up to 4 months.

This recipe was tested in a 6 L (6 quart) pressure cooker. If using an 8 L (8 quart) pressure cooker, increase the ingredients by 50%, and double the ingredients for a 10 L (10 quart) pressure cooker.

It is best to prepare meat stocks a day in advance so that you can skim off the fat that congeals on top after overnight refrigeration. Use the steaming basket if your cooker comes with one; lift it out when you're finished cooking for easy draining.

Potato Leek Soup

- 40 mL (2 Tbsp) olive oil
- ¼ cup unsalted butter
- 4 large leeks, white part only, thinly sliced
- 2 cloves garlic, crushed
- 1 large carrot, diced
- 4 large potatoes, thinly diced
- ¼ cup fresh parsley, minced
- 3 Tbsp plain (all-purpose) flour
- 1 L (4 cups) chicken stock (broth)
- 1 Tbsp dried bouquet garni
- 1 tsp sea salt (Kosher salt)
- ¼ tsp ground white pepper
- 80 mL (⅓ cup) light sour cream

Pressure Cooker

8 L (8 quart)

Serves 6

Heat oil and butter in pressure cooker. Add leeks and garlic and sauté for 2 minutes. Add carrot, potatoes and parsley; sprinkle vegetables with flour. Sauté, stirring occasionally for 2 minutes. Stir in stock (broth) and bouquet garni, salt and pepper.

Lock the lid in place. Over high heat bring to high pressure. Adjust heat to maintain high pressure and cook for 8 minutes. Let the pressure drop naturally. Remove the lid, tilting it away from you to allow any excess steam to escape.

Temper sour cream with stock (broth), a little at a time, if using; then add to soup pot. Bring almost to a boil, then let simmer for 5 minutes, stirring occasionally. Serve hot.

Thai Chicken Soup

- **750 mL (3 cups) chicken stock (broth)**
- **400 g (13½ oz) can unsweetened coconut milk**
- **¾ cup green onions (shallots, scallions), chopped**
- **2½ Tbsp green curry paste**
- **1½ Tbsp fresh lemongrass, minced**
- **1 Tbsp fresh ginger, peeled and minced**
- **4 large chicken thighs with bone**
- **60 mL (3 Tbsp) fish sauce**
- **180 g (6 oz) baby spinach leaves**
- **60 mL (3 Tbsp) fresh lime juice**

Pressure Cooker

6–8 L (6–8 quart)

Serves 4

Combine chicken stock (broth), coconut milk, green onions (shallots, scallions), green curry paste, lemongrass and ginger in pressure cooker. Add chicken thighs.

Lock the lid in place. Over high heat bring to high pressure. Adjust heat to maintain high pressure and cook for 8 minutes. Let the pressure drop naturally. Remove the lid, tilting it away from you to allow any excess steam to escape.

Remove chicken and transfer to cutting board, cool briefly. Remove bones and cut up chicken. Return chicken to soup and add fish sauce and spinach. Simmer until spinach wilts, about 1 minute. Add lime juice and season soup to taste with salt and pepper.

Tips and Techniques
You can also add pre-softened rice or egg noodles to soup when adding the spinach.

Turkey Vegetable Soup

- 20 mL (1 Tbsp) olive oil
- 2 cloves garlic, finely minced
- 1 kg (35 oz) can tomatoes, coarsely chopped, with juice
- 750 g (1½ lb) small potatoes, scrubbed
- 2 large carrots, peeled and cut in chunks
- 300 g (10 oz) small white onions, peeled
- 3 stalks celery, finely chopped
- ⅓ cup loosely packed dried mushrooms
- 1 tsp dried oregano
- ½ tsp dried rosemary leaves
- 1 bay leaf
- 2 strips orange zest
- ½ tsp salt
- 1 turkey drumstick, skinned
- 1 turkey thigh, skinned
- 300 g (10 oz) defrosted frozen green beans
- 1½ cups corn kernels
- ⅓ cup fresh parsley or coriander (cilantro), finely minced
- salt and pepper to taste

Pressure Cooker

6–8 L (6–8 quart)

Serves 4

Heat the oil in pressure cooker and sauté the garlic for 10 seconds. Add the tomatoes, potatoes, carrots, onions, celery, mushrooms, oregano, rosemary, bay leaf, orange zest and salt. Settle the turkey pieces into the soup.

Lock the lid in place. Over high heat bring to high pressure. Adjust heat to maintain the high pressure and cook for 12 minutes. Let the pressure drop naturally or use the quick-release method. Remove the lid, tilting it away from you to allow any excess steam to escape.

Remove the turkey pieces and cut the meat from the bone into bite-size chunks, and then add to the cooker. Stir in the green beans, corn kernels, parsley or coriander (cilantro) and cook over medium heat until the vegetables are cooked, about 3 to 5 minutes. Remove the orange zest and bay leaf, and add salt and pepper to taste before serving.

Vegetable and Pasta Soup

- 1.25 L (5 cups) chicken stock (broth)
- 375 mL (1½ cups) tomato juice
- 1 large carrot, finely chopped
- 1 small zucchini (courgette), cut in 6 mm (¼ in) slices
- ¼ cup celery, finely chopped
- 1 medium onion, finely chopped
- 1½ cups cabbage, chopped
- ⅓ cup alphabet pasta, or pasta up to 3 mm (⅛ in) thick
- 2 cloves garlic, minced
- ½ tsp salt
- ¼ tsp pepper
- 1 small bay leaf
- 1 Tbsp fresh parsley, chopped

Pressure Cooker

6–8 L (6–8 quart)

Serves 8

Pour stock (broth) and tomato juice into pressure cooker. Bring to boil on high heat. Add remaining ingredients, except parsley. Stir.

Lock the lid in place. Over high heat bring to high pressure. Adjust heat to maintain the high pressure and cook for 10 minutes. Let the pressure drop naturally. Remove the lid, tilting it away from you to allow any excess steam to escape.

Remove bay leaf. Serve hot, garnished with the parsley.

Tips and Techniques
To cook smaller quantities reduce all ingredients proportionately.

Vichyssoise

- 3 Tbsp butter
- 1 small onion, sliced
- 1½ cups leeks, white part only, thinly sliced
- 3 cups potatoes, peeled and cut in 1.25 cm (½ in) slices
- 2¼ tsp salt
- 875 mL (3½ cups) hot water
- 750 mL (3 cups) hot milk
- 250 mL (1 cup) hot pouring cream
- 250 mL (1 cup) heavy cream
- 1 Tbsp chives, chopped

Pressure Cooker
6–8 L (6–8 quart)

Serves 10

Melt the butter in pressure cooker. Add onion and leeks. Cook on low heat until soft but not brown, stirring occasionally. Add potatoes, salt and water.

Lock the lid in place. Over high heat bring to high pressure. Adjust heat to maintain high pressure and cook for 3 minutes. Let the pressure drop naturally. Remove the lid, tilting it away from you to allow any excess steam to escape.

Add milk and pouring cream. Stir. Place cooker on medium heat and bring to boil, stirring frequently.

Puree the soup smooth in a blender or mash it through a sieve. Cool to room temperature, stirring occasionally. Strain soup through a fine sieve. Stir in heavy cream and refrigerate until well chilled (approximately 6 hours). Serve cold, garnished with chives.

Tips and Techniques
To cook smaller quantities, reduce all ingredients proportionally but not below one-fourth of original amount.

Zucchini Bisque with Tomatoes and Fresh Basil

- 10 mL (2 tsp) olive oil
- 1 tsp garlic, minced
- 1 cup onions, coarsely chopped
- 1 kg (2 lb) zucchini (courgette), cut in 2.5 cm (1 in) chunks
- 375 g (¾ lb) thin-skinned potatoes, scrubbed and cut in 2.5 cm (1 in) chunks
- 500 g (1 lb) fresh Roma tomatoes, diced
- 1 small red capsicum (pepper), seeded and diced
- 750 mL (3 cups) boiling water
- 2 large bay leaves
- ½ cup fresh basil, minced
- 40 mL (2 Tbsp) freshly squeezed lemon juice
- salt to taste

Pressure Cooker
6 L (6 quart)

Serves 6

Heat the oil in pressure cooker. Cook the garlic over medium-high heat, stirring constantly, until lightly browned. Add the onions and continue to cook, stirring frequently, for 1 minute. Add the zucchini (courgette), potatoes, tomatoes, red capsicum (pepper), water (stand back to avoid sputtering oil) and bay leaves.

Lock the lid in place. Over high heat bring to high pressure. Adjust heat to maintain the high pressure and cook for 12 minutes. Let the pressure drop naturally or use the quick-release method. Remove the lid, tilting it away from you to allow any excess steam to escape.

Allow the soup to cool slightly. Remove the bay leaves. Puree the soup in three or four batches in a blender (for a smoother soup) or a food processor.

If serving hot, return to the cooker to reheat. If serving cold, transfer to a large storage container, cover and chill. Just before serving, stir in the basil, lemon juice to taste and salt.

78

Sauces

Eggplant and Mushroom Pasta Sauce

- **4 cups eggplant (aubergine), peeled and cut in 2.5 cm (1 in) cubes**
- **2 cups fresh mushrooms, quartered**
- **1 cup onion, coarsely chopped**
- **2 cloves garlic, minced**
- **1 tsp salt**
- **1 tsp dried basil, crushed**
- **½ tsp dried oregano, crushed**
- **½ tsp dried thyme, crushed**

- **¼ tsp pepper**
- **1 bay leaf**
- **875 g (28 oz) can tomatoes, diced**
- **190 g (6 oz) jar tomato paste**
- **125 mL (½ cups) water**
- **4 cups hot cooked corkscrew (macaroni) pasta**
- **⅓ cup parmesan cheese, grated**

Pressure Cooker
4–6 L (4–6 quart)

Serves 6

In pressure cooker, combine the eggplant, mushrooms, onion, garlic, salt, basil, oregano, thyme, pepper, bay leaf, undrained tomatoes, tomato paste and water.

Lock the lid in place. Over high heat bring to high pressure. Adjust heat to maintain high pressure and cook for 2 minutes. Let the pressure drop using the quick-release method. Remove the lid, tilting it away from you to allow any excess steam to escape.

Serve over hot cooked pasta and sprinkle with cheese.

Bolognese Sauce

- **500 g (1 lb) minced (ground) beef**
- **1 large onion, chopped**
- **1 clove garlic, minced**
- **½ cup celery, chopped**
- **1 green capsicum (pepper), diced**
- **2 tsp salt**
- **250 mL (1 cup) water**
- **420 g (8 oz) can Napoletana sauce**
- **⅛ tsp red chilli pepper flakes**
- **1 tsp parsley flakes**
- **½ tsp oregano**
- **½ tsp sweet basil**
- **¼ tsp thyme**
- **2 tsp sugar**
- **3 drops Tabasco sauce**
- **190 g (6 oz) jar tomato paste**

Pressure Cooker

6 L (6 quart)

Serves 6

Heat pressure cooker and brown beef. Stir in remaining ingredients, except tomato paste.

Lock the lid in place. Over high heat bring to high pressure. Adjust heat to maintain high pressure and cook for 8 minutes. Let the pressure drop using the quick-release method. Remove the lid, tilting it away from you to allow any excess steam to escape.

Stir in tomato paste and simmer, uncovered to desired thickness.

Tip and Techniques
Prepare sauce. Cool, cover and chill up to 24 hours. Reheat before serving or transfer to freezer containers. Seal, label and freeze up to 1 month. Thaw overnight in refrigerator and reheat.

Serve sauce over your choice of al dente pasta or use to make lasagne.

Beef
and
Veal

Beef Roast with Amber Ale

- 1.5–2 kg (3–4 lb) chuck roast, trimmed of visible fat
- salt and pepper
- olive oil and butter for browning
- 1 onion, sliced
- 3 carrots, scrubbed and cut in rounds
- 3–4 stalks celery with leaves, scrubbed and sliced
- 3–4 cloves garlic, minced
- 1 Tbsp beef stock paste/bouillon dissolved in 30 mL (⅛ cup) of water
- 1 bay leaf
- 1–2 tsp thyme
- 1 packet dry onion soup/dip mix
- 1 bottle room temperature amber ale (beer)
- 4 large baking (or russet) potatoes, peeled and cut into 4 cm (1½ in) cubes

Pressure Cooker
6–8 L (6–8 quart)

Serves 6

Apply salt and pepper to outside of roast.

Heat the olive oil and butter in pressure cooker and brown roast on all sides. Remove roast to plate.

Sauté onions, carrots, celery and garlic for a few minutes, adding more oil if needed. Add beef stock/bouillon, bay leaf, thyme and onion soup mix. Stir and then place roast back into pressure cooker. Pour the beer over the roast.

Lock the lid in place. Over high heat bring to high pressure. Adjust heat to maintain high pressure and cook for 45 minutes. Let the pressure drop naturally. Remove the lid, tilting it away from you to allow any excess steam to escape.

Remove roast to warm platter. Cover with foil and let rest. Thicken gravy if needed with milk and cornflour (cornstarch). Serve with oven-roast baked potatoes (see below).

Tip and Techniques

For this recipe peel baking potatoes and cut them into about 4 cm (1¹/₂ in) cubes. Put the potatoes in a glass baking dish. Dot about 3 Tbsp of bacon fat over the potatoes along with a little olive oil. Bake uncovered in a 190°C (375°F) oven for about an hour, being sure to toss the potatoes every 15 minutes after the fat has melted. Cook until golden and crispy.

Barbecue Beef Short Ribs

- **1.5 kg (3 lb) beef short ribs, cut in pieces**
- **2 Tbsp bacon fat**
- **2 Tbsp onion, chopped**
- **1 Tbsp red capsicum (pepper)**
- **250 mL (1 cup) tomato sauce (ketchup)**
- **1 tsp salt**
- **1 tsp celery seed**
- **2 Tbsp brown sugar**
- **40 mL (2 Tbsp) lemon juice**
- **250 mL (1 cup) water**
- **2 tsp dry mustard**

Pressure Cooker

6–8 L (6–8 quart)

Serves 4

Brown the short ribs in the bacon fat in pressure cooker. Pour off excess fat. Mix remaining ingredients and pour over ribs.

Lock the lid in place. Over high heat bring to high pressure. Adjust heat to maintain high pressure and cook for 35 to 40 minutes. Let the pressure drop naturally for 5 minutes, then place under cold running water. Remove the lid, tilting it away from you to allow any excess steam to escape.

Remove ribs and serve.

Beef and Bean Chilli with Roasted Red Capsicum

- 250 g (½ lb) pinto beans, picked over and rinsed, soaked overnight in ample water to cover
- 2 cups onions, coarsely chopped
- 2 large cloves garlic, minced
- 20 mL (1 Tbsp) olive oil
- 1 kg (2¼ lb) top sirloin, minced (ground) coarse
- 1 tsp ground cumin
- 2 tsp chilli powder or more to taste
- 875 g (28 oz) container beef stock (broth)
- 1 large green capsicum (pepper), seeded and diced

- 1 large red capsicum (pepper), seeded and diced
- ¼ tsp ground cinnamon
- 2 dried chipotle (smoked jalapeño) peppers, stemmed, seeded and snipped into bits or ⅛ tsp cayenne pepper
- 185 g (6 oz) jar tomato paste
- 2 stalks celery, chopped
- 1 tsp paprika
- 1 tsp dried oregano
- 5 Tbsp masa harina
- 500–750 mL (2–3 cups) water (to cover)
- 1 tsp salt after cooking

Pressure Cooker

6–8 L (6–8 quart)

Serves 6

Brown onion and garlic in olive oil. Add meat and brown. Drain beans and add to pressure cooker together with remaining ingredients (except salt).

Lock the lid in place. Over high heat bring to high pressure. Adjust heat to maintain high pressure and cook for 22 minutes. Let the pressure drop naturally. Remove the lid, tilting it away from you to allow any excess steam to escape.

Add salt to taste, stirring well.

Serve in a bowl over rice or with crusty, fresh bread

Tips and Techniques
Masa harina is the flour normally used to make tortillas.

Munchen Beef and Cabbage Rolls

- **1 head cabbage**
- **500 g (1 lb) minced (ground) beef**
- **2 tsp salt**
- **¼ Tbsp pepper**
- **1 cup cooked rice**

- **250 mL (1 cup) milk**
- **2 Tbsp brown sugar**
- **1 can Napoletana sauce**
- **60 mL (¼ cup) water**

Pressure Cooker

6–8 L (6–8 quart)

Serves 4

Dip cabbage leaves in hot water for 5 minutes, then dry on paper towel.

Combine beef, salt, pepper, cooked rice, milk and half the sugar and mix well. Place a tablespoon of mixture into centre of each leaf. Roll leaf around mixture and fasten with a toothpick. Stack in pressure cooker. Sprinkle with rest of sugar and add Napoletana sauce and water.

Lock the lid in place. Over high heat bring to high pressure. Adjust heat to maintain high pressure and cook for 12 minutes. Let the pressure drop naturally. Remove the lid, tilting it away from you to allow any excess steam to escape.

Serve on a bed of rice or mashed potato with gravy spooned over the cabbage rolls.

Sunday Beef and Dumplings

Beef
- **2 Tbsp dripping**
- **1.5 kg (3 lb) short ribs of beef or stewing beef**
- **750 mL (3 cups) water**
- **1 packet dry onion soup mix**
- **½ cup celery, diced**
- **¼ Tbsp dried thyme leaves**
- **2 Tbsp plain (all-purpose) flour**
- **60 mL (¼ cup) water**

Dumplings
- **1⅓ cup sifted plain (all-purpose) flour**
- **2 tsp baking powder**
- **2 tsp salt**
- **1 egg**
- **125 mL (½ cup) milk**

Pressure Cooker
6 L (6 quart)

Serves 4

Beef
Melt the dripping in pressure cooker and brown meat. Pour off fat. Add water, onion soup mix, celery and thyme.

Lock the lid in place. Over high heat bring to high pressure. Adjust heat to maintain high pressure and cook for 45 minutes. Let the pressure drop naturally for 2 minutes, then use the quick-release method. Remove the lid, tilting it away from you to allow any excess steam to escape.

Dumplings

Mix flour, baking powder and salt. Beat egg and milk together. Add to flour mixture, stirring until dry ingredients are just moistened.

Grease rack and place over meat in pressure cooker. Drop dumpling batter by heaping tablespoonfuls on rack. Steam dumplings, uncovered, over medium-high heat for 5 minutes.

Cover, without locking the lid, and steam for 5 minutes. Remove dumplings, rack and meat.

Combine flour and water for gravy. Stir into liquid in cooker until gravy is thickened and smooth.

Best served with the traditional roast vegetables and a green such as peas or French beans. Spoon generous amount of gravy over meat.

Boeuf Bourgegnone

- 3 slices bacon, diced
- 500 g (1 lb) boned beef stew meat, cut in 2.5 cm (1 in) pieces
- 2 cloves garlic, minced
- ½ tsp salt
- ¼ tsp freshly ground pepper
- 375 g (12 oz) mushrooms, halved
- 310 g (10 oz) small white pickling onions, peeled (about 12)
- 420 g (14 oz) container beef stock (broth)
- 375 mL (1½ cups) dry red wine, such as cabernet sauvignon
- 1½ tsp dried thyme or 1 sprig fresh thyme
- ¼ cup plain (all-purpose) flour
- 60 mL (¼ cup) water

Pressure Cooker

6 L (6 quart)

Serves 4–6

Cook the bacon in pressure cooker over medium heat until crisp. Transfer bacon with slotted spoon to a medium bowl and set aside. (Don't drain bacon drippings out of cooker.)

Brown beef with garlic, transferring it to a plate. Sprinkle evenly with salt and pepper. Add mushrooms to drippings in pan; cook 3 to 4 minutes or until mushrooms are browned, stirring frequently. Transfer mushrooms to bowl with bacon. Set aside. Return beef with any juices to cooker; add onions, stock (broth), wine and thyme.

Lock the lid in place. Over high heat bring to high pressure. Adjust heat to maintain high pressure and cook for 20 minutes. Let the pressure drop using the quick-release method. Remove the lid, tilting it away from you to allow any excess steam to escape.

Combine flour and water, mixing until smooth. Stir into meat mixture. Stir in reserved mushroom mixture. Bring to the boil, then reduce heat. Simmer uncovered for 10 minutes or until meat is tender and sauce thickens, stirring occasionally. Remove thyme sprig if fresh thyme was used.

Serve over fettuccine, rice or potatoes, if desired.

Beef in Beer with Dijon Gravy

- 250 mL (1 cup) water
- 3 Tbsp Dijon mustard
- 2 large onions, cut in thick slices
- 1 cup carrots, chopped
- 2 large bay leaves

- 1.5–2 kg (3–4 lb) well-trimmed boned beef chuck roast
- 375 mL (12 oz) bottle beer
- salt and freshly ground pepper

Pressure Cooker

6 L (6 quart)

Serves 10

In pressure cooker combine the water and mustard. Stir in onion, carrots and add bay leaves. Add meat and pour beer on top. Do not stir.

Lock the lid in place. Over high heat bring to high pressure. Adjust heat to maintain high pressure and cook for 45 to 55 minutes. Let the pressure drop naturally. Remove the lid, tilting it away from you to allow any excess steam to escape.

Transfer meat to a platter, tent with foil and let stand for 10 minutes before slicing.

Gravy

Strain and de-grease broth. Remove bay leaves. Puree the solids and return the puree and broth to cooker. To concentrate flavours, boil for 3 or 4 minutes. Add additional mustard and salt and pepper to taste.

91

Beef with Tomatoes and Chipotle Peppers

- 1.5 kg (3 lb) chuck roast, cut in large chunks
- salt and black pepper
- oil for searing
- 1 medium onion, chopped
- 5 cloves garlic, minced
- 2 bay leaves
- ½ tsp ground cumin
- 60 mL (¼ cup) red wine
- 2 chipotle (smoked jalapeño), peppers (or jalapeño peppers with seeds removed)
- 875 g (28 oz) can diced tomatoes in juice
- 4 large potatoes, cooked and mashed

Pressure Cooker

4–6 L (4–6 quart)

Serves 6

Season meat well with salt and black pepper. Heat pressure cooker over medium-high heat. Add oil and sear meat until well browned. Add the onion, garlic, bay leaves, cumin, wine, chipotle (smoked jalapeño) peppers and tomatoes with their juice. Stir well, scraping any bits from the bottom of the pan.

Lock the lid in place. Over high heat bring to high pressure. Adjust heat to medium-high and cook for 20 minutes. Let the pressure drop naturally. Remove the lid, tilting it away from you to allow any excess steam to escape.

Remove meat from pressure cooker with a slotted spoon and place alongside serves of mashed potatoes in large bowls. Spoon juices over meat.

Beef Stroganoff

- 60 mL (3 Tbsp) oil
- 1 kg (2 lb) beef stew meat or round steak cut in small cubes
- 2 Tbsp plain (all-purpose) flour
- 1 large onion, chopped
- 1 tsp garlic powder
- 250 mL (1 cup) beef stock (broth)

- 125 g (¼ lb) fresh mushrooms, sliced
- 2 Tbsp tomato paste
- 20 mL (1 Tbsp) Worcestershire Sauce
- 250 mL (1 cup) sour cream
- salt and pepper to taste
- 1 packet egg noodles, cooked

Pressure Cooker

4–6 L (4–6 quart)

Serves 4–6

Heat pressure cooker over medium-high heat. Add oil and brown meat. Add flour and mix well. Stir in onion, garlic powder, stock (broth), mushrooms, tomato paste and Worcestershire Sauce. Blend thoroughly.

Lock the lid in place. Over high heat bring to high pressure. Adjust heat to maintain high pressure and cook for 20 minutes. Let the pressure drop naturally. Remove the lid, tilting it away from you to allow any excess steam to escape.

Add salt and pepper, to taste. Stir in sour cream and blend well. Serve over hot egg noodles.

Bowtie, Beef Tips and Mushrooms

- **40 mL (2 Tbsp) olive oil**
- **750 g (1½ lb) boned beef chuck, cut in 2.5 cm (1 in) cubes**
- **310 g (10 oz) sliced mushrooms, use a variety in large pieces**
- **2 medium brown onions, coarsely chopped**
- **1 clove garlic, minced**

- **4 tsp paprika**
- **⅛ tsp dried thyme, crumbled**
- **125 mL (½ cup) white wine**
- **125 mL (1 cup) beef stock (broth)**
- **½ tsp salt**
- **¼ tsp black pepper**
- **125 mL (½ cup) sour cream**
- **bowtie pasta, cooked**

Pressure Cooker

4–6 L (4–6 quart)

Serves 4–6

Heat the oil in pressure cooker. Brown beef on all sides, in batches. After all meat is removed, add the mushrooms, onions and garlic. Sauté for 6 to 8 minutes or until the onions are soft and the mushrooms have released their liquid. Add the paprika, thyme, wine, stock, salt, pepper and the browned beef.

Lock the lid in place. Over high heat bring to high pressure. Adjust heat to maintain high pressure and cook for 22 minutes. Let the pressure drop naturally. Remove the lid, tilting it away from you to allow any excess steam to escape.

Stir in the sour cream over low heat and cook uncovered for 3 minutes or just until heated through. Do not allow to boil or the sauce will curdle. Serve over bowtie pasta.

Country-style Steak and Kidney Pudding

Filling
- **375 g (¾ lb) stewing steak, cubed**
- **125 g (¼ lb) sheep kidneys**
- **seasoned flour**
- **1 onion, chopped**
- **salt and pepper**
- **310 mL (1¼ cups) beef stock (broth)**

Suet Pastry
- **2 cups self-raising (self-rising) flour**
- **pinch salt**
- **1 cup shredded suet**
- **170 mL (⅔ cup) cold water**

Pressure Cooker
6–8 L (6–8 quart)

Serves 4

Coat the steak and sheep kidney pieces with seasoned flour. Place the meat, onion, salt and pepper and beef stock (broth) into pressure cooker.

Lock the lid in place. Over high heat bring to high pressure. Adjust heat to maintain high pressure and cook for 15 minutes. Let the pressure drop using the quick-release method. Remove the lid, tilting it away from you to allow any excess steam to escape.

Meanwhile, sieve the flour and salt together and stir in the suet. Mix with the cold water to form an elastic dough. Roll two-thirds of the dough into a circle and use it to line a greased 1¼ cup basin. Place the steak and kidney in the middle of the dough with half of the gravy. Dampen edges of the dough. Roll remaining dough into a circle and use it to cover the pudding. Press edges together firmly and trim. Cover securely with a piece of foil (make a pleat in the foil to allow the pudding to rise).

Pour in 60 mL (¼ cups) water into the pressure cooker, position the rack and stand the pudding on top. Close the pressure cooker (do not position the weight OR place on steam if using electric). When steam begins to escape from the vent in the lid, lower the heat and steam gently (without the weight) for 15 minutes. Increase the heat, bring to pressure and cook for 15 minutes. Reduce pressure slowly. Serve the pudding from the basin. Heat remaining gravy and serve separately.

Tips and Techniques
Presteaming is important since this helps give a light result to the suet pastry.

In this dish you can substitute mushrooms for the kidneys.

Blanquette de Veau

- **1 kg (2½ lb) boned veal shoulder or breast, trimmed and cut in 2.5 cm (1 in) cubes**
- **375 mL (1½ cups) chicken stock or bouillon**
- **375 mL (½ cup) dry white wine or vermouth**
- **4 sprigs fresh parsley**
- **1 bay leaf**
- **1 tsp minced garlic**
- **1 large pinch ground allspice**
- **375 g (¾ lb) small white onions (8–10), peeled**
- **375 g (½ lb) mushrooms, quartered**
- **¼ cup plain (all-purpose) flour**
- **¼ cup butter, room temperature**
- **3 large egg yolks**
- **375 g (¾ cup) heavy cream**
- **½ tsp salt or to taste**
- **freshly ground white pepper to taste**
- **egg noodles or rice, cooked**

Pressure Cooker

6 L (6 quart)

Serves 6

Combine the veal, stock, wine, parsley, bay leaf, garlic, allspice, onions and mushrooms in pressure cooker.

Lock the lid in place. Over high heat bring to high pressure. Adjust heat to maintain high pressure and cook for 10 minutes if using veal shoulder, or 15 minutes if using breast. Let the pressure drop naturally or use the quick-release method. Remove the lid, tilting it away from you to allow any excess steam to escape. Remove the parsley sprigs and bay leaf.

While maintaining the sauce at a gentle boil, slowly whisk in the flour-butter mixture (made by mashing the flour into the butter). Lightly beat the egg yolks and cream in a bowl. Slowly whisk 125 mL (½ cup) of the hot sauce into the yolk-cream mixture. The object is to prevent the yolks from curdling from contact with the hot liquid.

Continue whisking an additional 250 mL (1 cup) of the hot sauce into the yolk mixture, about 125 mL (½ cup) at a time. Slowly whisk this mixture back into the blanquette, which should be cooking at just below the simmering point.

Add salt and pepper to taste. Continue to cook below the simmering point until the sauce is thick enough to lightly coat the back of a spoon, about 2 to 3 minutes. Serve immediately in soup plates over egg noodles or rice. Wild rice is especially good.

Tips and Techniques

This dish is traditionally made with the economical breast of veal, which has a uniquely chewy texture. You might prefer the more tender shoulder cut. Either way, it's a satisfying dish of French rural cuisine.

Calabacita: Spanish Steak

- ¼ cup plain (all-purpose) flour
- 2 tsp salt
- ¼ tsp pepper
- 1 kg (2 lb) round steak cut 2.5 cm (1 in) thick
- 3 Tbsp melted dripping
- 1 cup canned tomatoes

- 2¾ cup onions, sliced
- ⅔ cup celery, diced
- 1 large green capsicum (pepper), cut in 6 mm (¼ in) strips
- 1 small clove garlic, chopped
- 40 mL (2 Tbsp) Worcestershire Sauce

Pressure Cooker

6 L (6 quart)

Serves 3

Combine flour, salt and pepper. Cut steak into 6 pieces and tap about half flour mixture onto steak with sharp edge of knife.

Heat the shortening in pressure cooker, without rack, on high heat. Add meat and cook until well browned on both sides. Remove meat and blend remaining flour mixture with shortening.

Place rack in pressure cooker. Add meat, tomatoes, onions, celery, green capsicum (pepper), garlic and Worcestershire Sauce. Cover with lid, leaving pressure control open. When steam escapes, close pressure control and when steam escapes again, adjust heat to cook for 20 to 25 minutes at high pressure. Remove pressure cooker from heat and cool quickly with cold running water. Remove the lid, tilting it away from you to allow any excess steam to escape.

Serve immediately.

Costa Azzura Osso Buco

- 20 mL (1 Tbsp) olive oil
- 1 kg (2 lb) veal shoulder steaks with bone
- 500 g (16 oz) baby carrots
- 500 g (8 oz) small onions
- 1 medium celery stalk, cut crosswise into 1.25 cm (½ in) pieces
- 3 cloves garlic, minced
- ½ tsp salt
- ¼ tsp black pepper
- ¼ tsp dried thyme
- 420 g (14½ oz) diced tomatoes
- 125 mL (½ cup) dry white wine
- 60 mL (¼ cup) water
- ½ cup fresh parsley, loosely packed
- 2 tsp lemon zest
- rice or pasta, cooked

Pressure Cooker

6 L (6 quart)

Serves 6

In pressure cooker heat oil over high heat. Add half the veal and cook until browned on both sides. Transfer veal to bowl; repeat with remaining veal. Add carrots, onions, celery, garlic, salt, pepper and thyme, and stir for 1 minute. Stir in tomatoes, wine and water and heat to boiling over high heat. Return veal to pressure cooker.

Lock the lid in place. Over high heat bring to high pressure. Adjust heat to maintain high pressure and cook for 15 minutes. Let the pressure drop using the quick-release method. Remove the lid, tilting it away from you to allow any excess steam to escape.

In a cup, mix parsley with lemon zest; sprinkle over stew just before serving. Serve over rice or pasta.

Chicago Steak Rollups

- 1 kg (2½ lb) round steak cut 1.25 cm (½ in) thick
- 1 cup plain (all-purpose) flour
- 1 tsp salt
- ½ tsp black pepper
- 1 cup fresh breadcrumbs
- 1¼ cups onion, chopped
- ¼ cup green capsicum (pepper), chopped
- ¼ cup celery, chopped
- 1 tsp salt
- 1 egg, beaten
- 2 Tbsp butter, melted
- ¼ cup butter, for browning
- 250 mL (1 cup) beef stock (broth)
- 375 g (12 oz) jar ready-made beef gravy
- 6 serves potatoes, mashed

Pressure Cooker

4–6 L (4–6 quart)

Serves 6

Cut meat into 8 pieces and pound between two sheets of plastic with smooth side of mallet to 6 mm (¹/₄ in) thickness. Combine flour, salt and pepper. Coat steak with the seasoned flour. Mix together breadcrumbs, onion, green capsicum (pepper) and celery, salt, egg and melted butter. Spread mixture over tops of each piece of steak. Roll up and fasten with wooden picks.

In a frying pan, melt butter. When melted butter is frothing, brown meat rolls on all sides, two at a time. Remove rolls from pan.

Place a rack in the bottom of pressure cooker and add beef stock (broth). Place meat rolls on rack. Lock the lid in place. Over high heat bring to high pressure. Adjust heat to maintain high pressure and cook for 15 minutes. Let the pressure drop using the quick-release method. Remove the lid, tilting it away from you to allow any excess steam to escape.

Transfer meat rolls to warm serving platter. Pour jar of gravy into juices remaining in cooker. You can thicken juices and gravy with cornflour (cornstarch) dissolved in water, or reduce to gravy consistency by cooking and constantly stirring. Serve beef rolls with mashed potatoes covered with gravy.

Chinese Beef, Rice and Baby Meatballs

- **500 g (1 lb) beef, chopped or minced (ground)**
- **4 scallions (green onions, shallots), white bottoms and green tops minced**
- **1 tsp fresh ginger, finely minced (or ½ tsp ground ginger if fresh is not available)**
- **2 whole eggs, lightly beaten**
- **¼ cup water chestnuts, finely minced**
- **2 tsp sugar**
- **80 mL (4 Tbsp) dark soy sauce**
- **60 mL (3 Tbsp) dry sherry**
- **1 cup standard rice, soaked for 30 minutes in warm water**
- **190 mL (¾ cup) dry white wine**
- **60 mL (3 Tbsp) vinegar**
- **2 to 3 drops Tabasco**
- **1 clove garlic, minced**
- **40 mL (2 Tbsp) light soy sauce**
- **5 mL (1 tsp) sesame seed oil**

Pressure Cooker

6 L (6 quart)

Serves 4

In a mixing bowl, lightly but thoroughly work together the beef, scallions (green onions, shallots), ginger, eggs, water chestnuts and a teaspoon of the sugar. Dribble over and blend in the dark soy sauce and up to 2 Tbsp (40 mL) of the sherry. You should have a mixture that remains just firm enough for the balls to hold together. Dip your hands in warm water and shape the mixture into balls about the size of cherry tomatoes. Spread the cup of rice out evenly on a tray and roll each ball into the rice until it is fully covered.

Place the base rack in pressure cooker, pour in the wine and arrange the balls about 6 mm (¼ in) apart. Lock the lid in place. Over high heat bring to high pressure. Adjust heat to maintain high pressure and cook for 6 minutes.

Meanwhile, prepare the sweet and sour sauce. In a mixing bowl, blend together the vinegar, Tabasco, garlic, light soy sauce, sesame seed oil, the remaining tablespoon of sherry and the final teaspoon of sugar. Taste and adjust the flavour by adding a tiny bit more of any or all of the ingredients. Reserve the sauce until the balls are ready.

Let the pressure drop using the quick-release method. Remove the lid, tilting it away from you to allow any excess steam to escape.

Transfer the meatballs to a serving dish and drizzle with sauce. Serve hot.

Sydney Cove Beef Dinner

- **1.5 kg (3 lb) beef brisket**
- **125 mL (½ cup) teriyaki sauce**
- **500 mL (2 cups) water**
- **4 small red potatoes, unpeeled**
- **3 medium carrots, peeled and quartered**
- **2 cups turnips, peeled and sliced**
- **2 large onions, quartered**
- **500 g (1 lb) cabbage, cut in 6–8 wedges**

Pressure Cooker
4–6 L (4–6 quart)

Serves 8

Place beef brisket and teriyaki sauce in a large plastic bag or a glass dish. Refrigerate, turning two or three times, for 1 to 2 days.

Place half of the water and cooking rack or steamer basket in the pressure cooker. Remove brisket from sauce and put on rack or in basket. Discard sauce.

Lock the lid in place. Over high heat bring to high pressure. Adjust heat to maintain high pressure and cook for 40 minutes. Let the pressure drop naturally. Remove the lid, tilting it away from you to allow any excess steam to escape. Remove meat and keep warm.

Add final cup of water to cooker. Place vegetables on rack or in basket. Lock the lid in place. Over high heat bring to high pressure. Adjust heat to maintain high pressure and cook for 3 minutes. Let the pressure drop using the quick-release method. Remove the lid, tilting it away from you to allow any excess steam to escape.

Serve brisket thinly sliced, surrounded by vegetables.

Corned Beef with Vegetables

- 1–1.5 kg (2½–3 lb) corned beef brisket, trimmed of excess fat and rinsed
- 1 L (4 cups) water
- 1 medium onion, peeled, halved and stuck with 4 whole cloves
- 2 stalks celery, cut in thirds
- 4 sprigs fresh parsley
- ½ tsp whole black peppercorns
- 2 bay leaves
- 1 medium head green cabbage, cut in 6 wedges and partially cored (leave enough to retain shape)
- 6 small red potatoes
- 6 medium carrots, peeled and cut in thirds
- horseradish or mustard sauce to serve

Pressure Cooker

4–6 L (4–6 quart)

Serves 8

Place the brisket in pressure cooker. Add water and bring to the boil over high heat. Skim foam from surface. Add onion, celery, parsley, peppercorns and bay leaves.

Lock the lid in place. Over high heat bring to high pressure. Adjust heat to maintain high pressure and cook for 60 minutes. Let the pressure drop using the quick-release method. Remove the lid, tilting it away from you to allow any excess steam to escape.

Remove brisket and vegetables. Add cabbage, potatoes and carrots to broth. Do not fill over two-thirds full. If necessary, remove some broth. Lock the lid in place. Over high heat bring to high pressure. Adjust heat to maintain high pressure and cook for 5 to 7 minutes. Let the pressure drop using the quick-release method. Remove the lid, tilting it away from you to allow any excess steam to escape.

Remove the brisket, cut across the grain into thin slices and arrange down the centre of a warm platter. Using a slotted spoon, remove vegetables from cooker and place around corned beef. Spoon a few tablespoons of broth over the corned beef. Serve with horseradish or mustard sauce.

Far East Pepper Steak

- 20 mL (1 Tbsp) sesame oil
- 40 mL (2 Tbsp) olive oil
- 1 large onion, sliced
- 2 cloves garlic, sliced
- 500 g (1 lb) beef round steak, cut in 3 × 1.25 cm (½ in) strips
- 125 mL (½ cup) beef stock (broth)
- 20 mL (1 Tbsp) sherry
- 1 tsp light brown sugar
- ½ tsp salt
- 1 tsp fresh ginger, grated
- ½ tsp red chilli pepper flakes
- 2 tomatoes, cut in eighths
- 1 green capsicum (pepper), sliced
- 4 green onions (shallots, scallions), coarsely chopped
- 60 mL (3 Tbsp) soy sauce
- 40 mL (2 Tbsp) water
- 2 Tbsp cornflour (cornstarch) or potato starch
- basmati rice, cooked

Pressure Cooker

4–6 L (4–6 quart)

Serves 4

Heat the oils in pressure cooker. Add onion and garlic and sauté for 2 minutes. Add beef strips, stir well, and cook over high heat for 1 minute. Stir in stock (broth), sherry, brown sugar, salt, ginger and red chilli pepper flakes.

Lock the lid in place. Over high heat bring to high pressure. Adjust heat to maintain high pressure and cook for 10 minutes. Let the pressure drop naturally. Remove the lid, tilting it away from you to allow any excess steam to escape.

Stir in tomatoes, green capsicum (pepper) and green onions (shallots, scallions). Lock the lid in place. Over high heat bring to high pressure. Adjust heat to maintain high pressure and cook for 2 minutes. Let the pressure drop using the quick-release method. Remove the lid, tilting it away from you to allow any excess steam to escape.

Combine soy sauce, water and cornflour (cornstarch) or potato starch in a small bowl. Blend until smooth. Gradually add to beef and vegetables, stirring gently until thickened and creamy. Serve beef and vegetables over rice.

French Country Beef

- 750 g (1½ lb) lean boned beef chuck roast, cut in 2.5 cm (1 in) pieces
- 4 medium carrots, peeled and cut in thirds
- 2⅔ cups fresh mushrooms, halved
- 1 medium onion, cut in wedges
- 2 cloves garlic, minced
- 1 bay leaf
- ¾ tsp salt
- ½ tsp dried thyme, crushed
- ¼ tsp black pepper

- 170 mL (⅔ cup) beef stock (broth) or water
- 170 mL (⅔ cup) dry red wine
- 2 Tbsp tomato paste
- 2 Tbsp plain (all-purpose) flour
- 60 mL (¼ cup) water
- ¼ cup snipped fresh parsley
- 6 cups dried pasta, cooked al dente in salt water (try spaghetti, linguine, noodles or other pasta of your choice)

Pressure Cooker

4–6 L (4–6 quart)

Serves 6

In pressure cooker combine beef, carrots, mushrooms, onion, garlic, bay leaf, salt, thyme, black pepper, beef stock (broth) or water, wine and tomato paste.

Lock the lid in place. Over high heat bring to high pressure. Adjust heat to maintain high pressure and cook for 12 minutes. Let the pressure drop naturally. Remove the lid, tilting it away from you to allow any excess steam to escape.

Remove the bay leaf and discard. In a small bowl stir together flour and water until well combined. Add to mixture in cooker. Stir until thickened and bubbly, and then stir for 1 minute more. Stir in parsley. Serve over pasta.

Traditional French Beef

- 40 mL (2 Tbsp) peanut oil
- 1 beef arm (chuck) roast, cut 2.5–5 cm (1–2 in) thick
- 1 large onion, finely diced
- 4 large cloves garlic, finely minced
- 250 mL (1 cup) dry white wine
- 250 mL (1 cup) beef stock (broth)
- 1 tsp salt
- 1 tsp coarse ground black pepper
- ½ tsp crushed thyme leaves
- 250 g (8 oz) fresh mushrooms, thinly sliced
- 500 g (1 lb) baby carrots, washed well
- 4–6 serves rice, steamed
- equal amounts of olive oil or butter and plain (all-purpose) flour for dark brown roux

Pressure Cooker
4–6 L (4–6 quart)

Serves 4–6

Add the peanut oil to a very hot pressure cooker pot. Brown meat on all sides. Remove meat to a platter.

Make roux (see below for instructions). Add onions and garlic to roux and continue stirring and cooking for 3 minutes. Remove pot from burner. Add the wine, stock (broth), salt, pepper and thyme leaves to the pot of roux. Stir until well blended. Return meat to pressure cooker pot.

Lock the lid in place. Over high heat bring to high pressure. Adjust heat to maintain high pressure and cook for 25 minutes. Let the pressure drop naturally. Remove the lid, tilting it away from you to allow any excess steam to escape.

Turn the heat to high to bring the liquid back to a boil. Add the sliced mushrooms and baby carrots. Simmer for just long enough for vegetables to become tender. Cook longer if gravy isn't thick enough. Serve over hot fluffy rice in shallow bowls.

Roux
Make a roux using equal amounts of olive oil and flour, or butter and flour. Use the highest heat possible without burning the ingredients. Stir constantly until the flour and oil mixture becomes a very dark brown. When the roux is the right shade of brown, remove from heat and cool quickly. Store in refrigerator indefinitely to use as needed.

Tips and Techniques
Hot buttered French bread and a green salad completes this dish.

Greek Beef

- 40 mL (2 Tbsp) peanut or canola oil
- 750 g (1½ lb) lean beef chuck, cut in 4 cm (1½ in) cubes
- 310 g (10 oz) small white onions, peeled
- 1 large clove garlic, minced
- 60 mL (¼ cup) port wine
- 60 mL (¼ cup) tomato puree
- 125 mL (½ cup) beef stock (broth)
- 40 mL (2 Tbsp) red wine vinegar
- 125 mL (½ cup) water
- 1½ tsp brown sugar
- 1 bay leaf
- ½ tsp ground cumin
- ½ tsp dried oregano
- ¼ tsp ground cinnamon
- ¼ tsp dried rosemary
- ⅛ tsp ground cloves
- salt and fresh pepper to taste

Pressure Cooker

6 L (6 quart)

Serves 4–6

Heat the oil in pressure cooker. Add half the beef and cook until well browned. Remove with a slotted spoon and set aside. Brown the remaining meat and set aside.

Add onions and garlic to cooker and cook for 1 minute. Add port wine and stir up any browned bits from the bottom of the cooker. Add the remaining ingredients, including the meat, stirring up well so that the tomato puree dissolves.

Lock the lid in place. Over high heat bring to high pressure. Adjust heat to maintain high pressure and cook for 35 minutes. Let the pressure drop naturally. Remove the lid, tilting it away from you to allow any excess steam to escape.

Adjust seasoning and serve.

Tips and Techniques
This stew can be refrigerated for several days or frozen. Reheat on stove or in microwave oven.

Hungarian Goulash

- 1 large onion, coarsely chopped
- 3 beef ribs, trimmed of excess fat
- 1 kg (2 lb) boned sirloin, 2.5 cm (1 in) thick or more, cut in 2.5 cm (1 in) cubes
- 2 Tbsp sweet paprika
- ½ tsp salt or to taste
- 2 Tbsp minced garlic or 2 garlic cloves, finely minced
- 2 × 420 g (14 oz) container beef stock (broth)
- 1 Tbsp cornflour (cornstarch) dissolved in 60 mL (3 Tbsp) cold water
- 4 serves egg noodles, cooked and buttered

Pressure Cooker

6 L (6 quart)

Serves 4

Heat pressure cooker. Add meat and brown well. Remove meat and set aside. Add onions and garlic to pot and sauté until soft but not browned. Return meat to pot and add paprika and salt. Add stock (broth). Taste and add more seasoning if needed.

Lock the lid in place. Bring pressure cooker up to speed and cook on medium heat with medium rocking motion for 30 minutes. Let the pressure drop naturally. Remove the lid, tilting it away from you to allow any excess steam to escape.

Resume heating opened pressure cooker over medium flame. Add cornflour (cornstarch) mixture when goulash begins bubbling and stir gently to thicken. Meanwhile cook egg noodles. Drain and butter noodles. Serve goulash over noodles.

Tuscan Beef Roast

- **40 mL (2 Tbsp) olive oil**
- **1.5–2 kg (3–4 lb) pot roast**
- **1 large onion, finely diced**
- **4 cloves garlic, finely minced**
- **250 mL (1 cup) chianti wine**
- **250 mL (1 cup) beef stock (broth)**
- **4 Tbsp tomato paste**
- **1 Tbsp sugar**
- **1 tsp red chilli pepper flakes**
- **1 Tbsp dried basil leaves**
- **1 tsp salt**
- **4–6 serves linguine, cooked al dente**
- **parmesan or romano cheese**

Pressure Cooker

6–8 L (6–8 quart)

Serves 4–6

Add the olive oil to very hot pressure cooker. Brown the roast on both sides. If your roast is too large to fit in the bottom of your cooker, cut in half to brown. Remove the meat from the pot to a platter and set aside.

Add the onions and garlic to the pot and sauté until they begin to turn brown. Add the rest of the ingredients and stir well to blend into a smooth sauce. Return meat to the pot.

Lock the lid in place. Over high heat bring to high pressure. Adjust heat to maintain high pressure and cook for 20 to 25 minutes. Let the pressure drop naturally. Remove the lid, tilting it away from you to allow any excess steam to escape.

Transfer the roast to a platter, and check the consistency of the sauce. If it is too thick, add a little more stock (broth) or wine and simmer a few minutes longer. Pour sauce into a serving bowl and serve it over some cooked pasta and slices of roast beef. Top with the cheese.

Tips and Techniques
Garlic bread and a tossed green salad is a perfect accompaniment.

Rosemary and Orange Beef

- **1.5–2 kg (3–4 lb) chuck roast, cut in 8 × 8 cm (3 × 3 in) or 10 × 10 cm (4 × 4 in) pieces**
- **40 mL (2 Tbsp) olive oil**
- **1 medium onion, peeled and finely chopped**
- **1 clove garlic, peeled and minced**
- **250 mL (1 cup) beef stock (broth)**
- **250 mL (1 cup) dry red wine**
- **2 Tbsp tomato paste**
- **3 sprigs fresh rosemary**
- **4 strips orange peel, each about 5 cm (2 in) long**
- **1 bouquet garni**
- **¼ tsp black pepper or to taste**

Pressure Cooker
8 L (8 quart)

Serves 8

In pressure cooker brown beef in oil over medium-high heat. Remove with a slotted spoon and set aside. Reduce heat and add onion, garlic and 40 mL (2 Tbsp) of the stock (broth). Cook, stirring, for about 1 minute. And remaining ingredients (except the beef). Stir well to dissolve the tomato paste. Add beef.

Lock the lid in place. Over high heat bring to high pressure. Adjust heat to maintain high pressure and cook for 45 minutes. Let the pressure drop naturally. Remove the lid, tilting it away from you to allow any excess steam to escape.

Remove rosemary sprigs and bouquet garni. Remove beef pieces from stew mixture and set aside in deep serving dish. Pour the base over the beef pieces and serve.

Tips and Techniques
Add a small amount of cornflour (cornstarch) to the stew base to thicken it a little.

Garlic mash potato makes a great addition to this dish.

Dill Pickle Beef Roast

- 40 mL (2 Tbsp) peanut oil
- 1 beef arm (chuck) roast cut about 5 cm (2 in) thick
- 1 large onion, finely chopped
- 4 large cloves garlic, minced
- 250 mL (1 cup) dry white wine
- 250 mL (1 cup) beef stock (broth)
- 1 tsp salt
- ½ tsp coarse ground black pepper
- 2 large Polish dill pickles (sour pickled cucumbers), coarsely chopped
- fresh mushrooms, thinly sliced
- 2 Tbsp plain (all-purpose) flour
- 250 mL (1 cup) sour cream
- 4 serves of either potato pancakes, mashed potatoes or hot buttered noodles

Pressure Cooker
4 L (4 quart)

Serves 4

Add the oil to very hot pressure cooker. Brown beef on both sides. Transfer beef from pot to a platter and set aside.

Add onions and garlic to the pot and sauté until they begin to colour. Add wine, stock (broth), salt, pepper, pickles and mushrooms and stir well to blend into a smooth sauce. Return meat to the pot.

Lock the lid in place. Over high heat bring to high pressure. Adjust heat to maintain high pressure and cook for 25 minutes depending on the size of your meat. Let the pressure drop naturally. Remove the lid, tilting it away from you to allow any excess steam to escape.

Combine the flour and sour cream. Stir some hot liquid from pot into the sour cream mixture, stirring constantly to blend. Pour sour cream mixture into pot and stir to blend. Simmer for 5 minutes while continuing to stir. Serve over potato pancakes, mashed potatoes or hot buttered noodles.

'Ye Olde' Beef Roast

- 1 kg (2–2 ½ lb) beef roast
- plain (all-purpose) flour for dredging
- salt and pepper to taste
- 20 mL (1 Tbsp) vegetable oil
- 1 large onion, cut in chunks
- 3 stalks celery, cut in chunks
- 1 tsp dried thyme
- 1 tsp dried rosemary
- 3 Tbsp honey
- 40 mL (2 Tbsp) cider vinegar
- 125 mL (½ cup) red wine
- 625 mL (2½ cups) vegetable juice blend (such as V8 juice)

Pressure Cooker
6–8 L (6–8 quart)

Serves 4–6

Dust beef with flour that has been seasoned liberally with salt and pepper.

In large pressure cooker heat the oil over high heat. Brown the meat on all sides and remove. Reduce heat to medium. Add the onion and celery and cook until soft, about 1 minute, stirring frequently. Add the thyme, rosemary, honey, vinegar and wine. Bring to the boil. Add the vegetable juice and heat until simmering. Adjust seasoning with salt and pepper. Return the beef to the pot.

Lock the lid in place. Over high heat bring to high pressure. Adjust heat to maintain high pressure and cook for 40 minutes. Remove from heat and let rest for 10 minutes. Release remaining steam through escape valve. Remove the lid, tilting it away from you to allow any excess steam to escape.

Slice meat and serve with the gravy and juices from the cooker.

Beef Roast with Vegetables

- **500 g (1 lb) beef round steak cut 1.25 cm (½ in) thick**
- **40 mL (2 Tbsp) cooking oil**
- **6 large carrots, cut in 5 cm (2 in) pieces**
- **6 whole new potatoes, halved**
- **1 large onion, cut in wedges**
- **1 tsp dried rosemary, crushed**
- **1 tsp dried thyme, crushed**
- **¼ tsp salt**
- **⅛ tsp black pepper**
- **190 mL (¾ cup) beef stock (broth)**
- **2 Tbsp plain (all-purpose) flour**
- **60 mL (3 Tbsp) water**

Pressure Cooker

4–6 L (4–6 quart)

Serves 4

Trim any visible fat from the meat. Set aside.

In pressure cooker heat 20 mL (1 Tbsp) of the oil over medium heat. Cook meat until brown on all sides. Add more oil, if needed. Remove the meat and set aside. Drain off fat and put meat back in cooker. Add carrots, potatoes, onion, rosemary, thyme, salt, black pepper and beef stock (broth).

Lock the lid in place. Over high heat bring to high pressure. Adjust heat to maintain high pressure and cook for 8 minutes. Let the pressure drop naturally. Remove the lid, tilting it away from you to allow any excess steam to escape.

With a slotted spoon remove meat and vegetables to a serving platter and keep warm. In a small mixing bowl stir together flour and water. Stir into broth. Cook until thickened and bubbly, and then cook and stir for 1 minute more. Serve over meat and vegetables.

113

Sauerbraten

- **2–2.5 kg (4–5 lb) chuck roast**
- **salt and pepper to taste**
- **60 mL (3 Tbsp) vegetable oil**
- **250 mL (1 cup) water**
- **125 mL (½ cup) red wine vinegar**
- **125 mL (½ cup) dry red wine or beef stock (broth)**
- **½ cup brown sugar**
- **½ tsp ground cloves**

- **1 tsp salt**
- **2 bay leaves**
- **4 carrots, chopped**
- **2 stalks celery, chopped**
- **2 onions, chopped**
- **2 cloves garlic, minced**
- **1 cup finely crushed Ginger Nut biscuits (Gingersnap cookies)**

Pressure Cooker

8–10 L (8–10 quart)

Serves 8–10

Pat roast dry with paper towel and rub with salt and pepper. Place oil in pressure cooker and brown the roast on all sides.

In small bowl, combine water, vinegar, wine, sugar, cloves, salt and bay leaves. When roast is browned, place the chopped vegetables and Ginger Nut biscuits (Gingersnap cookies) around the meat and pour the vinegar mixture over all.

Lock the lid in place. Over high heat bring to high pressure. Adjust heat to maintain high pressure and cook for 80 minutes. Let the pressure drop naturally. Remove the lid, tilting it away from you to allow any excess steam to escape.

Transfer the meat to a platter and cover with foil. Remove bay leaves. Pour sauce and cooked vegetables into a blender or food processor and blend until smooth. Serve with the sliced beef.

Short Ribs in Coconut Milk

- 4 beef short ribs, thick cut, about 170 g (6 oz) each
- oil for sautéing
- 380 mL (1½ cups) coconut milk
- 20 mL (1 Tbsp) fish sauce

- 1 cinnamon stick
- 4 whole cloves
- 1 knob fresh ginger, 2.5 cm (1 in) length, peeled and finely sliced
- 1 pod star anise

Pressure Cooker
4–6 L (4–6 quart)

Serves 2

Add the oil to pressure cooker and sauté beef until well browned. Add coconut milk, fish sauce, cinnamon stick, cloves, ginger and star anise.

Lock the lid in place. Over high heat bring to high pressure. Adjust heat to maintain high pressure and cook for 40 minutes. Let the pressure drop using the quick-release method. Remove the lid, tilting it away from you to allow any excess steam to escape.

To serve, lift two ribs on to warmed plates and spoon over sauce.

Tips and Techniques
Beef short ribs do exceptionally well in the pressure cooker, emerging nicely defatted, rich and succulent. This recipe is basically a modified version of Vietnamese beef stew. When it first emerges from the cooker, the sauce is thick like caramel. If you chill it overnight, the fat will separate and leave you with a much thinner sauce.

Garlic mash potato makes a great addition to this dish.

Shredded Beef Tacos

- 1 kg (2 lb) boned beef chuck roast cut 5 cm (2 in) thick
- 40 mL (2 Tbsp) cooking oil
- ¾ cup green or red capsicum (pepper), chopped
- ½ cup onion, chopped
- 2 to 3 cloves garlic, minced
- 2 dried chipotle (smoked jalapeño) peppers, seeded and chopped, or 2 jalapeño peppers, seeded and chopped

- 1 Tbsp chilli powder
- 190 mL (¾ cup) beef stock (broth)
- 8 taco shells
- guacamole, optional
- sour cream, optional
- cheddar cheese (American cheese), grated, optional
- lettuce, shredded, optional

Pressure Cooker

4–6 L (4–6 quart)

Serves 8

Trim any visible fat from the meat. Set aside.

In pressure cooker heat 20 mL (1 Tbsp) of the oil over medium heat. Cook meat until brown on all sides. Add more oil, if needed. Remove the meat and set aside. Drain off fat. Place the rack in the pressure cooker. Return the meat to cooker and add the capsicum (pepper), onion, garlic, chipotle or jalapeño peppers, chilli powder and beef stock (broth).

Lock the lid in place. Over high heat bring to high pressure. Adjust heat to maintain high pressure and cook for 35 minutes. Let the pressure drop naturally. Remove the lid, tilting it away from you to allow any excess steam to escape.

Meanwhile, heat taco shells according to package directions. Transfer meat to a cutting board. Using the tines of two forks, pull the meat across the grain to form shreds. With a slotted spoon remove the vegetables to a serving platter. Combine with meat.

Spoon about half a cup of the meat mixture into each taco shell. If desired, top with guacamole, sour cream, cheese and lettuce. Serve tacos.

Porcupine Meatballs

- **500 g (1 lb) minced (ground) beef**
- **1 cup uncooked white rice**
- **1 small onion, finely chopped**
- **salt and pepper to taste**
- **1 egg, beaten with 40 mL (2 Tbsp) of warm water**
- **2 × 420 g (15 oz) cans Campbell's tomato soup**
- **40 mL (2 Tbsp) Worcestershire Sauce**
- **190 mL (¾ cup) water**
- **40 mL (2 Tbsp) tomato sauce (ketchup)**
- **6 serves mashed potatoes and green or yellow vegetables**

Pressure Cooker

4 L (4 quart)

Serves 6

In large mixing bowl, combine meat, rice, onion, salt and pepper and egg. (Makes about 50 small meatballs.) Place meatballs in pressure cooker.

In separate bowl, mix soup, Worcestershire Sauce, water and tomato sauce (ketchup). Pour over meatballs. Roll meatballs in sauce to coat.

Secure lid of pressure cooker. Place over medium-high heat. When cooker starts to sizzle, lower heat to medium for 9 minutes. Remove from heat, wait 5 minutes. Let the pressure drop using the quick-release method. Remove the lid, tilting it away from you to allow any excess steam to escape.

Serve with mashed potatoes and a green or yellow vegetable.

New Mexico Tomato Brisket

- 1 onion, minced
- 2 cloves garlic, minced
- 1 serrano chilli, seeded and minced
- 1½ Tbsp brown sugar
- 1 Tbsp chilli powder
- 20 mL (1 Tbsp) apple cider vinegar
- ½ tsp ground cumin

- 1 tsp salt
- 40 mL (2 Tbsp) vegetable oil
- 1.5 kg (3 lb) beef brisket
- 300 g (10 oz) can diced tomatoes, undrained
- 1 onion, cut in wedges

Pressure Cooker

8 L (8 quart)

Serves 8

Combine onion, garlic, chilli, sugar, chilli powder, apple cider vinegar, cumin and salt in a small bowl. Rub this mixture over all sides of beef brisket, then transfer meat to a glass dish. Cover and marinate in refrigerator for 24–36 hours.

Heat oil in a pressure cooker over medium-high heat. Cook meat uncovered for 6 to 8 minutes, turning to brown all sides. Add tomatoes, lifting meat to let some tomatoes fall underneath. Add onion wedges.

Lock the lid in place. Over high heat bring to high pressure. Adjust heat to maintain high pressure and cook for 60 minutes. Let the pressure drop naturally or use the quick-release method. Remove the lid, tilting it away from you to allow any excess steam to escape.

Slice meat across the grain. Serve pan juices with the meat.

Milwaukee-style Spareribs

- **1 kg (2½ lb) spareribs**
- **250 mL (1 cup) beer**
- **80 mL (⅓ cup) honey**
- **10 mL (2 tsp) lemon juice**
- **1 tsp salt**
- **1½ tsp dry mustard**

- **½ tsp ground ginger**
- **⅛ tsp nutmeg**
- **20 mL (1 Tbsp) cooking oil**
- **2 tsp cornflour (cornstarch)**
- **40 mL (2 Tbsp) cold water**

Pressure Cooker

6–8 L (6–8 quart)

Serves 2–3

Cut spareribs into serving pieces; place in shallow dish. Combine beer, honey, lemon juice, salt, dry mustard, ginger and nutmeg. Pour over ribs. Cover and chill for several hours or, preferably, overnight.

Heat pressure cooker. Add the oil and brown spareribs. Pour 125 mL (½ cup) marinade into pressure cooker.

Lock the lid in place. Over high heat bring to high pressure. Adjust heat to maintain high pressure and cook for 15 minutes. Let the pressure drop naturally. Remove the lid, tilting it away from you to allow any excess steam to escape.

Remove ribs to serving platter.

Thicken gravy by mixing cornflour (cornstarch) and cold water and stirring into simmering juices. When suitably thickened, spoon gravy over ribs.

Steak and Onions

- **1 kg (2½ lb) round steak**
- **20 mL (1 Tbsp) olive oil**
- **320 g (10½ oz) can condensed cream of mushroom soup**
- **2 large onions, sliced 6 mm (¼ in) thick**
- **125 mL (½ cup) beef stock (broth)**
- **salt and pepper to taste**
- **½ tsp garlic powder**
- **2 Tbsp dried chives**
- **4 serves steamed rice**

Pressure Cooker

6–8 L (6–8 quart)

Serves 4

Cut steak into serving size pieces. Heat the oil in hot pressure cooker. Add the steak a few pieces at a time and brown on both sides. Remove from pot and set aside. Lightly brown onion slices in drippings left from steak. Remove from pot.

Mix soup, stock (broth), salt, pepper, garlic powder and chives together. Place steak pieces back into pot and put onions on top of meat. Pour soup mixture over meat and onions.

Lock the lid in place. Over high heat bring to high pressure. Adjust heat to maintain high pressure and cook for 15 minutes. Let the pressure drop naturally or use the quick-release method. Remove the lid, tilting it away from you to allow any excess steam to escape.

Serve steak and onions with the gravy over hot fluffy rice.

St Patrick's Day Corned Beef Dinner

- 250 mL (1 cup) water
- 1.5 kg (3 lb) corned beef brisket
- 4 small white turnips, peeled and halved
- 500 g (1 lb) small carrots
- 1 large sweet onion, cut in eighths
- 8 small red potatoes, halved
- 500 g (1 lb) green cabbage, cut in eighths

Sauce
- 420 g (14 oz) container chicken stock (broth)
- 2 Tbsp horseradish
- 2 Tbsp German mustard

Pressure Cooker
6–8 L (6–8 quart)

Serves 8

Place the cooking rack on the bottom of the pressure cooker and add the water. Trim the corned beef and place it on the rack.

Lock the lid in place. Over high heat bring to high pressure. Adjust heat to maintain high pressure and cook for 35 minutes. Let the pressure drop using the quick-release method. Remove the lid, tilting it away from you to allow any excess steam to escape.

Transfer the corned beef onto a platter and discard the liquid in the cooker. Replace the cooking rack and place the turnips, carrots, onion wedges, potatoes and cabbage in the pressure cooker. Place the corned beef on top. Combine the chicken stock (broth), horseradish and mustard, mix well, and pour over the vegetables and meat.

Lock the lid in place. Over high heat bring to high pressure. Adjust heat to maintain high pressure and cook for 8 minutes. Let the pressure drop using the quick-release method. Remove the lid, tilting it away from you to allow any excess steam to escape.

Arrange meat and vegetables on a warm serving platter. Thicken sauce, if desired, by boiling rapidly, uncovered. Season to taste with salt and pepper. Pour sauce over meat and vegetables. Serve additional horseradish and mustard(s) on the side.

Tips and Techniques
This cooking time is suitable for a square-cut brisket. A thicker cut of the same weight may take 5 to 10 minutes longer to cook.

You cannot always get a corned beef with the seasonings, and this recipe will work just as well without them, as the sauce and vegetables flavour the meat.

Traditional Beef Stew

- 40 mL (2 Tbsp) olive or vegetable oil
- 1 kg (2½ lb) beef roast, trimmed of fat and cut in 5 cm (2 in) cubes
- sea salt (Kosher salt) and fresh coarse ground pepper
- 1 cup plain (all-purpose) flour
- 2 Tbsp butter
- 2 Tbsp molasses (black treacle)
- 2 medium onions, cut in sixths
- 5 cloves garlic, minced
- 1 Tbsp tomato paste
- 2 L (8 cups) beef stock (broth), homemade or preprepared
- ¼ cup snipped fresh parsley
- 6 sprigs fresh thyme or ½ tsp dried thyme
- 2 bay leaves
- 1 tsp salt
- 1 tsp pepper
- 625 g (1¼ lb) medium red potatoes, quartered
- 4 medium carrots, cut in 2.5 cm (1 in) pieces
- 2 stalks celery, cut in 2.5 cm (1 in) pieces
- 420 g (14 oz) can peeled tomatoes, lightly crushed, with juice
- 20 mL (1 Tbsp) red wine vinegar
- salt and pepper to taste

Pressure Cooker

6–8 L (6–8 quart)

Serves 6–8

In pressure cooker heat oil until pan is hot, but not smoking. Season beef generously with salt and pepper and dredge in flour. Sauté the meat in three separate batches, uncovered, stirring only occasionally, until well browned. Meat should cover bottom of pot without layering to allow meat to brown. Transfer the beef to a plate.

Return pot to stove and melt butter over medium-high heat. Add onions and cook, stirring until lightly browned, for about 5 minutes; do not burn or they will be bitter. Add garlic and stir for about 1 minute. Add tomato paste and cook, stirring, until lightly browned, about 1 minute.

Return the beef to the pot, add the beef stock (broth) and bring to a simmer. Using a piece of kitchen twine, tie the parsley, thyme and bay leaves up in a piece of cheesecloth, and put in pot. Season with salt and pepper.

Lock the lid in place. Over high heat bring to high pressure. Adjust heat to maintain high pressure and cook for 30 minutes. Let the pressure drop using the quick-release method. Remove the lid, tilting it away from you to allow any excess steam to escape.

Add potatoes, carrots, celery and tomatoes, close lid and lock down. Bring cooker back to high pressure and cook for 6 minutes. Let the pressure drop using the quick-release method. Remove the lid, tilting it away from you to allow any excess steam to escape.

Stir in red wine vinegar and season with salt and pepper to taste. Serve in bowls immediately.

Tips and Techniques
This dish is excellent with a salad and some warmed Italian bread with butter on the side.

Scandinavian Beef Roast

- **750 g (3 lb) boned chuck roast**
- **½ tsp ground nutmeg**
- **½ tsp ground ginger**
- **1 tsp ground cinnamon**
- **salt and pepper to taste**
- **20 mL (1 Tbsp) cooking oil**

- **2 medium brown onions, thinly sliced**
- **1 clove garlic, crushed**
- **½ cup light brown sugar**
- **125 mL (½ cup) dry red wine**
- **250 mL (1 cup) water**
- **4 serves egg noodles**

Pressure Cooker

4 L (4 quart)

Serves 4

Combine nutmeg, ginger, cinnamon, salt and pepper, and sprinkle over both sides of roast.

In hot pressure cooker add oil and brown meat well on all sides. Add onions and garlic. Dissolve brown sugar in red wine and water, and pour over meat.

Lock the lid in place. Over high heat bring to high pressure. Adjust heat to maintain high pressure and cook for 35 minutes. Let the pressure drop naturally. Remove the lid, tilting it away from you to allow any excess steam to escape.

Serve with noodles.

Kylie Jayne's Texas Barbecue Beef Roast

- 125 mL (½ cup) tomato sauce (ketchup)
- ½ cup apricot preserve
- ¼ cup dark brown sugar
- 60 mL (¼ cup) white vinegar
- 125 mL (½ cup) teriyaki sauce or light soy sauce
- 1 tsp crushed dried red chilli pepper
- 1 tsp dry mustard
- ¼ tsp pepper
- 2 kg (4 lb) eye of round, bottom round, boned chuck roast or pork loin roast
- 375 mL (1½ cups) water for beef, or 500 mL (2 cups) water for pork
- 1 large onion, sliced

Pressure Cooker

6–8 L (6–8 quart)

Serves 8–10

Prepare barbecue sauce by mixing together tomato sauce (ketchup), apricot preserve, brown sugar, vinegar, teriyaki, red chilli pepper, dry mustard and pepper. Place roast and barbecue sauce in a large plastic bag or glass dish. Refrigerate overnight.

Place the water and cooking rack in pressure cooker. Cover rack with half of the sliced onions. Remove roast from sauce (reserve sauce). Place roast over onions and cover with remaining onions.

Lock the lid in place. Over high heat bring to high pressure. Adjust heat to maintain high pressure and cook for the following doneness: 8 to 10 minutes per 500 g (1 lb) for rare; 10 to 12 minutes per 500 g (1 lb) for medium; and at least 12 to 15 minutes per 500 g (1 lb) for well-done meat. Cook pork 15 minutes per 500 g (1 lb) until well done. Let the pressure drop naturally. Remove the lid, tilting it away from you to allow any excess steam to escape.

Meanwhile, place reserved barbecue sauce in a saucepan and simmer until reduced by about half, stirring occasionally. Remove roast and keep warm. Discard cooking water or use for making soup. Puree onions in a blender or food processor and add to reduced barbecue sauce. Serve sauce with sliced roast.

Veal and Mushroom Cream

- **750 g (1½ lb) veal shoulder cut in cubes**
- **seasoned flour**
- **¼ cup butter**
- **1 onion, chopped**
- **1 clove garlic, crushed**

- **pinch dried thyme**
- **310 mL (1¼ cups) dry cider**
- **salt and pepper**
- **2 cups sliced mushrooms**
- **190 mL (¾ cup) cream**
- **watercress for garnish**

Pressure Cooker

4 L (4 quart)

Serves 4

Coat the veal with seasoned flour. Heat the butter in pressure cooker and lightly brown the veal. Add the onion and garlic, and cook for a further minute. Add the thyme, cider and salt and pepper, then stir in the mushrooms.

Lock the lid in place. Over high heat bring to high pressure. Adjust heat to maintain high pressure and cook for 12 minutes. Let the pressure drop naturally. Remove the lid, tilting it away from you to allow any excess steam to escape.

Stir in the cream just before serving. Garnish with watercress.

Veal Paprika

- 1 kg (2 lb) boned veal shoulder, trimmed and cut in bite-size cubes
- 3 Tbsp plain (all-purpose) flour
- 2 Tbsp butter, divided
- 20 mL (1 Tbsp) oil
- 1 clove garlic, minced
- 2 shallots (green onions, scallions), minced, optional
- 2 medium onions, coarsely chopped
- 125 mL (½ cup) dry white wine or vermouth
- 125 mL (½ cup) chicken stock or bouillon
- 1 Tbsp paprika
- 1 bay leaf
- 1 tsp dried thyme
- 1 Tbsp tomato paste
- ½ tsp salt or to taste
- freshly ground black pepper to taste
- ¼ cup fresh parsley, minced
- 250 mL (1 cup) sour cream or plain yoghurt

Pressure Cooker
6–8 L (6–8 quart)

Serves 6

Rinse the veal, pat dry and dredge in flour, pressing the flour into the veal with the heel of your hand. Shake off extra flour. In pressure cooker heat 1 Tbsp butter and the oil. Over medium heat, brown the veal on all sides in 2 to 3 batches. Remove the browned veal and set aside on a platter.

Add the remaining butter to the cooker and sauté the garlic, shallots (green onions, scallions), if desired, and onions until the onions are soft; about 2 to 3 minutes. Pour in the wine, and while cooking for 1 to 2 minutes over a medium-high flame, scrape up any browned bits from the bottom of the pot. Add the reserved veal and any juices that have collected in the platter, the stock, paprika, bay leaf, thyme, tomato paste and salt and pepper to taste.

Lock the lid in place. Over high heat bring to high pressure. Adjust heat to maintain high pressure and cook for 10 minutes. Let the pressure drop naturally or use the quick-release method. Remove the lid, tilting it away from you to allow any excess steam to escape.

Remove the bay leaf and stir in the parsley and sour cream. Adjust the seasoning before serving.

Tips and Techniques
For pressure cookers requiring a 500 mL (2 cup) liquid minimum to come up to pressure, add an additional cup of stock. When the veal is done, remove it with a slotted spoon and boil the sauce vigorously until reduced. Return the veal to the cooker and stir in the parsley and sour cream.

Veal with Dumplings

Veal
- **750 g (1½ lb) veal cut in 5 cm (2 in) cubes**
- **3 Tbsp dripping**
- **1 tsp salt**
- **pinch pepper**
- **½ bay leaf**
- **375 mL (1½ cups) water**
- **4 medium onions**
- **4 medium carrots**

Dumplings
- **1⅓ cups plain (all-purpose) flour, sifted**
- **2 tsp baking powder**
- **1 tsp salt**
- **1 egg**
- **125 mL (½ cup) milk**

Gravy
- **2 Tbsp plain (all-purpose) flour**
- **80 mL (⅓ cup) cold water**
- **250 mL (1 cup) boiling stock from pressure cooker juices**

Pressure Cooker
4–6 L (4–6 quart)

Serves 4

Veal
In pressure cooker brown meat in hot dripping. Add salt, pepper, bay leaf and water.

Lock the lid in place. Over high heat bring to high pressure. Adjust heat to maintain high pressure and cook for 8 minutes. Let the pressure drop naturally. Remove the lid, tilting it away from you to allow any excess steam to escape.

Add onions and carrots. Wipe inside of lid with paper towels to remove excess moisture. Lock the lid in place. Over high heat bring to high pressure. Adjust heat to maintain high pressure and cook for 8 minutes. Let the pressure drop using the quick-release method. Remove the lid, tilting it away from you to allow any excess steam to escape.

Dumplings

Sift flour with baking powder and salt. In a separate bowl, beat egg, then add milk. Combine mixtures.

Drop dumpling batter from spoon into the simmering juices. Cook uncovered for 5 minutes. Cover, steam for 5 minutes without control on vent. Remove dumplings to a hot platter.

Gravy

Thicken gravy by blending flour with cold water until smooth. Gradually add boiling stock, stirring constantly. Slowly add this mixture to the rest of the gravy, stirring constantly. Cook over medium heat, stirring, until gravy is smooth and thickened.

Brunswick Beef

- 2 slices bacon, diced
- 3 Tbsp plain (all-purpose) flour
- 1 tsp salt
- ½ tsp pepper
- pinch cayenne pepper
- 1.5 kg (3 lb) rabbit or chicken, cut up with giblets
- 3 onions, sliced
- 750 mL (3 cups) water
- 4 ripe tomatoes, peeled and chopped
- 1 red capsicum (pepper), chopped
- ½ tsp dried thyme
- 2 cups fresh lima beans
- 2 cups corn kernels
- 250 g (½ lb) okra, sliced
- 2 Tbsp fresh parsley, chopped
- 20 mL (1 Tbsp) Worcestershire Sauce

Pressure Cooker

6 L (6 quart)

Serves 4

In pressure cooker fry bacon. Remove bacon and set aside. Combine flour, salt, pepper, cayenne pepper and dredge rabbit or chicken. Brown the pieces in the bacon fat with the onions. Add water, tomatoes, red capsicum (pepper), thyme, lima beans, corn and okra.

Lock the lid in place. Over high heat bring to high pressure. Adjust heat to maintain high pressure and cook for 15 minutes. Let the pressure drop using the quick-release method. Remove the lid, tilting it away from you to allow any excess steam to escape.

Add the bacon, Worcestershire Sauce and parsley. Cover and cook for 10 minutes, not under pressure. Let stand, covered, for 10 to 15 minutes to blend flavours.

To serve, spoon on to warmed plates, ensuring that rabbit or chicken pieces are distributed evenly.

Tips and Techniques
Although not technically a beef recipe, this recipe has been included in this section as rabbit is, of course, known as underground beef!

Pork

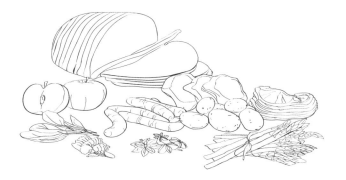

'Barbecued' Spareribs

- **40 mL (2 Tbsp) safflower oil or olive oil**
- **2.5 kg (5 lb) spareribs (about 3–4 ribs each) cut in servings**
- **170 mL (⅔ cup) cider vinegar**
- **60 mL (3 Tbsp) soy sauce**
- **125 mL (½ cup) dry sherry**
- **250 mL (1 cup) water**

- **250 mL (1 cup) tomato sauce (ketchup)**
- **1 Tbsp dry mustard**
- **⅓ cup brown sugar**
- **1 Tbsp garlic, minced**
- **½ tsp salt or to taste**
- **1 green capsicum (pepper), diced**
- **1 cup onion, coarsely chopped**

Pressure Cooker

6 L (6 quart)

Serves 4

In the pressure cooker heat 20 mL (1 Tbsp) of oil. Over high heat, brown the spareribs well in several batches, about 3 to 5 minutes on the meaty side and 1 to 2 minutes on the fatty side. Add more oil as needed. (Use a large frying pan in addition to the cooker to speed up this process.)

In a bowl, combine the remaining ingredients for the sauce. When the ribs are browned, tip off any excess fat and pour the sauce into the cooker, taking care to scrape up any browned bits that are sticking to the bottom of the pot. Add the ribs, and stir to coat well with the sauce. Don't be concerned if some of the ribs aren't actually sitting in the sauce.

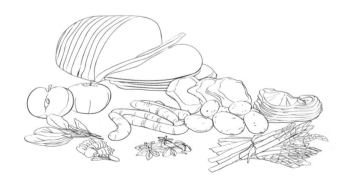

Lock the lid in place. Over high heat bring to high pressure. Adjust heat to maintain high pressure and cook for 12 minutes. Let the pressure drop using the quick-release method. Remove the lid, tilting it away from you to allow any excess steam to escape.

The pork is cooked if the meat can be separated easily from the bone when poked with a fork. Transfer the ribs to a serving platter. If the sauce is too thin, boil vigorously over high heat until it reaches a glazing consistency. Adjust the seasonings and pour over the ribs. Serve immediately.

Tips and Techniques

Add some Tabasco or chilli peppers for a sauce that's fiery hot, or for a milder sauce substitute your favourite barbecue sauce for the tomato sauce (ketchup).

For ribs on a griller (broiler), skip the browning and cook in the sauce as directed, then grill for 2 to 3 minutes on each side, basting frequently with additional sauce. For ribs under a griller, skip the browning and cook in the sauce as directed, then set the cooked ribs under a griller to achieve a crispy crust.

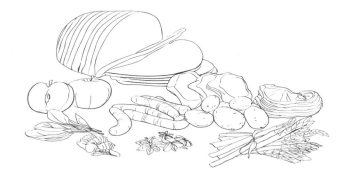

'Barbecued' Pork with Sweet Potatoes

- 190 mL (¾ cup) chilli sauce
- 2 Tbsp spicy mustard or Dijon mustard
- 40 mL (2 Tbsp) Worcestershire Sauce
- 1 Tbsp maple syrup or brown sugar
- 1 kg (2 lb) pork shoulder, cut in 2 cm (¾ in) cubes
- 20 mL (1 Tbsp) olive oil
- 2 cups onion, coarsely chopped
- 2 large green capsicums (peppers), seeded and diced
- 125 mL (½ cup) water
- 1 kg (2½ lb) sweet potatoes, peeled and cut in 5 cm (2 in) cubes
- salt to taste
- black pepper, freshly ground, to taste

Pressure Cooker
6 L (6 quart)

Serves 4

In a large bowl, blend the chilli sauce, mustard, Worcestershire Sauce and maple syrup. Add the pork and toss to coat. Set aside for a few moments at room temperature or marinate, covered, in the refrigerator overnight or up to 16 hours.

In pressure cooker heat the oil over medium-high heat. Cook the onions, stirring frequently, for 2 minutes. Add the green capsicums (peppers) and cook for another minute. Stir in the water, taking care to scrape up any browned bits sticking to the bottom of the cooker. Cut four pieces of sweet potato into thin slices and add them to the broth. Transfer the sauce-coated pork plus any unabsorbed marinade to the cooker. Do not stir. Set the remaining sweet potatoes on top.

Lock the lid in place. Over high heat bring to high pressure. Adjust heat to maintain high pressure and cook for 10 minutes. Let the pressure drop using the quick-release method. Remove the lid, tilting it away from you to allow any excess steam to escape.

If the pork is not sufficiently tender, remove the large chunks of sweet potatoes and return to high pressure for 5 minutes more. If you wish, cut the sweet potatoes into smaller chunks. Stir the stew well. Add salt and freshly ground pepper. Serve in large shallow bowls.

Tips and Techniques
In this dish, a quickly made barbecue sauce infuses the pork with a slightly sweet irresistible flavour. The sweet potatoes dissolve and thicken the sauce.

Black Beans and Sausage (Jeijoada)

- **500 g (1 lb) dried black beans**
- **1 hot Portuguese sausage (chorizo)**
- **1 mild Polish sausage**
- **250 g (½ lb) salt pork or slab bacon, diced**
- **1 onion, finely chopped**
- **6 cloves garlic, smashed with flat of knife**
- **salt to taste**
- **60 mL (3 Tbsp) oil**
- **6 serves steamed rice**

Pressure Cooker

4 L (4 quart)

Serves 6

Soak beans overnight covered in cold water. Discard water and put beans in pressure cooker with clean water to cover. Add sausages (whole) and bacon or salt pork.

Lock the lid in place. Over high heat bring to high pressure. Adjust heat to maintain high pressure and cook for 15 minutes. Let the pressure drop naturally. Remove the lid, tilting it away from you to allow any excess steam to escape.

Add more water to just cover beans. Add the onion, garlic, salt and oil, which have been sautéed until lightly browned.

Lock the lid in place. Over high heat bring to high pressure. Adjust heat to maintain high pressure and cook for 20 minutes. Let the pressure drop using the quick-release method. Remove the lid, tilting it away from you to allow any excess steam to escape.

Serve hot, over rice. The beans will be soupy.

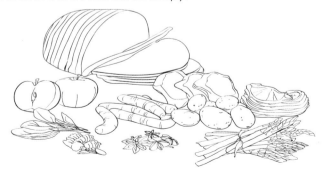

Crispy Pork with Avocado and Tomato Salsa

Pork

- **2 kg (4lb) boned pork ribs (boil in salted water for 30 minutes and drain well to remove excess fat)**
- **500 mL (2 cups) chicken stock (broth)**
- **375 mL (1½ cups) orange juice**
- **1 tsp orange zest**
- **6 cloves garlic, mashed, peeled and finely minced**
- **1 tsp sea salt (Kosher salt)**
- **60 mL (¼ cup) brandy**
- **4 tortillas, to serve**

Salsa

- **2 ripe avocados, diced**
- **2 large ripe tomatoes, seeded and diced**
- **1 tsp ground cumin**
- **60 mL (3 Tbsp) lime juice**
- **30 mL (1½ Tbsp) olive oil**
- **2 cloves garlic, finely minced**
- **2 fresh or bottled jalapeño peppers, finely minced**

Pressure Cooker

6 L (6 quart)

Serves 4

Pork

Cut pork pieces into thirds. In hot pressure cooker combine pork, chicken broth, orange juice, orange zest, garlic and salt.

Lock the lid in place. Over high heat bring to high pressure. Adjust heat to maintain high pressure and cook for 30 minutes. Let the pressure drop naturally. Remove the lid, tilting it away from you to allow any excess steam to escape.

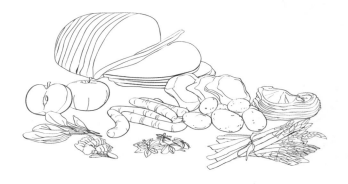

Remove meat from pressure cooker. Cook liquid until it has almost evaporated. Stir often and keep at low boil. Stir in brandy and return meat to pot. Stirring often, keep at a low boil until liquid evaporates and meat browns and begins to get crispy, about 15 minutes.

Cool meat slightly and tear into strips, return to pot. Using two forks, shred meat. Transfer to a bowl. Serve with warm flour tortillas and avocado and tomato salsa.

Salsa
Mix everything together, cover and refrigerate until ready to serve.

Tips and Techniques
This pork dish can be made the day before. After meat is finally cooked, cool, cover and refrigerate. To warm, add 40 mL (2 Tbsp) water to a frying pan, cover and reheat pork over medium-low heat, stirring every 5 minutes.

You can make a delicious tortilla wrap by filling a warm flour tortilla with meat and salsa, fold half of tortilla over filling, fold in sides a good 2.5 cm (1 in) and roll tortilla over.

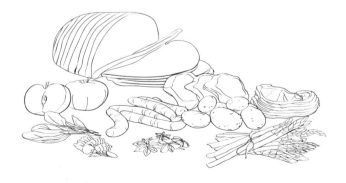

Carolina Barbecue Pork

- 1½ cups brown onion, chopped
- 435 g (14½ oz) can diced tomatoes
- 1 Tbsp molasses (black treacle)
- ½ cup firmly packed dark brown sugar
- 60 mL (3 Tbsp) cider vinegar
- 2 Tbsp coarse Dijon mustard
- 20 mL (1 Tbsp) Worcestershire Sauce
- ¾ tsp celery salt
- 1¼ tsp ground black pepper
- 4 cloves garlic, peeled and minced
- 1.5 kg (3 lb) pork shoulder roast, trimmed and cut in strips, bone reserved
- 2 Tbsp tomato paste
- 40 mL (2 Tbsp) pure maple syrup
- ½ tsp mesquite-flavoured liquid smoke
- 6 serves green salad

Pressure Cooker

6 L (6 quart)

Serves 6

Combine the onion, tomatoes, molasses (black treacle), brown sugar, cider vinegar, Dijon mustard, Worcestershire Sauce, celery salt and half of the pepper in the pressure cooker. Stir in the garlic. Add the pork strips and the reserved bone.

Lock the lid in place. Over high heat bring to high pressure. Adjust heat to maintain high pressure and cook for 25 minutes. Let the pressure drop naturally. Remove the lid, tilting it away from you to allow any excess steam to escape.

Discard bone and break up the meat. Mix in the tomato paste, maple syrup, liquid smoke and remaining half of the pepper. Bring sauce to the boil for approximately 10 minutes or until thickened.

This is delicious served with a green salad.

Tips and Techniques
When cooled, shred the pork and use as a filling in buttered rolls.

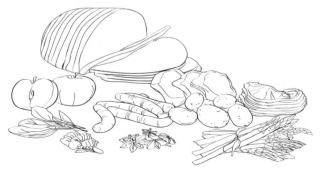

Chop Suey

- **20 mL (1 Tbsp) canola oil or olive oil**
- **500 g (1 lb) round steak, diced in 1.25 cm (½ in) cubes**
- **500 g (1 lb) lean pork, such as pork loin, diced in 1.25 cm (½ in) cubes**
- **salt and pepper to taste**
- **2 large onions, diced in small pieces**
- **60 mL (3 Tbsp) soy sauce**
- **2 tsp molasses (black treacle)**
- **2 cups celery, diced in small pieces**
- **1 can Chinese vegetables**
- **1 can bean sprouts**
- **4 serves steamed rice**

Pressure Cooker

6 L (6 quart)

Serves 4

In pressure cooker heat the oil and brown meat. Season with salt and pepper. Add onion, soy sauce, molasses, celery and liquid drained from canned vegetables.

Lock the lid in place. Over high heat bring to high pressure. Adjust heat to maintain high pressure and cook for 8 minutes. Let the pressure drop naturally. Remove the lid, tilting it away from you to allow any excess steam to escape.

Add vegetables and bean sprouts and simmer, stirring occasionally while you prepare rice for serving.

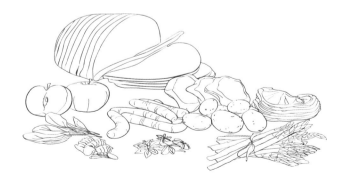

Ham and Pineapple Slice

- 1 tsp bacon fat
- 1.5–2 kg (3–4 lb) ham, sliced
- cloves, if desired
- 250 mL (1 cup) water
- 1 Tbsp brown sugar
- 375 g (8 oz) canned pineapple

Pressure Cooker

6 L (6 quart)

Serves 6–8

Heat pressure cooker and add bacon fat. Sear ham on both sides until golden brown. Place ham on plate and score fat in diamond shapes with sharp knife. Insert cloves in ham. Place ham on rack in cooker. Add water, brown sugar and pineapple.

Lock the lid in place. Over high heat bring to high pressure. Adjust heat to maintain high pressure and cook for 3 minutes. Let the pressure drop naturally. Remove the lid, tilting it away from you to allow any excess steam to escape.

Cook syrup until thick in open cooker and pour over ham.

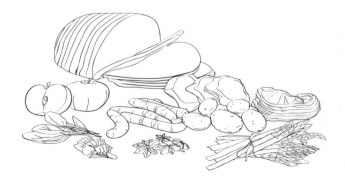

Mexican-style Pork

- 80–120 mL (4–6 Tbsp) oil
- 1 kg (2½ lb) pork shoulder, cut in 4 cm (1½ in) cubes
- 1 cup onion, coarsely chopped
- 2–8 jalapeño peppers or other fresh chillies, seeded and cut in strips
- 420 g (14 oz) can tomatoes, coarsely chopped, with juice
- 60 mL (¼ cup) chicken stock (broth)
- 1 tsp minced garlic
- 2 tsp ground cinnamon
- ¼–½ tsp ground cloves
- ½ tsp dried oregano
- ½ tsp salt or to taste
- ½ tsp ground black pepper
- ⅔–1 cup sliced pimiento-stuffed green olives
- ½ cup crushed pineapple
- ½ cup prunes cut in half
- 2 Tbsp plain (all-purpose) flour, for gravy if desired
- 2 Tbsp room-temperature butter, for gravy if desired

Pressure Cooker

6–8 L (6–8 quart)

Serves 6

In the pressure cooker heat 40 mL (2 Tbsp) of the oil and brown the meat. This may need to be done in 2 or 3 batches and you may need to add more oil. Remove the meat and sauté the onions and jalapeño peppers until soft. Scrape up any of the brown bits that are sticking to the pot; this is easier to do if you add the juice from the tomatoes. Add the remaining ingredients.

Lock the lid in place. Over high heat bring to high pressure. Adjust heat to maintain high pressure and cook for 10 minutes. Let the pressure drop naturally. Remove the lid, tilting it away from you to allow any excess steam to escape.

Thicken sauce if desired by making a paste of 2 Tbsp of flour and 2 Tbsp of room-temperature butter and then whisking spoonfuls of this into the stew until it achieves the thickness you like. (Alternatively, mix the flour with cold water to make a smooth liquid and just pour that in while the stew is boiling.) Adjust seasonings and serve.

Mongolian Pork Roast

Pork
- **40 mL (2 Tbsp) olive oil**
- **1 kg (2 lb) pork roast (shoulder roast)**
- **1 tsp garlic, minced**
- **¼ tsp dried ginger**
- **¼ tsp dried thyme**
- **½ tsp lemon pepper**
- **salt and pepper to taste**

Sauce
- **60 mL (¼ cup) olive oil**
- **2 Tbsp brown sugar**
- **40 mL (2 Tbsp) water**
- **60 mL (3 Tbsp) soy sauce**

Pressure Cooker
6 L (6 quart)

Serves 6

In the pressure cooker heat the olive oil. Place the roast in the hot oil and brown on all sides. In a bowl, stir the sauce ingredients together. Add garlic, dried ginger, dried thyme and lemon pepper with the sauce mixture. Add salt and pepper to taste. Pour sauce over meat.

Lock the lid in place. Over high heat bring to high pressure. Adjust heat to maintain high pressure and cook for 35 minutes. Let the pressure drop naturally. Remove the lid, tilting it away from you to allow any excess steam to escape.

Check if cooked. If not cooked to your liking, repeat steps above and cook for 10 minutes more. Remove meat from cooker. Let meat set for 15 minutes before slicing as thinly as you can. Serve the juices hot and drizzle over the servings of meat.

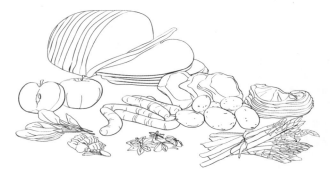

142

Pork in Beer and Onions

- **2 tsp garlic, finely minced**
- **20 mL (1 Tbsp) soy sauce**
- **2 Tbsp brown sugar, packed**
- **¼ tsp ground allspice**
- **¼ tsp cayenne pepper**
- **½ tsp salt or to taste**
- **2 kg (4½ lb) pork shoulder, bone and rind removed (trimmed weight)**

- **625 mL (2½ cups) beer**
- **2 bay leaves**
- **6 cups onion, sliced and tightly packed**
- **2 Tbsp cornflour (cornstarch) dissolved in 60 mL (3 Tbsp) water**

Pressure Cooker

6–8 L (6–8 quart)

Serves 4–6

In a small bowl, make a paste by mashing together the garlic, soy sauce, sugar, allspice, cayenne pepper and salt. Rub into the pork.

Pour the beer into pressure cooker and add the bay leaves. Set the rack in place. Arrange half the onions on the rack and set the pork on top. Spread the remaining onions over the pork.

Lock the lid in place. Over high heat bring to high pressure. Adjust heat to maintain high pressure and cook for 55 minutes. Let the pressure drop naturally. Remove the lid, tilting it away from you to allow any excess steam to escape.

Check the pork is cooked with a meat thermometer inserted into the centre. It should register 77°C (170°F). If not, relock the lid and return the pork to high pressure for a few more minutes. Remove pork to a platter and set aside in a warm place. Remove the rack.

If there is more than 2 cups of sauce, boil vigorously over high heat to reduce. Whisk in just enough of the cornflour (cornstarch) solution to thicken the gravy while cooking at a low boil for 2 to 3 minutes. Remove the bay leaves, carve the pork and pour the gravy over it. Serve.

Pork Ragù

- **500 g (1 lb) boned pork loin**
- **125 g (4 oz) link hot Italian sausage**
- **1 cup onion, chopped**
- **1 Tbsp fresh rosemary, chopped, or 1 tsp dried rosemary**
- **¼ tsp salt**
- **¼ tsp black pepper**
- **190 mL (¾ cup) chicken stock (broth)**
- **190 mL (¾ cup) dry red wine**
- **840 g (28 oz) can Italian-style whole tomatoes, undrained and chopped**
- **4 cups hot cooked penne; about 250 g (8 oz) uncooked**
- **2 Tbsp butter**
- **¼ cup romano cheese, freshly grated**
- **fresh rosemary sprigs, optional**

Pressure Cooker

6 L (6 quart)

Serves 4

Trim fat from pork. Cut pork into 6 mm (¹/₄ in) cubes. Remove casing from sausage. Cook sausage in open pressure cooker over medium-high heat until browned; stir to crumble. Remove sausage from cooker with slotted spoon.

Add onion to cooker and sauté for 4 minutes or until lightly browned. Add pork and sauté for 5 minutes. Add sausage, rosemary, salt and pepper. Stir in stock (broth) and wine, scraping the bottom of cooker to loosen browned bits. Bring to boil and cook for 5 minutes. Add tomatoes.

Lock the lid in place. Over high heat bring to high pressure. Adjust heat to maintain high pressure and cook for 30 minutes.

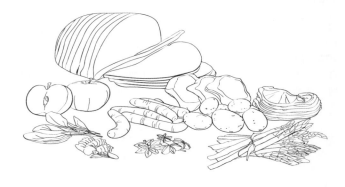

While the ragù is cooking, cook your pasta, drain and stir in butter. Mix thoroughly until butter is melted and covers pasta well. Cover the bowl with cling wrap until ragù is done.

When 30 minutes is up, let the pressure drop using the quick-release method. Remove the lid, tilting it away from you to allow any excess steam to escape. Check for seasoning and doneness.

Serve ragù ladled over the pasta. Sprinkle with cheese. Garnish with rosemary sprigs, if desired.

Tips and Techniques
Put some shredded mixed Italian cheeses on the table with a green tossed salad and some hot buttered garlic bread.

To freeze the ragù, place in a large heavy-duty zip-lock plastic bag. Cool completely in refrigerator, then freeze for up to 1 month. To reheat, place bag in a large pot of boiling water (do not unseal bag). Cook for 15 minutes or until thoroughly heated. Remove bag from water using tongs. While ragù is reheating, grate cheese and cook pasta according to package instructions, omitting salt and fat.

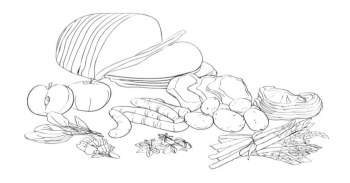

Pork Roast

- **1–1.5 kg (2½–3 lb) pork shoulder roast**
- **1 tsp caraway seeds, crushed**
- **½ tsp salt**
- **½ tsp black pepper**
- **40 mL (2 Tbsp) vegetable oil**
- **1 onion, cut in wedges**
- **250 mL (1 cup) water**
- **190 mL (¾ cup) apple cider or apple juice**
- **3 medium cooking apples, cut in wedges**

Pressure Cooker

4–6 L (4–6 quart)

Serves 8

Trim any visible fat from the meat and pat dry with paper towels. Set aside. In a small mixing bowl combine caraway seeds, salt and pepper; rub this mixture over roast.

In a pressure cooker heat 20 mL (1 Tbsp) of the oil over medium heat. Cook meat until brown on all sides, adding more oil, if necessary. Remove the meat from the cooker and set aside. Drain off fat.

Place the rack or an ovenproof rack in the cooker. Return the meat to the cooker and add the onion, water and apple cider.

Lock the lid in place. Over high heat bring to high pressure. Adjust heat to maintain high pressure and cook for 45 minutes. Let the pressure drop naturally. Remove the lid, tilting it away from you to allow any excess steam to escape.

Transfer meat and onion to a serving platter; keep warm by covering with foil. Add apples to cooker and bring to boil. Cover loosely (do not lock lid) and cook over medium heat for about 5 minutes or until apples are crisp-tender. With a slotted spoon, remove apples to serving platter with pork roast and onions.

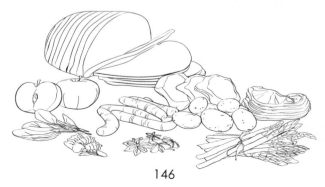

Simply Pork Chops

- 40 mL (2 Tbsp) vegetable oil
- 1 small onion, chopped
- 4 pork chops, trimmed and cut 2.5 cm (1 in) thick
- 170 mL (⅔ cup) beef stock (broth)
- 125 mL (½ cup) dry red wine or grape juice or tomato juice
- ½ tsp dried thyme
- ½ tsp sugar
- ½ tsp salt
- hot, cooked rice to serve

Pressure Cooker

6 L (6 quart)

Serves 4

Heat oil in the pressure cooker. Sauté onion until tender. Set aside.

Brown the chops evenly on both sides. Arrange chops in a single layer in the cooker. Add the stock, wine, thyme, sugar, salt and onion.

Lock the lid in place. Over high heat bring to high pressure. Adjust heat to maintain high pressure and cook for 9 minutes. Let the pressure drop using the quick-release method. Remove the lid, tilting it away from you to allow any excess steam to escape.

Remove chops and thicken juices as desired for gravy. Serve over hot cooked rice.

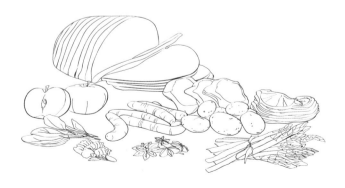

Smoked Sausage Supper

- **750 g (1½ lb) smoked sausage**
- **500 g (16 oz) can sauerkraut**
- **4 medium or large potatoes**
- **60 mL (¼ cup) water**
- **1 tsp sugar, if desired**

Pressure Cooker

4 L (6 quart)

Serves 4

Cut sausage into 10 cm (4 in) lengths and then cut in half lengthwise. Brown sausage, cut side down, in pressure cooker. While browning sausage, peel and quarter potatoes. Drain off drippings.

Layer sauerkraut, potatoes and sausage in cooker; add water. A teaspoon of sugar may be added to sauerkraut if desired.

Lock the lid in place. Over high heat bring to high pressure. Adjust heat to maintain high pressure and cook for 10 minutes. Let the pressure drop using the quick-release method. Remove the lid, tilting it away from you to allow any excess steam to escape.

Lift out of pressure cooker with a slotted spoon, being careful to keep the layers as intact as possible.

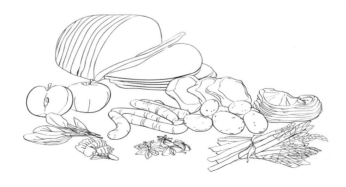

Spareribs and Sauerkraut

- **1 kg (2 lb) spareribs cut in serving size pieces**
- **20 mL (1 Tbsp) vegetable oil**
- **salt and pepper**

- **1 litre (1 quart) sauerkraut**
- **1 Tbsp brown sugar**
- **375 mL (1½ cups) water**
- **4 serves mashed potato**

Pressure Cooker

4 L (4 quart)

Serves 4

Heat the pressure cooker, add oil and brown ribs on all sides. Season with salt and pepper. Pour sauerkraut over ribs and sprinkle with brown sugar. Add water.

Lock the lid in place. Over high heat bring to high pressure. Adjust heat to maintain high pressure and cook for 15 minutes. Let the pressure drop using the quick-release method. Remove the lid, tilting it away from you to allow any excess steam to escape.

Serve on warmed plates with mashed potato.

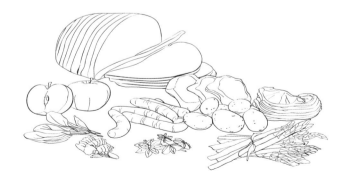

Stuffed Pork Chops

- **4 double pork chops, cut 3 cm (1¼ in) thick**
- **70 g (5 Tbsp) butter**
- **1 medium onion, finely chopped**
- **¼ cup celery, finely chopped**
- **1½ cups fresh bread, crumbled**
- **¼ tsp dried sage**
- **¼ tsp ground basil**
- **¼ tsp coarse ground anise seed**
- **¼ cup fresh parsley, chopped**
- **½ tsp salt**
- **¼ tsp pepper**
- **40 mL (2 Tbsp) heavy cream**
- **250 mL (1 cup) dry white wine**

Pressure Cooker

6 L (6 quart)

Serves 4

Trim excess fat off chops. Slit chops at lower end to make pockets.

In pressure cooker melt 3 Tbsp butter. Add onion and celery. Stir-fry until onion is light brown. Add bread, sage, basil, anise seed, parsley, salt and pepper. Stir.

Remove cooker from heat. Allow to cool. Add cream. Mix well. Divide mixture into four portions. Stuff each chop, securing pockets with toothpicks.

Wipe cooker with paper towel. Melt remaining butter (2 Tbsp) in cooker. Brown chops on both sides and remove. Pour wine into cooker. Put the rack in cooker, placing the chops on rack.

Lock the lid in place. Over high heat bring to high pressure. Adjust heat to maintain high pressure and cook for 10 minutes. Let the pressure drop naturally. Remove the lid, tilting it away from you to allow any excess steam to escape.

Place chops on serving dish. Remove toothpicks. Serve hot.

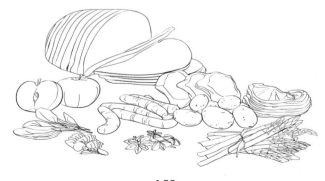

Sweet and Sour Pork Spareribs

- **1 kg (2 lb) pork spareribs**
- **salt and pepper to taste**
- **60 mL (3 Tbsp) cooking oil (not olive oil)**
- **60 mL (¼ cup) water**
- **60 mL (¼ cup) pineapple juice**

- **40 mL (2 Tbsp) cooking sherry**
- **¾ cup crushed pineapple, drained**
- **¼ cup brown sugar**
- **60 mL (¼ cup) sweet and sour sauce**
- **4 serves of either steamed rice or French fries and green salad**

Pressure Cooker
6 L (6 quart)

Serves 4

Cut spareribs in sections and season with salt and pepper. Brown spareribs in oil in pressure cooker. Drain off fat and add water, juice and sherry to cooker. Place ribs on pressure cooker rack. Cover ribs with pineapple and brown sugar. Spread sweet and sour sauce over sugar.

Lock the lid in place. Over high heat bring to high pressure. Adjust heat to maintain high pressure and cook for 35 minutes. Let the pressure drop naturally. Remove the lid, tilting it away from you to allow any excess steam to escape.

May be served with rice or French fried potatoes and salad.

Tips and Techniques
Venison may be used instead of spareribs.

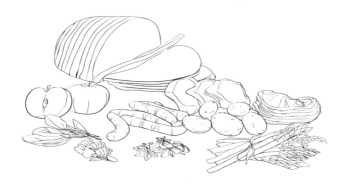

151

Pork Vindaloo with Spinach and Potatoes

- 7 mL (1½ tsp) Indian mustard oil, vegetable oil or ghee
- ½ large onion, peeled, halved and thinly sliced
- 500 g (1 lb) boned pork loin or pork loin chops, cut in 1.3 cm (1 in) cubes and well trimmed of fat
- 1 tsp cumin seeds
- additional oil, if needed
- 1.25 cm (½ in) cube ginger, thinly sliced, smashed and minced
- 3 large cloves garlic, smashed and minced
- 1 small serrano chilli, seeded and minced
- ¾ tsp sweet paprika
- ¾ tsp black mustard seeds
- 1½ tsp ground turmeric
- 1 small bay leaf
- ⅓ tsp freshly ground black pepper
- ¼ tsp ground cardamom

- ¼ tsp ground coriander
- ⅛ tsp ground cloves
- ⅛ tsp cayenne pepper, or more to taste
- 40 mL (2 Tbsp) water
- 20 mL (1 Tbsp) cider vinegar
- 220 mL (⅞ cup) unsweetened light coconut milk
- 1 Tbsp coarse-grained mustard
- 1 tsp sea salt (Kosher salt)
- 320 g (10 oz) box frozen chopped spinach (still frozen)
- 375 g (¾ lb) bintje, desiree or red pontiac potatoes, peeled and cut in 5 cm (2 in) chunks
- 1 Tbsp plain (all-purpose) flour, optional
- 40 mL (2 Tbsp) cool water, chicken broth or coconut milk, optional
- fresh coriander (cilantro), coarsely chopped, for garnish, optional

Pressure Cooker

6 L (6 quart)

Serves 6

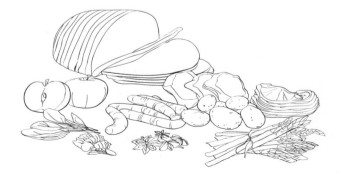

Heat 20 mL (1 Tbsp) oil in pressure cooker over medium-high heat. Cook the onion, stirring frequently, for 2 minutes. Add the pork and cumin seeds, adding more oil if needed, and cook until the pork loses its pink colour, stirring frequently, for 2 to 3 minutes. (The pork doesn't have to brown.)

Add the ginger, garlic and spices and sauté for 30 seconds more, being careful that the spices do not burn on the bottom of the cooker. (The spices need to sauté a bit to achieve their fullest flavour.) Add the water and cider vinegar. Stir well, taking care to scrape up any browned bits stuck to the bottom of the cooker. Add the coconut milk and blend in the mustard and salt. Add the frozen block of spinach. Set the potatoes on top.

Lock the lid in place. Over high heat bring to high pressure. Adjust heat to maintain high pressure and cook for 18 to 20 minutes. Let the pressure drop using the quick-release method. Remove the lid, tilting it away from you to allow any excess steam to escape.

If you wish, cut the potatoes into bite-size pieces. Stir the stew well, adding more cayenne pepper, mustard and salt if needed. If desired, thicken sauce. (In a small bowl, whisk the flour and water until smooth. Slowly stir as much as needed into the simmering stew to thicken the sauce slightly, so it coats the back of a spoon. Simmer for 1 to 2 minutes in order to cook the flour.) Sprinkle with coriander (cilantro), if desired, and serve.

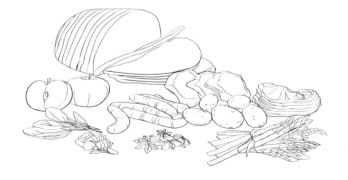

Jambalaya with a Difference

- 40 mL (2 Tbsp) olive oil
- 3 cloves garlic, minced
- 2 cups onion, coarsely chopped
- 250 g (½ lb) garlic sausage, cut in 6 mm (¼ in) slices
- 1¼ cups raw short grain brown rice
- 250 g (½ lb) cooked country ham, cut in 1.25 cm (½ in) cubes
- 4 stalks celery, cut in 1.25 cm (½ in) slices
- 1 large green capsicum (pepper), cut in 2.5 cm (1 in) strips
- 500 mL (2 cups) water
- 1 bay leaf
- 2 Tbsp tomato paste
- ½ tsp salt or to taste
- Tabasco sauce or cayenne pepper to taste
- 1 cup tightly packed fresh coriander (cilantro), minced

Pressure Cooker
4–6 L (4–6 quart)

Serves 4

Heat the oil in pressure cooker. Sauté the garlic and onion for 3 minutes. Push the onions aside, and brown the sausage slices for about 30 seconds on each side. Stir in the rice, coating the grains with the fat. Add the ham, celery, green capsicum (pepper), water, bay leaf, tomato paste, and salt and Tabasco sauce to taste.

Lock the lid in place. Over high heat bring to high pressure. Adjust heat to maintain high pressure and cook for 15 minutes. Let the pressure drop naturally for 10 minutes, then quick release any remaining pressure. Remove the lid, tilting it away from you to allow any excess steam to escape.

If the rice is slightly undercooked, cover and simmer over low heat for another 2 to 3 minutes; stir in a few tablespoons of water if the mixture is dry. Stir in the coriander (cilantro), adjust seasonings, and serve.

Tips and Techniques
Remove the casings of the garlic sausage, if necessary. If the sausage is thick, cut the slices into two to three pieces.

Long grain brown rice can also be used in this recipe.

Poultry

Arroz con Pollo

- 1 cup long grain white rice
- 375 mL (1½ cups) water
- 250 mL (1 cup) water
- 1.5 kg (3 lb) chicken, cut in serving pieces
- paprika
- salt and pepper
- 40 mL (2 Tbsp) vegetable oil or olive oil
- 2 medium onions, chopped
- 1 clove garlic, minced
- 1 bay leaf
- ½ tsp crushed red chilli pepper
- ¼ tsp saffron powder
- 410 g (13½ oz) container chicken stock (broth)
- 1 tomato, peeled and chopped
- 310 g (10 oz) frozen green peas
- 1 cup green olives, sliced
- 125 g (4 oz) jar pimiento, sliced

Pressure Cooker
4–6 L (4–6 quart)

Serves 4–6

Steamed Rice
Combine rice and 375 mL (1½ cups) water in a metal bowl. Use a 1.25 L (5 cup) capacity bowl, 8 cm (3 in) high or less, which will fit loosely into a 4 to 6 L (4 to 6 quart) pressure cooker. Place 250 mL (1 cup) water, cooking rack and bowl in pressure cooker.

Lock the lid in place. Over high heat bring to high pressure. Adjust heat to maintain high pressure and cook for 5 minutes. Let the pressure drop naturally. Remove the lid, tilting it away from you to allow any excess steam to escape, and allow rice to steam, uncovered, for 5 minutes.

Chicken

Sprinkle chicken with paprika, salt and pepper. Heat the oil in pressure cooker. Brown chicken a few pieces at a time, then set aside. Sauté onions and garlic until tender. Return all chicken to pressure cooker, and add bay leaf, crushed red chilli pepper, saffron and chicken stock (broth).

Lock the lid in place. Over high heat bring to high pressure. Adjust heat to maintain high pressure and cook for 8 minutes. Let the pressure drop using the quick-release method. Remove the lid, tilting it away from you to allow any excess steam to escape.

Remove chicken and stir in rice, tomato, green peas, green olives and pimiento. Return chicken to pressure cooker and heat to a simmer, uncovered.

Serve spooned into warmed bowls.

Beauy Chicken

- **salt and pepper**
- **1.5 kg (3½ lb) chicken pieces (with bone)**
- **2 rashers bacon, cut in 2.5 cm (1 in) pieces**
- **2 medium potatoes, cut in 3–5 cm (1½–2 in) pieces**

- **125 g (¼ lb) mushrooms**
- **½ onion, diced**
- **1 tsp plain (all-purpose) flour**
- **20 mL (1 Tbsp) brandy**
- **60 mL (¼ cup) white wine or sherry**
- **60 mL (¼ cup) chicken stock (broth)**

Pressure Cooker

4–6 L (4–6 quart)

Serves 4

Salt and pepper the chicken pieces. In pressure cooker sauté the bacon. Remove the bacon and set aside. Add the potato pieces and brown for several minutes, then remove. Brown the chicken pieces on all sides and remove. Add the mushrooms and onions and sauté for 1 minute. Sprinkle in the flour and add the brandy, white wine or sherry and chicken stock (broth). Return the chicken, bacon and potatoes to the cooker.

Lock the lid in place. Over high heat bring to high pressure. Adjust heat to maintain high pressure and cook for 8 minutes. Let the pressure drop using the quick-release method. Remove the lid, tilting it away from you to allow any excess steam to escape.

Serve chicken and spoon sauce over.

Braised Turkey Breast

- salt and pepper
- 2–2.5 kg (4–5 lb) whole turkey breast, wings removed, rinsed under cold water and patted dry
- 40 mL (2 Tbsp) vegetable oil
- 1 onion, thinly sliced
- 2 cloves garlic, crushed
- 2 carrots, peeled and thinly sliced
- 2 stalks celery, thinly sliced
- 250 mL (1 cup) chicken stock (broth)
- 250 mL (1 cup) dry red wine
- 1 Tbsp cornflour (cornstarch)
- 40 mL (2 Tbsp) water

Pressure Cooker
6–8 L (6–8 quart)

Serves 6

Generously salt and pepper the turkey breast. Heat the oil in pressure cooker over medium-high heat. Add the turkey breast and brown on all sides. Remove and set aside. Add the onion, garlic, carrots and celery. Cook until the onion is soft. Add the stock (broth) and wine. Cook for 2 minutes. Place the turkey breast in cooker.

Lock the lid in place. Over high heat bring to high pressure. Adjust heat to maintain high pressure and cook for 40 minutes. Let the pressure drop using the quick-release method. Remove the lid, tilting it away from you to allow any excess steam to escape.

Carefully remove the turkey and place on a large plate. Cover with foil. Strain the cooking liquid. Pour it back into the cooker and boil it down by a third. Combine the cornflour (cornstarch) and water. Add to the cooking liquid and whisk until thickened. Season to taste with salt and pepper. Slice the turkey off the carcass. Serve with the gravy.

Anchor Bar Chicken Wings

Chicken Wings
- **24 chicken wings**
- **80 mL (⅓ cup) Tabasco sauce or other hot pepper sauce**
- **pinch of cayenne pepper**
- **¼ tsp salt**
- **celery sticks, to serve**

Blue Cheese Dipping Sauce
- **1 cup plain yoghurt**
- **60 mL (¼ cup) mayonnaise**
- **2 tsp cider vinegar**
- **½ cup crumbled blue cheese**

Pressure Cooker
6–8 L (6–8 quart)

Serves 4

Chicken Wings
Rinse and pat dry the chicken wings. If desired, cut off the wing tips and reserve for stock. Combine the Tabasco sauce, cayenne pepper and salt. Add the wings, toss to coat and refrigerate to marinate for at least 30 minutes (overnight is best). Place the wings and sauce in pressure cooker.

Lock the lid in place. Over high heat bring to high pressure. Adjust heat to maintain high pressure and cook for 15 minutes. Let the pressure drop naturally for 5 minutes, then use the quick-release method. Remove the lid, tilting it away from you to allow any excess steam to escape.

Arrange the chicken wings on a platter and pour the sauce over them. Serve with Blue Cheese Dipping Sauce and celery sticks on the side.

Blue Cheese Dipping Sauce
Combine the yoghurt, mayonnaise and cider vinegar in a small bowl and whisk to smooth. Stir in the cheese and use right away or refrigerate, covered, for up to 1 week.

Chicken and Dumpling Casserole

- **8 chicken thighs, boned and skinned**
- **500 mL (2 cups) chicken stock (broth)**
- **250 mL (1 cup) dry white wine**
- **2 tsp garlic, minced (about 4 cloves)**
- **2 cups wholegrain scone (biscuit) mix**
- **⅔ cup skim milk**
- **1 Tbsp dried dill**

Pressure Cooker

4 L (4 quart)

Serves 4

Add the chicken thighs, stock (broth), wine and garlic to pressure cooker.

Lock the lid in place. Over high heat bring to high pressure. Adjust heat to maintain high pressure and cook for 6 minutes. Let the pressure drop using the quick-release method. Remove the lid, tilting it away from you to allow any excess steam to escape.

Combine scone mix, skim milk and dill and drop large spoonfuls into boiling chicken broth. Cook uncovered for 6 minutes.

When dumplings are cooked, spoon casserole into warmed bowls and top with dumplings.

Jambalaya

- 20 mL (1 Tbsp) vegetable oil
- 250 g (½ lb) chicken breasts, boned and skinned
- 250 g (½ lb) fully cooked andouille or bratwurst sausage sliced, with skin removed
- 250 g (½ lb) uncooked small frozen prawns (shrimp)
- 2 tsp Cajun seasoning
- 2 tsp dried thyme
- 2 tsp cayenne pepper
- 1 onion, chopped
- 3 cloves of garlic, minced
- 1 green capsicum (pepper), chopped
- 3 stalks celery, sliced
- 1 cup long grain white rice
- 500 g (16 oz) can chopped tomatoes, undrained
- 1 cup chicken stock (broth)
- 3 Tbsp fresh parsley, minced
- 4–6 serves of either cooked pasta or couscous

Pressure Cooker

6 L (6 quart)

Serves 4–6

Heat the oil in pressure cooker over medium-high heat or use brown function. Add chicken, sausage and frozen prawns. Sprinkle meats with half the Cajun seasoning, half the thyme and half the cayenne pepper. Cook for 3 to 5 minutes uncovered, stirring frequently, until chicken and prawns are thoroughly cooked. Remove chicken, sausage and prawns with a slotted spoon and set aside.

Add onion, garlic, capsicum (pepper), celery and remaining Cajun seasoning, thyme and cayenne pepper to cooker. Cook for 4 to 5 minutes, stirring frequently until vegetables are crisp-tender. Add rice, tomatoes with their juice and stock (broth).

Lock the lid in place. Over high heat bring to high pressure. Adjust heat to maintain high pressure and cook for 8 minutes. Let the pressure drop using the quick-release method. Remove the lid, tilting it away from you to allow any excess steam to escape.

Stir in chicken, sausage, prawns and parsley. Cover tightly and let stand for 5 minutes before serving. Stir, and serve with hot cooked pasta or couscous.

Chicken and Rice with Gravy

- 1.5 kg (3 lb) chicken pieces
- 40 mL (2 Tbsp) lemon juice
- 1 cup plain (all-purpose) flour
- ½ tsp salt
- ¼ tsp coarse ground black pepper
- 1 tsp sweet paprika
- 60 mL (3 Tbsp) olive oil

- ¼ tsp dried rosemary
- 625 mL (2½ cups) chicken stock (broth)
- 1 cup uncooked long grain white rice
- 325 g (10½ oz) can cream of mushroom soup
- 250 mL (1 cup) sour cream

Pressure Cooker

6 L (6 quart)

Serves 4

Sprinkle chicken with lemon juice. Set aside for 15 minutes. Combine flour, salt, pepper and paprika, and mix thoroughly. Coat chicken with flour mixture.

Heat the oil in pressure cooker and add chicken a few pieces at a time. Brown well on all sides. Add rosemary, stock (broth) and rice.

Lock the lid in place. Over high heat bring to high pressure. Adjust heat to maintain high pressure and cook for 15 minutes. Let the pressure drop naturally. Remove the lid, tilting it away from you to allow any excess steam to escape.

Place rice and chicken on platter to serve. Add cream of mushroom soup to cooker and stir with heat on simmer, until smooth. Gradually stir in sour cream, mixing well to blend. Pour gravy over chicken and rice.

Chicken and Vegetable Chilli

- cooking spray
- 375 g (12 oz) skinned, boned chicken thighs or breast, cut in bite-size pieces
- 1 cup onion, chopped
- 1 cup red capsicum (pepper), chopped
- ¼ cup seeded jalapeño pepper, chopped
- ¼ cup sun-dried tomatoes, packed without oil, chopped
- 1½ Tbsp chilli powder
- 1 Tbsp ground cumin
- 2 tsp dried oregano
- ¼ tsp cayenne pepper
- 3 cloves garlic, minced
- 500 mL (2 cups) boiling water
- 1 cup dried pinto beans
- 1 cup tomatoes, chopped
- 1 cup fresh corn kernels (about 2 ears)
- ½ tsp salt

Pressure Cooker
6 L (6 quart)

Serves 6

Coat inside of pressure cooker with cooking spray and warm over medium-high heat. Add chicken and onion and sauté for 2 minutes. Add capsicum (pepper), jalapeño peppers, tomatoes, chilli powder, cumin, oregano, cayenne pepper and garlic, and sauté for 1 minute. Stir in boiling water and pinto beans.

Lock the lid in place. Over high heat bring to high pressure. Adjust heat to maintain high pressure and cook for 25 minutes. Let the pressure drop using the quick-release method. Remove the lid, tilting it away from you to allow any excess steam to escape.

Stir in tomato, corn and salt. Bring to the boil. Cook, uncovered, for 5 minutes, stirring frequently.

Serve in large warmed bowls.

Chicken Cacciatore

- 1.5 kg (3 lb) chicken, cut up
- 3 Tbsp plain (all-purpose) flour
- 1 tsp salt
- ⅛ tsp pepper
- 40 mL (2 Tbsp) vegetable oil or olive oil
- ¼ cup salt pork, diced
- 1½ cups onions, sliced
- 2 cloves garlic, minced
- 2 Tbsp fresh parsley, minced
- ½ tsp fresh oregano, chopped, or ¼ tsp dried oregano
- ½ cup carrots, chopped
- ½ cup celery, chopped
- 420 g (14 oz) can Italian tomatoes, chopped
- salt and pepper
- 125 mL (½ cup) white wine
- 180 g (6 oz) tomato paste

Pressure Cooker

4–6 L (4–6 quart)

Serves 4–6

Coat chicken in mixture of flour, salt and pepper, then set aside. Heat the oil in pressure cooker. Sauté pork until crisp. Add onions and sauté until light brown, then remove and set aside. Brown chicken a few pieces at a time, then set aside.

Pour off excess drippings. Stir garlic, parsley and oregano into remaining drippings. Return chicken and onion to cooker. Add carrots, celery, tomatoes, salt, pepper and white wine.

Lock the lid in place. Over high heat bring to high pressure. Adjust heat to maintain high pressure and cook for 8 minutes. Let the pressure drop using the quick-release method. Remove the lid, tilting it away from you to allow any excess steam to escape.

Place chicken on a warm platter. Stir tomato paste into sauce in cooker. Simmer until thickened. Pour over chicken and serve.

Chicken Curry

Chicken Curry

- 0.5–1 kg (1–2 lb) chicken pieces, boned and skinned
- 80 mL (4 Tbsp) oil or butter
- 2 jalapeño peppers, seeded and coarsely chopped
- 3 cloves garlic, finely chopped
- 2.5 cm (1 in) cube fresh ginger, finely chopped (leave the peel on)
- 1 large red onion, finely chopped
- 3 tsp curry spice mix (see opposite)
- 1 tsp garam masala spice mix (see opposite)
- 20 mL (1 Tbsp) soy sauce
- 250 mL (1 cup) chicken stock (broth)
- 250 mL (1 cup) canned coconut milk, divided
- 125 mL (½ cup) buttermilk
- 80 mL (⅓ cup) plain yoghurt
- fresh coriander (cilantro) leaves as garnish

Garam Masala Spice Mix

- ¼ cup coriander seeds
- 2 Tbsp cumin seeds
- 1 Tbsp black peppercorns
- 2 tsp cardamom pods
- 2 cinnamon sticks, broken into small pieces
- 1 tsp whole cloves
- 1 whole nutmeg

Curry Spice Mix

- 2 Tbsp ground coriander
- 2 Tbsp ground cumin
- 2 tsp ground cardamom
- 2 tsp ground cinnamon
- 1 tsp ground cloves
- 1 tsp ground nutmeg
- 1 tsp ground turmeric
- ½ tsp cayenne pepper
- 1 tsp freshly ground black pepper

Pressure Cooker

4–6 L (4–6 quart)

Serves 4

166

Chicken Curry

Trim fat, wash and cut chicken into small pieces. Heat the oil in pressure cooker, add jalapeño peppers and then garlic, ginger and red onion (beware, it will splutter). After onion is fried, add soy sauce, curry spice mix and garam masala mix and stir well. Add chicken pieces, increase heat and brown chicken on both sides. Add chicken stock (broth) and half the coconut milk.

Lock the lid in place. Over high heat bring to high pressure. Adjust heat to maintain high pressure and cook for 6 minutes. Let the pressure drop naturally. Remove the lid, tilting it away from you to allow any excess steam to escape and bring to the boil, reducing broth by half.

Add buttermilk, remaining coconut milk and yoghurt, mixing well until the chicken is coated and heated through. Adjust seasoning to taste. Garnish with coriander (cilantro) and serve over rice.

Garam Masala Spice Mix

Dry roast the coriander seeds in a small frying pan over medium heat, sliding the pan back and forth over the burner to prevent burning, until the seeds exude a pleasant aroma, about 1 to 2 minutes. Transfer to a bowl and set aside.

Repeat the process, one at a time, with the cumin seeds, peppercorns, cardamom pods, cinnamon pieces and cloves. Let cool completely. Put all the ingredients except the nutmeg in a spice grinder and grind to a fine powder. Transfer to a bowl. Grate the nutmeg over the mixture. Stir to mix well.

Transfer to a glass jar with a tight-fitting lid. The garam masala will keep at room temperature for at least a month. This recipe makes about half a cup.

Curry Spice Mix

Combine all ingredients. Stir well. Store in an airtight container.

Chicken with Cracked Pepper

- 2 chicken breasts, boned, skinned and cut in half
- 1 tsp cracked mixed peppercorns
- 20 mL (1 Tbsp) olive oil or vegetable oil
- ¼ cup chives or green onion (shallots, scallions) tops, chopped

- 1 small garlic clove, minced
- 40 mL (2 Tbsp) brandy, optional
- 250 mL (1 cup) chicken stock (broth)
- ¼ cup packaged breadcrumbs
- 20 mL (1 Tbsp) lemon juice
- 5 mL (1 tsp) Worcestershire Sauce
- 1 Tbsp fresh parsley, chopped

Pressure Cooker

4–6 L (4–6 quart)

Serves 4

Sprinkle chicken with pepper, pressing it into the flesh. Heat pressure cooker, add oil and brown chicken. Remove chicken from pan. Add chives, garlic, brandy and stock (broth). Stir well. Place cooking rack in cooker. Put chicken on cooking rack.

Lock the lid in place. Over high heat bring to high pressure. Adjust heat to maintain high pressure and cook for 3 minutes. Let the pressure drop using the quick-release method. Remove the lid, tilting it away from you to allow any excess steam to escape.

Remove chicken and keep warm. Remove rack. Stir breadcrumbs, lemon juice, Worcestershire Sauce and parsley into sauce. Thicken, if desired.

168

Chicken with Lentils and Spinach

- 40 mL (2 Tbsp) olive oil
- 1 large onion, coarsely chopped
- 1 Tbsp whole cumin seeds
- 1 Tbsp ginger, finely minced
- 1½ cups dried lentils
- 1 kg (2–2½ lb) chicken parts, skinned (dark meat remains moister)
- 2 large carrots, peeled and cut in 3 to 4 chunks
- 875 mL (3½ cups) water
- ¼ tsp ground allspice
- ½ tsp ground cinnamon
- ⅔ cup raisins
- 310 g (10 oz) box frozen spinach, defrosted
- ¾ tsp salt or to taste
- 4–6 serves rice, steamed
- mango chutney, to serve

Pressure Cooker

4–6 L (4–6 quart)

Serves 4–6

In pressure cooker heat the oil and sauté the onion until lightly browned, about 3 to 4 minutes. Stir in the cumin seeds and ginger and sauté for 1 minute more. Add the lentils, chicken, carrots, water, allspice, cinnamon and raisins. Stir to scrape up any brown bits sticking to the bottom of the cooker.

Lock the lid in place. Over high heat bring to high pressure. Adjust heat to maintain high pressure and cook for 9 minutes. Let the pressure drop using the quick-release method. Remove the lid, tilting it away from you to allow any excess steam to escape.

Squeeze the spinach to get rid of the excess water. Stir in the spinach and taste for salt. Simmer until the spinach is cooked, about 2 minutes.

Serve this with rice and mango chutney on the side. You don't really need anything else with it. The lentils are filling enough to make this a one dish meal.

Coq au Vin

- **1.5 kg (3–3.5 lb) chicken breasts**
- **flour for dusting**
- **40 mL (2 Tbsp) olive oil**
- **3 rashers bacon, minced**
- **1 large onion, chopped**
- **2 cloves garlic, minced**
- **1 carrot, scraped and diced**
- **1 Tbsp plain (all-purpose) flour**

- **250 mL (1 cup) dry red wine**
- **½ tsp thyme**
- **2 Tbsp fresh parsley, minced**
- **1 bay leaf**
- **salt and pepper to taste**
- **125 g (¼ lb) fresh mushrooms, cleaned and sliced**

Pressure Cooker

6 L (6 quart)

Serves 4–6

Dust the chicken parts with flour. Heat the oil in pressure cooker until very hot and brown chicken on all sides (don't crowd pot). Transfer chicken to a warm platter. Add bacon, onion, garlic and carrot, and sauté until onion is wilted. Stir in the flour, then gradually add the wine and stir until thickened a little bit (3 to 4 minutes.) Add thyme, parsley, bay leaf, salt and pepper, then return chicken to cooker.

Lock the lid in place. Over high heat bring to high pressure. Adjust heat to maintain high pressure and cook for 8 minutes. Let the pressure drop using the quick-release method. Remove the lid, tilting it away from you to allow any excess steam to escape.

Add mushrooms and simmer for 3 minutes. Discard bay leaf. Serve.

Cypriot Chicken

- ¼ cup butter
- 4 chicken joints
- 1 medium onion, chopped
- 2 cups mushrooms, sliced
- 170 mL (⅔ cup) medium dry sherry
- salt
- pepper
- 310 mL (1¼ cup) thickened cream
- 1 tsp paprika
- 2 Tbsp fresh parsley, chopped

Pressure Cooker

4 L (4 quart)

Serves 4

In pressure cooker heat the butter and brown the chicken joints well on all sides. Remove the chicken. In the same butter, sauté the onion gently for 2 to 3 minutes. Stir in the mushrooms and sherry and season with salt and pepper. Add the browned chicken joints.

Lock the lid in place. Over high heat bring to high pressure. Adjust heat to maintain high pressure and cook for 7 minutes. Let the pressure drop using the quick-release method. Remove the lid, tilting it away from you to allow any excess steam to escape.

Lift the chicken joints onto a serving dish and keep warm. Stir the remaining ingredients into the sherry mixture. Adjust the seasonings if necessary and then reheat, without boiling, and pour over the chicken. Serve.

East Indian Chicken

- **1.5 kg (3 lb) chicken, cut into pieces**
- **250 mL (1 cup) water**
- **125 mL (½ cup) plain yoghurt**
- **20 mL (1 Tbsp) lemon juice**
- **2 cloves garlic, minced**
- **2 tsp fresh ginger, grated, or ½ tsp ground ginger**
- **1 tsp turmeric**
- **1 tsp salt**
- **1 tsp paprika**
- **1 tsp curry powder**
- **¼ tsp pepper**
- **40 mL (2 Tbsp) vegetable oil or olive oil**
- **2 tsp cornflour (cornstarch)**
- **40 mL (2 Tbsp) cold water**

Pressure Cooker

4–6 L (4–6 quart)

Serves 6

Place chicken in a single layer in a glass or pottery dish. Combine water, yoghurt, lemon juice, garlic, ginger, turmeric, salt, paprika, curry powder and pepper; pour over chicken and marinate at room temperature for 1 hour. Remove chicken from marinade, brushing off as much of marinade as possible (reserve marinade).

Heat the oil in pressure cooker. Brown chicken, a few pieces at a time, then set aside. Return all chicken to cooker. Pour marinade over chicken.

Lock the lid in place. Over high heat bring to high pressure. Adjust heat to maintain high pressure and cook for 8 minutes. Let the pressure drop using the quick-release method. Remove the lid, tilting it away from you to allow any excess steam to escape.

Transfer chicken pieces to a warm platter. Mix cornflour (cornstarch) with cold water, then blend into hot liquid. Cook and stir until mixture boils and thickens. Pour sauce over chicken and serve.

Italian Chicken Pockets

- **430 g (14½ oz) can Italian diced tomatoes, undrained**
- **1 cup assorted capsicums (peppers), red, green, yellow**
- **2 cups fresh mushrooms, sliced**
- **70 g (2¼ oz) jar sliced ripe olives, drained**
- **½ cup onion, chopped**
- **1 Tbsp plain (all-purpose) flour**
- **½ tsp garlic salt**
- **¼ tsp pepper**
- **4 chicken breasts, boned and skinned**
- **1 tsp Italian seasoning**
- **4 serves either pasta, cooked al dente, or garlic toast**

Pressure Cooker

6–8 L (6–8 quart)

Serves 4

Use a regular size foil cooking bag (fold up a doubled sheet of foil). Combine tomatoes, capsicums (peppers), mushrooms, olives, onion, flour, garlic salt and pepper. Open foil bag. Spread tomato mixture in foil bag in an even layer. Arrange chicken on top, then sprinkle with Italian seasoning. To seal, double fold open end of foil bag.

Place foil bag on the rack inside pressure cooker. Add water to reach just to the top of the rack. Be sure to leave enough space around the packet for steam to move freely.

Lock the lid in place. Over high heat bring to high pressure. Adjust heat to maintain high pressure and cook for 12 minutes. Let the pressure drop using the quick-release method. Remove the lid, tilting it away from you to allow any excess steam to escape.

Use oven mitts to transfer the foil bag to a serving bowl. Open the bag with scissors or a sharp knife. Carefully fold back top of foil bag, allowing steam to escape and empty into bowl. Serve with pasta and garlic toast.

JB's Chicken and Mushroom Casserole

- **60 mL (3 Tbsp) olive oil**
- **1 kg (2 lb) chicken breasts, boned and skinned**
- **1 tsp salt**
- **1 onion, chopped**
- **250 g (8 oz) button mushrooms, cut in half**
- **2 × 300 g (10 oz) cans cream of mushroom soup**
- **125 mL (½ cup) chicken stock (broth)**
- **4–6 serves of either hot cooked pasta or couscous**

Pressure Cooker

4–6 L (4–6 quart)

Serves 4–6

In pressure cooker heat the oil over medium-high heat or use brown function. Brown the chicken breasts, two at a time, on both sides. Remove browned pieces and add more, continuing until all breasts are browned. Sprinkle chicken with salt.

Sauté onion and mushrooms in drippings remaining in cooker, about 3 to 5 minutes. Return chicken to cooker, add soup and stock (broth), and stir.

Lock the lid in place. Over high heat bring to high pressure. Adjust heat to maintain high pressure and cook for 15 minutes. Let the pressure drop naturally, about 30 minutes. Remove the lid, tilting it away from you to allow any excess steam to escape.

Stir and serve with hot cooked pasta or couscous.

174

Lemon Herbed Chicken

- 1.5 kg (3 lb) chicken, cut up
- salt to taste
- freshly ground black pepper to taste
- 40 mL (2 Tbsp) vegetable oil or olive oil
- 1 onion, chopped
- 1 Tbsp garlic, chopped
- 250 mL (1 cup) chicken stock (broth)
- 60 mL (¼ cup) lemon juice
- 1 cup fresh parsley, chopped
- ½ cup celery leaves, chopped
- 2 tsp fresh oregano, chopped, or 1 tsp dry oregano
- 1 tsp fresh basil, chopped, or ½ tsp dry basil
- 1 cup pitted black olives
- 2 Tbsp plain (all-purpose) flour
- 40 mL (2 Tbsp) cold water

Pressure Cooker
4–6 L (4–6 quart)

Serves 4

Sprinkle chicken with salt and pepper. Heat oil in pressure cooker. Sauté onion and garlic until tender, then remove. Brown chicken a few pieces at a time and set aside. Return all chicken to cooker with onion and garlic. Add remaining ingredients except black olives, flour and cold water.

Lock the lid in place. Over high heat bring to high pressure. Adjust heat to maintain high pressure and cook for 8 minutes. Let the pressure drop using the quick-release method. Remove the lid, tilting it away from you to allow any excess steam to escape.

Transfer chicken to a warm dish. Add olives to liquid and heat. Blend together flour and cold water; add to hot broth. Cook and stir liquid until thickened. Pour sauce over chicken.

Tips and Techniques
The ancient Greeks were the first to discover chicken's splendid possibilities for the banquet table. The Mediterranean landscape of Greece is rich with the fragrant lemons and herbs that are essential to Greek cooking. Serve this dish with Greek pasta (orzo) and a green salad topped with feta cheese. For dessert, serve another speciality of the Greek Isles, honey-drenched baklava.

If desired, do not thicken sauce and prepare the Greek pasta (orzo) in the remaining liquid.

Poulet Cocotte Grandmaman

- 1.5 kg (3 lb) chicken
- 1 lemon
- 1 medium onion, peeled and thickly sliced
- 20 mL (1 Tbsp) olive oil
- 125 mL (½ cup) dry red wine
- 2 stalks celery, coarsely chopped
- 2 medium carrots, coarsely chopped
- 5 cloves garlic, peeled
- several sprigs fresh rosemary
- salt and pepper to taste
- 500 g (1 lb) carrots, peeled
- 8 small red potatoes, halved
- 6 small shallots (green onions, scallions), peeled and trimmed

Pressure Cooker

4–6 L (4–6 quart)

Serves 4

Wash and dry the chicken. Slice the lemon into 5 or 6 pieces and place it and half the onion in the cavity. Truss the chicken.

In pressure cooker heat oil over medium-high heat. Add the chicken and turn as needed to brown on all sides. Reduce heat if the oil begins to burn. When browned, carefully lift the chicken out of the pot and set aside on a platter. Discard excess oil and add the wine, scraping up any brown bits left on the bottom of the pan. Add a bit more oil and the remaining vegetables to the pan and place the chicken on top. Cover the chicken with the salt, pepper and rosemary.

Lock the lid in place. Over high heat bring to high pressure. Adjust heat to maintain high pressure and cook for 5 minutes per 500 g (1 lb). Let the pressure drop using the quick-release method. Remove the lid, tilting it away from you to allow any excess steam to escape.

Remove the chicken and place on a heated platter to carve. Remove the rosemary stems from the sauce. Using a fat skimmer, remove excess grease from cooking liquid. Puree the vegetables with resulting broth to make a sauce for the chicken. (A hand-held blender is ideal for this). Place the sauce back in cooker and add the carrots, shallots (green onions, scallions) and potatoes.

Lock the lid in place. Over high heat bring to high pressure. Adjust heat to maintain high pressure and cook for 4 minutes. Let the pressure drop using the quick-release method. Remove the lid, tilting it away from you to allow any excess steam to escape.

Check consistency of the sauce and reduce to thicken as needed to intensify flavour. Taste and correct seasoning. Place chicken pieces back in the sauce to warm them slightly if needed; otherwise, nap the sauce over the chicken.

Tips and Techniques
To add a richness to the sauce, pour $1/4$ cup of flaming brandy over the sauce in cooker just before serving.

Roast Chicken

- **40 mL (2 Tbsp) olive oil**
- **1 kg (2½ lb) whole chicken (small enough to fit in your pressure cooker)**
- **1 small onion, diced**
- **4 cloves garlic, peeled, crushed and minced**
- **2 small tart apples, cored, seeded and chopped**
- **½ tsp salt**
- **⅛ tsp ground black pepper**
- **2 Tbsp fresh parsley, snipped**

- **4 sprigs fresh rosemary or 1 tsp dried rosemary**
- **125 mL (½ cup) white wine**
- **125 mL (½ cup) chicken stock (broth)**
- **40 mL (2 Tbsp) olive oil**
- **2 Tbsp plain (all-purpose) flour**
- **420 g (14 oz) container chicken stock (broth)**
- **4–6 serves of mashed potatoes or other vegetables**

Pressure Cooker
4–6 L (4–6 quart)

Serves 4–6

Heat the oil in pressure cooker. Place chicken in cooker and carefully brown on all sides as well as you can. Remove chicken from pot. Add onion, garlic and apples to pot and sauté for 3 minutes. With slotted spoon, remove mixture to a bowl.

Mix together salt, pepper, parsley and rosemary. Rub chicken inside and out with seasoning. Mix up more if needed. When chicken is thoroughly seasoned, place apple, onion and garlic mixture inside of chicken cavity. Place a rack in the bottom of cooker and gently place chicken on the rack. Add wine and chicken stock (broth) mixed together.

Lock the lid in place. Over high heat bring to high pressure. Adjust heat to maintain high pressure and cook for 30 minutes. Let the pressure drop using the quick-release method. Remove the lid, tilting it away from you to allow any excess steam to escape.

Stick a fork into the leg or thigh, not hitting the bone, to check for doneness. If juices run clear, it's time to eat. If not, replace lid and lock down. Bring back to pressure and cook for an additional 5 minutes. After releasing steam, remove lid and transfer chicken to platter.

Add olive oil to cooker. Mix flour and 125 mL (1/2 cup) chicken broth together. Add container of chicken stock (broth) to cooker. Heat oil and broth mixture to a slow boil and stir in flour thickener. Keep stirring constantly until a nice gravy consistency is produced. Remove from heat and cover.

Serve your chicken and gravy with mashed potatoes and another vegetable of your choice.

Raspberry Chicken

- **125 mL (½ cup) sweet red wine**
- **125 mL (½ cup) vinegar**
- **125 mL (½ cup) raspberry jam (can be low sugar or sugarless)**
- **40 mL (2 Tbsp) soy sauce**
- **40 mL (2 Tbsp) honey**

- **1 tsp Dijon mustard**
- **1 clove garlic, minced**
- **1 frying chicken, skinned and cut in pieces**
- **strips of orange zest for garnish**

Pressure Cooker

6 L (6 quart)

Serves 4

Mix all ingredients together except chicken and orange zest. Stir until well combined. Taste and adjust sweetness to your personal preference. Pour mixture over chicken and let it marinate for up to 4 hours in the refrigerator.

Place chicken with marinade in pressure cooker and bring to the boil.

Lock the lid in place. Over high heat bring to high pressure. Adjust heat to maintain high pressure and cook for 12 minutes. Let the pressure drop naturally. Remove the lid, tilting it away from you to allow any excess steam to escape.

Remove chicken, leaving marinade in pot. If a thicker sauce is desired, boil sauce in uncovered pot until it thickens. Pour thickened sauce over chicken and sprinkle with orange zest.

Tips and Techniques

This is an absolutely delicious chicken recipe, but depending on the type of jam used, it can take on a very dark colour. Enhance the appearance by garnishing with fine shreds of orange peel.

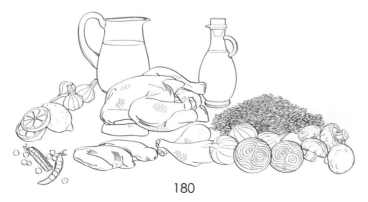

Soy Chicken

- **2 chicken breasts, boned and skinned**
- **½ cup mushrooms, sliced**
- **½ medium onion, sliced**
- **½ cup celery, sliced**
- **60 mL (¼ cup) low sodium soy sauce**

- **250 mL (1 cup) water**
- **3 Tbsp brown sugar**
- **4 serves steamed rice and/or cooked vegetables**

Pressure Cooker

4–6 L (4–6 quart)

Serves 4

Place all ingredients in pressure cooker.

Lock the lid in place. Over high heat bring to high pressure. Adjust heat to maintain high pressure and cook for 5 minutes. Let the pressure drop naturally. Remove the lid, tilting it away from you to allow any excess steam to escape.

Serve with rice and/or vegetables.

Fruity Rock Chicken

- **20 mL (1 Tbsp) oil**
- **2 chickens, 750 g (1½ lb) each**
- **12 pitted prunes**
- **8 dried apricots**
- **½ small lemon, cut in 6 thin slices**
- **¼ cup shallots (green onions, scallions) or onions, finely minced**
- **2 stalks celery, finely minced**
- **1 Tbsp fresh ginger, finely minced**

- **250 mL (1 cup) chicken stock or bouillon**
- **¼ tsp salt (less if using preprepared stock or bouillon)**
- **750 g (1½ lb) sweet potatoes, peeled and halved**
- **1 Tbsp orange zest**
- **60 mL (¼ cup) Grand Marnier**

Pressure Cooker

6–8 L (6–8 quart)

Serves 2–4

Heat the oil in pressure cooker. Brown the chickens well on both sides. Stuff each chicken with 6 prunes and 4 apricots, interspersing the lemon slices among the dried fruits. Truss the chickens and set aside.

In the fat remaining in cooker, sauté the shallots (green onions, scallions), celery and ginger for 2 minutes. Stir in the stock or bouillon and salt; scrape up any browned bits that are sticking to the bottom of the pan. Place the chickens side by side in the sauce. (You may need to put one chicken on its side.) Place the sweet potatoes on top.

Lock the lid in place. Over high heat bring to high pressure. Adjust heat to maintain high pressure and cook for 10 minutes. Let the pressure drop using the quick-release method. Remove the lid, tilting it away from you to allow any excess steam to escape.

Check for doneness by inserting a knife into the drumstick joint; if the meat is still pink, lock the lid back in place, return to high pressure and cook for another 1 to 2 minutes. Transfer the chickens to a platter and remove the trussing. Reserve in a warm place.

Add the orange zest and Grand Marnier and boil the sauce over high heat until the alcohol burns off and the sauce is reduced slightly, about 3 to 4 minutes. Transfer sauce to a sauce boat and pour over the stuffed chickens, then serve.

Tips and Techniques
For the chickens to hold their shape during cooking, you'll need some kitchen string to truss them. Depending upon your appetite and the number of accompaniments, two stuffed chickens will serve either two or four people.

Sweet 'n' Sour Chicken

Chicken

- 20 mL (1 Tbsp) vegetable oil or olive oil
- 1.5 kg (3 lb) chicken, cut up
- ½ cup celery, sliced
- 1 green or red capsicum (pepper), cut in chunks
- 600 g (20 oz) can pineapple chunks, drained and juice reserved
- 250 mL (1 cup) reserved pineapple juice (add water if necessary)
- ¼ cup brown sugar
- 125 mL (½ cup) vinegar
- 40 mL (2 Tbsp) soy sauce
- 20 mL (1 Tbsp) tomato sauce (ketchup)
- ½ tsp Worcestershire Sauce
- ¼ tsp ground ginger
- 2 Tbsp cornflour (cornstarch)
- 40 mL (2 Tbsp) cold water

Steamed Rice

- 1 cup long grain white rice
- 375 mL (1½ cups) water
- 250 mL (1 cup) water

Pressure Cooker

4–6 L (4–6 quart)

Serves 4–6

184

Chicken

Heat the oil in pressure cooker. Brown chicken a few pieces at a time; set aside. Return all chicken to cooker, and add celery and capsicum (pepper). Combine pineapple juice, brown sugar, vinegar, soy sauce, tomato sauce (ketchup), Worcestershire Sauce and ginger; pour over chicken.

Lock the lid in place. Over high heat bring to high pressure. Adjust heat to maintain high pressure and cook for 8 minutes. Let the pressure drop using the quick-release method. Remove the lid, tilting it away from you to allow any excess steam to escape.

Transfer chicken and vegetables to a warm platter. Mix cornflour (cornstarch) with cold water; blend into hot liquid. Cook and stir until mixture boils and thickens. Add pineapple chunks and heat. Pour sauce over chicken. Serve with steamed rice.

Steamed Rice

Combine rice and 250 mL (1 cup) water in a metal bowl. Use a 1.25 L (5 cup) capacity bowl, 8 cm (3 in) high or less, which will fit loosely into a 4 to 6 L (4 to 6 quart) pressure cooker.

Place 250 mL (1 cup) water, cooking rack and bowl in cooker.

Lock the lid in place. Over high heat bring to high pressure. Adjust heat to maintain high pressure and cook for 5 minutes. Let the pressure drop naturally. Remove the lid, tilting it away from you to allow any excess steam to escape. Let rice steam, uncovered, for 5 minutes.

Stuffed Chicken Breasts

- **4 chicken breast halves, boned and skinned**
- **75 g (2½ oz) jar sliced mushrooms, drained**
- **½ cup fine dry breadcrumbs**
- **½ tsp dried sage, crushed**
- **¼ tsp dried marjoram, crushed**
- **dash garlic salt**
- **dash black pepper**
- **125 mL (½ cup) chicken stock (broth)**
- **1 Tbsp cornflour (cornstarch)**
- **20 mL (1 Tbsp) dry white wine**

Pressure Cooker

4–6 L (4–6 quart)

Serves 4

Rinse chicken and pat dry. Place each chicken breast half between two sheets of cling wrap. Working from the centre to the edges, pound lightly with the flat side of a meat mallet to 3 mm (¹/₈ in) thickness. Set aside.

In a small mixing bowl, stir together mushrooms, breadcrumbs, sage, marjoram, garlic salt, pepper and 40 mL (2 Tbsp) chicken stock (broth). Spoon a quarter of the mixture onto the short end of each chicken breast. Fold in long sides of chicken and roll up, starting from the short edge. Secure with wooden toothpicks. Place in pressure cooker and add ¹/₂ cup of chicken stock (broth).

Lock the lid in place. Over high heat bring to high pressure. Adjust heat to maintain high pressure and cook for 5 minutes. Let the pressure drop using the quick-release method. Remove the lid, tilting it away from you to allow any excess steam to escape.

Transfer chicken to a serving platter and keep warm.

To make sauce, strain liquid in cooker through a sieve. Return liquid to cooker. In a small bowl, stir together cornflour and wine. Add to liquid in cooker. Cook and stir until thickened and bubbly, and then cook and stir for 2 minutes more. Serve sauce over chicken.

Tips and Techniques
You can prepare the chicken rolls in advance and chill until time to pressure cook them.

Turkey and Vegetable Hot Pot

- 20 mL (1 Tbsp) olive oil
- 1 clove garlic, finely minced
- 1 kg (35 oz) can tomatoes with juice, coarsely chopped
- 750 g (1½ lb) small potatoes, scrubbed
- 2 large carrots, peeled and cut in 4 to 5 chunks
- 8 small onions, peeled
- 3 stalks celery, finely chopped
- ⅓ cup dried mushrooms
- 1 tsp dried oregano
- ½ tsp dried rosemary leaves
- 1 bay leaf
- 2 strips orange zest
- ½ tsp salt or to taste
- 2 turkey drumsticks, skinned
- 310 g (10 oz) fresh or frozen green beans, thawed
- 1½ cups corn kernels
- ⅓ cup fresh parsley or coriander (cilantro), finely minced
- salt and pepper to taste

Pressure Cooker

6–8 L (6–8 quart)

Serves 4

Ensure the two turkey drumsticks will fit into your pressure cooker. There's no harm if the end of the bone touches the lid of the cooker, as long as it doesn't block the vent.

Heat the oil in cooker and sauté the garlic for 10 seconds. Add the tomatoes, potatoes, carrots, onion, celery, mushrooms, oregano, rosemary, bay leaf, orange zest and salt. Stand the two drumsticks, meaty side down, in the soup.

Lock the lid in place. Over high heat bring to high pressure. Adjust heat to maintain high pressure and cook for 12 minutes. Let the pressure drop naturally. Remove the lid, tilting it away from you to allow any excess steam to escape.

Remove the drumsticks and cut the meat from the bone. Cut the meat into 2.5 cm (1 in) chunks and return to the pot. Discard the bones (or reserve them for stock). Stir in the green beans, corn and parsley, and cook over medium heat until the vegetables are cooked, about 3 to 5 minutes. Remove the orange zest and bay leaf and add salt and pepper to taste. Serve.

Warm Chicken Salad

- **4 chicken breasts, boned and skinned**
- **¾ cup dried apricots, snipped**
- **1 cinnamon stick**
- **½ tsp orange zest**
- **¼ tsp ground cloves**
- **190 mL (¾ cup) orange juice**

- **60 mL (¼ cup) water**
- **½ cup pecans, toasted (see below)**
- **½ cup mozzarella cheese, finely shredded**
- **8 cups torn leaf lettuce**

Pressure Cooker
4–6 L (4–6 quart)

Serves 4

Rinse chicken and pat dry. In pressure cooker combine chicken, apricots, cinnamon stick, orange zest, cloves, orange juice and water.

Lock the lid in place. Over high heat bring to high pressure. Adjust heat to maintain high pressure and cook for 4 minutes. Let the pressure drop using the quick-release method. Remove the lid, tilting it away from you to allow any excess steam to escape.

Remove chicken and apricots with a slotted spoon. Cut chicken in bite-size strips. Line four salad plates with lettuce; arrange chicken, apricots, pecans and mozzarella over lettuce. Remove cinnamon stick from the juices and discard. Drizzle cooking juices over each salad and serve.

Tips and Techniques
To toast pecans, spread the pecans into a thin layer in a shallow baking pan. Bake in a 175°C (350°F) oven for 5 to 10 minutes or until light golden brown, stirring once or twice.

Lamb

Irish Lamb Stew

- **1 kg (2½ lb) boneless lamb, cut in 4 cm (1½ in) cubes**
- **40 mL (2 Tbsp) oil**
- **750 mL (3 cups) water**
- **1½ tsp salt**
- **½ tsp ground pepper**
- **4 turnips, cut in 1.25 cm (½ in) slices**
- **4 carrots, cut in 1.25 cm (½ in) slices**
- **2 onions, sliced**
- **4 potatoes, peeled and quartered**
- **2 Tbsp plain (all-purpose) flour**
- **60 mL (¼ cup) water**
- **¼ cup fresh parsley, chopped**

Pressure Cooker

4–6 L (4–6 quart)

Serves 4

Brown the meat in oil in pressure cooker. Add water.

Lock the lid in place. Over high heat bring to high pressure. Adjust heat to maintain high pressure and cook for 15 minutes. Let the pressure drop naturally. Remove the lid, tilting it away from you to allow any excess steam to escape.

Add the salt, pepper, turnips, carrots, onions and potatoes to cooker. Cover and simmer, not under pressure, for 30 minutes.

Blend flour with the water until it forms a paste. Slowly add to the stew, stirring constantly until slightly thickened. Stir in parsley and serve.

Lamb Hot Pot

- **8 lamb chops**
- **40 mL (2 Tbsp) oil**
- **250 g (½ lb) onions, sliced**
- **125 g (¼ lb) carrots, sliced**
- **500 g (1 lb) potatoes, sliced**
- **salt and pepper**
- **500 mL (2 cups) vegetable stock (broth)**

Pressure Cooker
4–6 L (4–6 quart)

Serves 4

Trim excess fat from the chops. Heat the oil in pressure cooker and brown the chops on all sides. Add the vegetables and cook gently for a further 3 to 4 minutes. Season well with salt and pepper and add the stock (broth).

Lock the lid in place. Over high heat bring to high pressure. Adjust heat to maintain high pressure and cook for 35 minutes. Let the pressure drop naturally. Remove the lid, tilting it away from you to allow any excess steam to escape.

If necessary, remove some of the surface fat with a paper towel. Arrange the chops, vegetables and stock (broth) in a serving dish, finishing with a layer of potatoes. Brown under your griller (broiler) before serving.

Seafood

Almond Cod with Peas

- 500 g (1 lb) frozen cod fillets
- 2 large cloves garlic, cut in half
- ½ cup lightly packed parsley sprigs
- 1 Tbsp fresh oregano sprigs or
  ½ tsp dried oregano
- 2 Tbsp slivered or sliced almonds
- ½ tsp paprika

- 20 mL (1 Tbsp) vegetable oil
- 250 mL (1 cup) chicken stock (broth)
  or white wine
- 310 g (10 oz) frozen peas
- 1 Tbsp cornflour (cornstarch)
- 20 mL (1 Tbsp) cold water

Pressure Cooker

4–6 L (4–6 quart)

Serves 4

Remove fish from freezer and let stand at room temperature while preparing herb mixture. Put garlic, parsley, oregano, 1 Tbsp almonds and paprika in food processor. Chop using intermittent switch.

Heat the oil in pressure cooker. Brown remaining almonds in hot oil. Remove from cooker and drain on paper towels; set aside.

Pour chicken stock (broth) or white wine into cooker and stir in herb mixture. Place cooking rack in cooker. Cut fish into four even pieces and place on rack.

Lock the lid in place. Over high heat bring to high pressure. Adjust heat to maintain high pressure and cook for 2 minutes. Let the pressure drop using the quick-release method. Remove the lid, tilting it away from you to allow any excess steam to escape.

Carefully remove fish and keep warm. Remove the rack from cooker. Add frozen peas to cooker.

Lock the lid in place. Over high heat bring to high pressure. Adjust heat to maintain high pressure and cook for 1 minute. Let the pressure drop using the quick-release method. Remove the lid, tilting it away from you to allow any excess steam to escape.

If desired, thicken mixture with cornflour (cornstarch) mixed with cold water. Pour peas into serving dish and place fish on top of peas. Sprinkle fish with browned almonds and serve.

Boston Clambake

- 375 mL (1½ cups) water
- 1 bay leaf
- 1 Tbsp each fresh chopped herbs such as parsley, chives, oregano, thyme, chervil (or substitute with ½ tsp dried herbs)
- 4 cloves garlic, slivered
- sea salt and freshly ground white pepper to taste
- 2–3 large red potatoes, washed and quartered
- 1 medium onion, quartered
- 16–20 fresh/live littleneck clams, thoroughly rinsed (or if clams are not available, use fresh, live mussels)
- 250–300 g (8–10 oz) cold water lobster tail (may substitute large prawns/ shrimp, deveined, shells left on)
- 4–6 large sea scallops
- 3 Tbsp butter, cut in thin slices
- 1 ear corn, cut in 4 × 4 cm (1½ in) pieces
- lemon wedges for garnish

Pressure Cooker

6 L (6 quart)

Serves 4

Pour the water into pressure cooker. Add bay leaf, herbs and garlic. Season with salt and pepper. Add potatoes and onion. Add clams or mussels; spread them evenly. Split lobster tail in half (leave in shell), lightly season and lay over clams. Lightly season sea scallops and layer in cooker. Place thinly sliced butter over the top of the lobster and scallops. Add corn-on-the-cob pieces.

Lock the lid in place. Over high heat bring to high pressure. Adjust heat to maintain high pressure and cook for 4 minutes. Let the pressure drop using the quick-release method. Remove the lid, tilting it away from you to allow any excess steam to escape.

Serve hot in large bowls with a lemon wedge.

Sweet and Sour Prawns

- **500 g (1 lb) small green prawns (shrimp), peeled**
- **125 g (¼ lb) snow peas**
- **60 mL (3 Tbsp) soy sauce**
- **40 mL (2 Tbsp) white vinegar**
- **125 mL (½ cup) pineapple juice**
- **2 Tbsp sugar**
- **250 mL (1 cup) chicken stock (broth)**
- **4 serves steamed rice**

Pressure Cooker

4 L (4 quart)

Serves 4

In pressure cooker combine all ingredients.

Lock the lid in place. Over high heat bring to high pressure. Adjust heat to maintain high pressure and cook for 3 to 5 minutes. Let the pressure drop using the quick-release method. Remove the lid, tilting it away from you to allow any excess steam to escape.

If sauce needs to be thickened, place back on stove and turn heat on low and stir constantly for a few minutes. Serve hot over rice.

Stuffed Snapper

- 4 cleaned snapper (small pinkies or baby snapper are best)
- salt and pepper
- 2 eating apples, grated
- 1 small onion, finely chopped
- 1 cup fresh breadcrumbs
- 1 cup cheddar cheese (American cheese), grated
- 80 mL (⅓ cup) melted butter
- 310 mL (1¼ cups) water
- lemon slices and chopped fresh parsley for garnish

Pressure Cooker

4–6 L (4–6 quart)

Serves 4

Wipe the inside of the snapper and season it inside and out with salt and pepper.

Mix together the apple, onion, breadcrumbs and grated cheese. Season to taste, then bind the mixture with 40 mL (2 Tbsp) of the melted butter. Stuff the fish and secure it with wooden cocktail sticks or toothpicks. Place each fish on a separate sheet of foil. Pour the remaining melted butter over the snapper. Fold the foil over and seal to make four parcels. Pour the water into the pressure cooker and position the rack. Place the parcels on the rack.

Lock the lid in place. Over high heat bring to high pressure. Adjust heat to maintain high pressure and cook for 6 minutes. Let the pressure drop using the quick-release method. Remove the lid, tilting it away from you to allow any excess steam to escape.

Serve with a parsley garnish and a slice of lemon.

Whiting in Creole Sauce

- **40 mL (2 Tbsp) oil**
- **1 small onion, chopped**
- **1 clove garlic, crushed**
- **1 stalk celery, chopped**
- **1 green capsicum (pepper), chopped and seeded**
- **500 g (1 lb) can tomatoes**
- **310 mL (1¼ cups) water (to make tomato juice)**

- **1 Tbsp tomato paste**
- **1 tsp sugar**
- **pinch of basil**
- **½ tsp chilli powder**
- **salt and pepper**
- **4 whiting fillets, skinned and cut in cubes**
- **4 side serves of green salad**

Pressure Cooker
4 L (4 quart)

Serves 4

Heat the oil in pressure cooker and sauté the onion, garlic, celery and capsicum (pepper) gently for 2 to 3 minutes. Stir in the tomatoes, including juice made up to 310 mL (1¹/₄ cups) using added water. Add the tomato paste, sugar, basil, chilli powder, seasoning and whiting pieces.

Lock the lid in place. Over high heat bring to high pressure. Adjust heat to maintain high pressure and cook for 4 minutes. Let the pressure drop using the quick-release method. Remove the lid, tilting it away from you to allow any excess steam to escape.

Serve on warmed plates with a green side salad.

Tips and Techniques
Haddock is a good substitute for the whiting fillets.

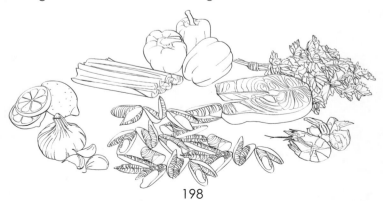

Pasta and Rice

Barley Risotto Primavera

- **40 mL (2 Tbsp) olive oil**
- **1 cup pearl or pot barley**
- **1 small onion, minced**
- **1 clove garlic, minced**
- **½ cup zucchini (courgette), finely chopped**
- **½ cup carrot, minced**
- **¼ cup celery, minced**
- **375 mL (1½ cup) vegetable stock (broth) or water**
- **1 tsp tamari (soy sauce)**
- **¼ cup parmesan cheese, freshly grated**
- **⅛ tsp freshly ground black pepper**

Pressure Cooker

4 L (4 quart)

Serves 4

In pressure cooker heat oil over medium heat. Add barley and sauté for 1 minute or until toasted. Add onions, garlic, zucchini (courgette), carrot and celery, and sauté for 1 minute longer or until vegetables begin to soften. Stir in the stock (broth) or water and tamari.

Lock the lid in place. Over high heat bring to high pressure. Reduce heat to medium-low, just to maintain even pressure and cook for 18 minutes. Remove from heat and let the pressure drop naturally. Remove the lid, tilting it away from you to allow any excess steam to escape.

Fluff risotto with a spoon. Stir in parmesan cheese and pepper. Serve immediately.

Basmati Salad with Corn and Roasted Red Capsicums

- 20 mL (1 Tbsp) olive oil
- 1 large garlic clove, peeled and finely chopped
- 1½ tsp cumin seeds
- 1 large onion, finely chopped
- 1 cup brown basmati rice
- 450 g (14½ oz) container chicken or vegetable stock (broth)
- 1 tsp sea salt (less if using preprepared stock)
- fresh kernels from 2 large ears of sweet corn
- 2 large roasted red capsicums (peppers), seeded and cut in 6 mm × 1.25 cm (¼ in × ½ in) strips
- freshly ground black pepper to taste
- 20 mL (1 Tbsp) balsamic vinegar
- ⅓ cup fresh coriander (cilantro), minced and tightly packed

Pressure Cooker

4–6 L (4–6 quart)

Serves 4

Heat the oil in pressure cooker and sauté the garlic, cumin seeds and onion for 1 minute, stirring frequently. Stir in the rice, making sure to coat it thoroughly with the oil. Add the stock (broth) and optional salt. Stir until the mixture reaches boiling over high heat.

Lock the lid in place. Over high heat bring to low pressure. Adjust the heat to maintain low pressure and cook for 15 minutes. Let the pressure drop using the quick-release method. Remove the lid, tilting it away from you to allow any excess steam to escape.

Stir in the corn, roasted capsicums (peppers), black pepper, balsamic vinegar and coriander (cilantro). Place the lid on the cooker and leave sitting off the heat for 3 more minutes. Serve immediately or chill to serve cold. Tastes great the second day!

Brown Rice and Lentil Stew

- **40 mL (2 Tbsp) olive oil**
- **3 cloves garlic, minced**
- **3 cups onions, coarsely chopped**
- **3 stalks celery, sliced**
- **2½ cups raw short grain brown rice, picked over and rinsed**
- **2 cups dried lentils**
- **250 g (½ lb) mushrooms, sliced**
- **1.2 L (4¾ cups) chicken or vegetable stock or bouillon**
- **2 bay leaves**
- **1½ tsp dried oregano**
- **1 Tbsp prepared mustard**
- **½ tsp salt or to taste**
- **250 mL (1 cup) Napoletana sauce**
- **1 cup fresh parsley, minced**

Pressure Cooker

6–8 L (6–8 quart)

Serves 6–8

Heat the oil in pressure cooker. Sauté the garlic and onions until the onions are lightly browned, about 4 to 5 minutes. Stir in the celery, brown rice and lentils and sauté for another minute. Add the mushrooms, stock or bouillon, bay leaves, oregano and mustard, and bring to the boil.

Lock the lid in place. Over high heat bring to high pressure. Adjust heat to maintain high pressure and cook for 20 minutes. Let the pressure drop naturally for 10 minutes and then quick-release any remaining pressure. Remove the lid, tilting it away from you to allow any excess steam to escape.

Remove the bay leaves and stir in the salt, Napoletana sauce and parsley. If the rice or lentils are not quite done, cover and simmer over low heat until desired consistency, stirring in a bit of boiling water if the mixture seems dry. Adjust seasonings and serve.

Tips and Techniques
This recipe calls for short grain brown rice, which has a delightfully chewy texture – a nice contrast to the pliant lentils.

Brown Rice and Vegetables

- 1 cup brown rice
- 500 mL (2 cups) chicken stock (broth)
- 60 g (2 oz) sliced blanched almonds
- ½ cup carrots, diced
- ½ cup celery, diced
- ½ cup green capsicum (pepper), diced
- ½ cup green onions (shallots, scallions), sliced
- 1 large tomato, peeled, seeded and chopped
- 375 mL (1½ cups) water
- ¼ cup fresh parsley, chopped

Pressure Cooker

4 L (4 quart)

Serves 4

Combine brown rice and stock (broth) in a metal bowl that fits loosely in a 6 L (6 quart) pressure cooker. Stir in almonds and vegetables. Place water, cooking rack or steamer basket, and bowl in cooker.

Lock the lid in place. Over high heat bring to high pressure. Adjust heat to maintain high pressure and cook for 10 minutes. Let the pressure drop naturally. Remove the lid, tilting it away from you to allow any excess steam to escape and allow rice to steam uncovered for 5 minutes.

Stir in parsley and serve.

Caribbean-style Rice and Beans

- 20 mL (1 Tbsp) oil
- 2 tsp garlic, minced
- 1 cup onions, coarsely chopped
- 1 hot red chilli pepper, seeded and chopped, or a generous pinch of crushed red chilli pepper flakes
- 1 cup red capsicum (pepper), diced
- 1 cup plum tomatoes, coarsely chopped
- 560 mL (2¼ cups) boiling water
- 1½ cups long grain brown rice
- ½ cup dried, unsweetened coconut, grated
- ½ tsp dried thyme or oregano leaves
- 1 tsp salt or to taste
- 1 cup cooked pigeon or black-eyed peas
- ¼ cup fresh coriander (cilantro), finely minced
- 2 very ripe plantains, peeled and cut on diagonal into thin slices and fried

Pressure Cooker

6–8 L (6–8 quart)

Serves 6

Heat the oil in pressure cooker. Add garlic, onions and chilli pepper. Cook over medium-high heat, stirring frequently, for 1 minute. Add capsicum (pepper), tomatoes, water, rice, coconut, thyme and salt.

Lock the lid in place. Over high heat bring to high pressure. Adjust heat to maintain high pressure and cook for 25 minutes. Let the pressure drop naturally. Remove the lid, tilting it away from you to allow any excess steam to escape.

Add cooked peas and coriander (cilantro). Stir well to distribute coconut. Serve topped with plantains.

Chana Dal Pilaf

- 125 mL (½ cup) vegetable oil
- 2 bay leaves
- 6 peppercorns
- 6 black cardamom pods (see Tips and Techniques below)
- 6 whole cloves
- ⅓ cinnamon stick
- 1½ tsp cumin seeds
- 1½ cups chana dal (see Tips and Techniques below), soaked in water for 2 hours and drained
- 2½ cups basmati rice
- 1 Tbsp salt
- 1.125 L (4½ cups) water
- yoghurt to serve

Pressure Cooker

4–6 L (4–6 quart)

Serves 6

Heat the oil in pressure cooker on medium-high heat. Add bay leaves, peppercorns, cardamom pods, cloves, cinnamon stick and cumin seeds. Stir for a few seconds until cumin seeds darken a few shades. Add chana dal. Stir for about 3 minutes. Add rice. Stir until rice turns opaque (approximately 3 minutes). Add salt and water. Stir.

Lock the lid in place. Over high heat bring to high pressure. Adjust heat to maintain high pressure and cook for 5 minutes. Let the pressure drop using the quick-release method. Remove the lid, tilting it away from you to allow any excess steam to escape.

Fluff up rice gently with a fork to separate grains. Discard bay leaves, cardamom pods and cinnamon stick. Serve hot, accompanied with yoghurt.

Tips and Techniques

Black cardamom pods and chana dal are available at East Indian food stores.

To cook smaller quantities, reduce all ingredients proportionately but not below one-fourth of original amount.

Chicken Biryani

- 1 Tbsp butter
- 1½ cups onions, chopped
- 2 tsp anise seed
- 2 tsp cumin seeds
- 2 Tbsp tomato paste
- 500 mL (2 cups) chicken stock (broth)
- 250 mL (1 cup) water
- 2 large bay leaves
- 1½ tsp table salt (½ tsp if using salty stock/broth)
- 4 tsp mild curry powder plus more to taste
- ¼ tsp ground cinnamon
- 1 pinch cayenne pepper, optional
- 750 g (1½ lb) chicken thighs, boned and skinned, cut in 2.5 cm (1 in) chunks, or chicken breast halves, boned and skinned (or a combination of breasts and thighs)
- 2 cups basmati rice or long grain white rice
- 1 cup frozen peas
- ½ cup toasted slivered almonds or chopped roasted cashews

Pressure Cooker

4 L (4 quart)

Serves 6

Heat the butter in pressure cooker. Add the onions, anise seeds and cumin seeds, and cook over medium-high heat, stirring frequently, until the onions begin to soften, about 2 minutes. Blend in the tomato paste and cook for 20 seconds longer. Stir in the stock (broth), water, bay leaves, salt, curry powder, cinnamon and cayenne pepper (if using). Taste the broth and, if there isn't a strong curry flavour, add more curry powder to taste. Stir in the chicken and rice.

Lock the lid in place. Over high heat bring to high pressure. Adjust heat to maintain high pressure and cook for 3 minutes. Turn off the heat. Let the pressure drop naturally for 7 minutes, then quick release any remaining pressure. Remove the lid, tilting it away from you to allow steam to escape.

Quickly stir in the peas and almonds and additional salt, if needed. Replace the cover and steam the mixture in the residual heat until the peas are defrosted, about 1 to 2 minutes. Stir well to fluff up rice. Remove the bay leaves. Serve with bowls of yoghurt toppings on the side (see page 207).

Tips and Techniques
For a variation add $1/3$ cup raisins along with rice.

Zesty, Sweet Yoghurt Topping
Blend 1 heaped Tbsp of sweet mango chutney into 1 cup plain yoghurt.

Spicy-Hot Yoghurt Topping
Blend 1 heaped Tbsp of eggplant relish into 1 cup plain yoghurt.

Lamb Biryani
Omit chicken stock (broth) and increase water to 750 mL (3 cups). Replace chicken with 750 g ($1^1/2$ lb) boned lamb shoulder, cut in 2 cm ($3/4$ in) chunks and trimmed. (If boned shoulder is not available, buy 1 kg/$2^1/2$ lb lamb shoulder chops; cut in cubes and trim yourself. Include bones for added flavour, then remove before serving.)

Before adding rice, cook lamb for 8 minutes at high pressure. Quick-release pressure and skim off any surface fat. Stir in rice and cook for 3 more minutes at high pressure, plus 7 minute using natural pressure release.

Vegetable Biryani
For a vegetarian option use vegetable instead of chicken stock (broth). Replace the chicken with $1^1/2$ cups cooked chickpeas (garbanzos) (or a 450 g/15 oz can, drained) and 500 g (1 lb) peeled butternut pumpkin (squash) cut in 2 cm ($3/4$ in) chunks. After cooking, stir in $1/4$ cup chopped fresh coriander (cilantro). Season with 20 to 40 mL (1 to 2 Tbsp) freshly squeezed lime juice.

Curried Rice with Chicken, Peas and Currants

- 1 packet frozen peas, slightly thawed
- 2 Tbsp butter
- 3 chicken breasts, boned and skinned
- 1 small onion, coarsely chopped
- 1 cup baby carrots
- 1 tsp cumin seeds
- 1 tsp fennel seeds
- 2 cups long grain white rice (jasmine or basmati)

- 420 g (14 oz) container chicken stock (broth)
- 420 g (14 oz) can unsweetened coconut milk
- 1½ Tbsp curry powder
- ¼ cup currants
- 1 tsp salt

Pressure Cooker

4–6 L (4–6 quart)

Serves 6

Take the peas out of the freezer and set aside to partially thaw.

Heat 1 Tbsp of butter in pressure cooker over medium-high heat. Add the chicken and brown on both sides. Transfer chicken to a plate and cover to keep warm. The chicken will still be pink in the middle. (Do not be tempted to overcook. You will finish the cooking later.)

Heat an additional tablespoon of butter in the cooker and sauté the onion and carrots for 1 to 2 minutes. Add cumin seeds, fennel seeds and rice, stirring to coat with the oil. (Be careful not to scorch the rice.) Add the stock (broth), coconut milk, curry powder, currants and salt. Stir the mixture well, making sure nothing is sticking to the bottom of cooker (coconut milk and rice will scorch). Keep stirring until the mixture begins to boil. This is a very important step!

Lock the lid in place. Over high heat, bring to medium pressure. Adjust the heat to maintain medium pressure and cook for 7 minutes. Let the pressure drop naturally. Remove the lid, tilting it away from you to allow any excess steam to escape.

While the rice is cooking, cut the chicken into small diced pieces. The chicken will still be a bit pink in the centre, but it will cook more when added to the rice. The coconut milk will have risen to the top, so stir it down into the mixture. Adjust for creamy consistency, adding water or stock (broth) if necessary, and adjust the spices. Add the chicken and peas to the rice and stir.

Put the lid on the cooker but do not bring under pressure. Let the chicken, peas and rice steam for an additional 1 to 2 minutes until the peas are warmed through and the rice is done. Stir well before serving.

Creamy Rice with Vegetables

- **20 mL (1 Tbsp) olive oil**
- **1 medium onion, peeled and finely chopped**
- **1 cup short grain or arborio rice**
- **2 small carrots, chopped**
- **250 g (½ lb) broccoli florets**
- **450 g (14½ oz) container chicken or vegetable stock (broth)**
- **1 tsp dried Italian herbs**
- **¼ cup parmesan cheese, freshly grated**

Pressure Cooker

4 L (4 quart)

Serves 4

In pressure cooker heat olive oil over medium-high heat. Add onion and sauté until transparent. Add rice, stirring often, until lightly golden. Add the vegetables and stock (broth). Stir to mix. Increase heat to high. Stir in herbs. Continue to stir until mixture comes to the boil to prevent sticking.

Lock the lid in place. Over high heat bring to medium pressure. Adjust heat to maintain medium pressure and cook for 7 minutes. Let the pressure drop using the quick-release method. Remove the lid, tilting it away from you to allow any excess steam to escape.

Stir in parmesan cheese and serve.

Macaroni with Steak

- **2 Tbsp peanut or canola oil**
- **500 g (1 lb) round steak, at least 2.5 cm (1 in) thick**
- **1 large onion, chopped**
- **1 red capsicum (pepper), chopped**
- **sweet paprika to taste**
- **2 cloves garlic, minced**
- **2 × 420 g (14 oz) cans Italian tomatoes, undrained**

- **1 tsp oregano flakes**
- **salt and pepper to taste**
- **3 Tbsp tomato paste**
- **190 g (6 oz) can mushroom stems and pieces**
- **250 g (8 oz) uncooked elbow macaroni**
- **1 cup grated cheddar cheese**

Pressure Cooker

4 L (4 quart)

Serves 4

Heat pressure cooker, add oil and place steak in hot oil in bottom of pot. Brown steak well on all sides. Add onions, capsicum (pepper), paprika and garlic, and stir-fry until onions and garlic are soft but not brown. Add tomatoes, oregano, salt and pepper. Add tomato paste and mushrooms. Place macaroni in pot and cover with rest of ingredients until pasta is submerged. (Top up with cold water if necessary).

Lock the lid in place. Over high heat bring to high pressure. Adjust heat to maintain high pressure and cook for 6 minutes. Let the pressure drop using the quick-release method. Remove the lid, tilting it away from you to allow any excess steam to escape.

Stir in cheese until it is melted and smooth. Serve in shallow bowls.

211

One Dish Pasta with Meat Sauce

- 20 mL (1 Tbsp) olive oil
- 350 g (¾ lb) minced (ground) turkey, beef, pork or lamb
- 1½ cups onions, coarsely chopped
- 1 tsp fennel seeds
- 125 mL (½ cup) dry red wine
- 375 mL (1½ cup) water
- ¾ tsp salt
- 1 tsp garlic powder
- 375 g (12 oz) spiral or other short tubular pasta that normally cooks in 9–13 minutes
- 840 g (28 oz) can crushed tomatoes with juice
- ¼ cup fresh parsley, chopped
- ¼ cup fresh grated parmesan
- ½ tsp crushed red chilli pepper flakes
- pinch of sugar, optional

Pressure Cooker
4–6 L (4–6 quart)

Serves 4

Heat oil in pressure cooker. Add meat and brown over high heat, stirring to break up clumps. Stir in onion and fennel seeds and cook for 1 minute. Stir in the wine, scraping up any browned bits on the bottom of the pan. Boil over high heat for 1 minute. Stir in water, salt and garlic. Bring back to the boil. Add the pasta and pour the tomatoes on top. Do not stir after adding the tomatoes.

Lock the lid in place. Over high heat bring to high pressure. Adjust heat to maintain high pressure and cook for 5 minutes. Let the pressure drop using the quick-release method. Remove the lid, tilting it away from you to allow any excess steam to escape.

Stir in parsley, parmesan cheese and red chilli pepper flakes. Add sugar, if using. Break up any clumps of pasta and let the dish rest, uncovered, for 3 to 5 minutes. If the pasta is not uniformly tender, replace the lid during the resting period and set the cooker on low heat, stirring occasionally, until the pasta is done. If desired, drizzle with a bit more olive oil and sprinkle with additional cheese when serving.

Noodle Goulash

- **40 mL (2 Tbsp) olive oil**
- **250 g (½ lb) minced (ground) beef**
- **¼ cup onion, sliced**
- **½ cup green capsicum (pepper), sliced**
- **½ cup celery, diced**
- **1 cup green beans, canned or frozen**
- **40 mL (2 Tbsp) cream of mushroom soup**
- **125 mL (½ cup) tomato puree, by pulsing some canned tomatoes in blender or food processor**
- **40 mL (2 Tbsp) Worcestershire Sauce**
- **1 tsp salt**
- **½ tsp fresh ground black pepper**
- **40 mL (2 Tbsp) preprepared or homemade beef stock (broth)**
- **1 Tbsp sweet paprika**
- **1 cup wide egg noodles**
- **butter for serving**

Pressure Cooker

4–6 L (4–6 quart)

Serves 4

Brown meat in hot oil in pressure cooker. Add onion, capsicum (pepper) and celery, and sauté for 1 minute. Add remaining ingredients except egg noodles.

Lock the lid in place. Over high heat bring to high pressure. Adjust heat to maintain high pressure and cook for 10 minutes. Let the pressure drop using the quick-release method. Remove the lid, tilting it away from you to allow any excess steam to escape.

Serve goulash over hot cooked buttered noodles.

Pasta e Fagioli

- 1½ cups dried cannellini beans, soaked overnight in water to cover
- 20 mL (1 Tbsp) olive oil
- 1 Tbsp garlic, coarsely chopped
- 2 cups onions, coarsely chopped
- 2 large stalks celery, diced
- 2 large carrots, halved lengthwise and cut in 1.25 cm (½ in) slices
- 1 large bay leaf
- 1½ tsp dried basil leaves
- 1 tsp dried rosemary leaves
- ¼ tsp crushed red chilli pepper flakes
- 1.25 L (5 cups) boiling water
- 3 Tbsp tomato paste
- 1 cup small dry pasta (orzo or spirals)
- 60 mL (3 Tbsp) balsamic vinegar
- 1 tsp salt
- 20 mL (1 Tbsp) olive oil
- freshly grated parmesan cheese

Pressure Cooker
6–8 L (6–8 quart)

Serves 6

Drain and rinse the beans, and set aside. Heat 20 mL (1 Tbsp) of the oil in pressure cooker. Cook the garlic over medium-high heat, stirring frequently, until lightly browned. Stir in the onions and continue cooking, stirring occasionally for 1 minute. Add the celery, carrots, bay leaf, basil, rosemary, red chilli pepper flakes, reserved beans and water.

Lock the lid in place. Over high heat bring to high pressure. Adjust heat to maintain high pressure and cook for 9 to 12 minutes. Let the pressure drop using the quick-release method. Remove the lid, tilting it away from you to allow any excess steam to escape.

If the beans are still hard, return to high pressure for a few more minutes, or leave the lid off and simmer until the beans are soft. Remove the bay leaf and stir in the tomato paste and pasta. Continue cooking over medium-high heat, stirring occasionally, until the pasta is tender, about 7 minutes. Stir in the vinegar, the additional tablespoon of olive oil and salt. Garnish individual servings with parmesan cheese.

Risotto Alfredo with Chicken and Peas

- 40 mL (2 Tbsp) extra virgin olive oil
- 1 Tbsp butter
- 2 chicken breasts, boned and skinned, cut in 2.5 cm (1 in) pieces
- 2 cloves garlic, finely chopped
- 1 small onion, minced
- 1 cup arborio or short grain white rice
- 2 × 420 g (14 oz) container chicken stock (broth)
- 60 mL (¼ cup) white wine
- 1 cup frozen green peas, thawed
- 250 mL (1 cup) bottled or fresh alfredo sauce
- ⅓ cup freshly grated parmigiano reggiano cheese
- salt and pepper to taste

Pressure Cooker

4 L (4 quart)

Serves 4

Heat the oil and butter in pressure cooker and sauté the chicken pieces, garlic and onion over medium-high heat, stirring frequently, until they start to turn a nice golden colour. Add the rice, stirring to coat with the oil. Let the rice cook in the oil for about 2 minutes, stirring constantly until it begins to look translucent. Add the stock (broth) and wine.

Lock the lid in place. Over high heat bring to medium pressure. Adjust the heat to maintain medium pressure and cook for 7 minutes. Let the pressure drop using the quick-release method. Remove the lid, tilting it away from you to allow any excess steam to escape.

The rice will be a bit al dente and should have a creamy consistency. Bring to a simmer and add the peas, alfredo sauce and parmigiano reggiano cheese. Stir until heated through and adjust salt and pepper to taste. Serve.

Risotto with Gruyere and Parmesan

- 2 Tbsp unsalted butter
- 20 mL (1 Tbsp) olive oil
- ⅓ cup onions, finely minced
- 1½ cup arborio rice
- 1 L (4 cups) vegetable or chicken stock or bouillon
- 1 cup gruyere cheese, grated
- ¼ cup parmesan cheese, grated
- salt to taste, if desired

Pressure Cooker

4–6 L (4–6 quart)

Serves 6 as an entree, 4 as a main course

Heat the butter and oil in pressure cooker. Sauté the onion until soft but not brown, about 2 minutes. Stir in the rice, making sure to coat it thoroughly with the oil. Stir in the stock or bouillon (watch for sputtering oil).

Lock the lid in place. Over high heat bring to high pressure. Adjust heat to maintain high pressure and cook for 6 minutes. Let the pressure drop using the quick-release method. Remove the lid, tilting it away from you to allow any excess steam to escape.

Taste the rice. If it's not sufficiently cooked, add a bit more stock as you stir. Cook over medium heat until the additional liquid has been absorbed and the rice is desired consistency, about 1 to 2 minutes. When the rice is ready, stir in the gruyere and parmesan cheese, add salt to taste and serve immediately.

Tips and Techniques

Traditionally arborio rice is not rinsed before cooking, since the water washes away starches that contribute to the velvety sauce enveloping each grain. The perfect risotto should be slightly soupy and properly chewy, with the rice offering just a pleasant resistance to the bite. For this reason, the pressure is always quick released and the risotto must be served as soon as it is finished.

Leftover risotto can be shaped into pancakes and warmed or pan-fried in a little butter, or reheated in the microwave.

Although classic risottos usually contain wine, this recipe is flavourful without it.

Risotto with Mushrooms Piédmontese

- **250 g (½ lb) mushrooms (porcini, cremini, chanterelles), sliced**
- **40 mL (2 Tbsp) olive oil**
- **½ Tbsp rosemary**
- **salt and fresh pepper**
- **1 Tbsp unsalted butter**

- **1 shallot (green onion, scallion), minced**
- **1 cup arborio rice**
- **¼ cup dry white wine**
- **2 cups chicken stock (broth)**
- **salt and pepper to taste**
- **grated parmesan cheese to serve**

Pressure Cooker

4 L (4 quart)

Serves 4

Trim the stems from the mushrooms and save. Slice the mushroom caps.

In pressure cooker heat the oil. Add the mushroom caps, rosemary, salt and pepper, and cook for 3 minutes. Stir. Add butter, shallot (green onion, scallion) and chopped mushroom stems. Cook for 2 minutes. Add rice, wine and stir. Add stock (broth).

Lock the lid in place. Over high heat bring to high pressure. Adjust heat to maintain high pressure and cook for 6 minutes. Let the pressure drop using the quick-release method. Let stand for 5 minutes, then remove the lid, tilting it away from you to allow any excess steam to escape.

Season with salt and pepper, and serve with parmesan cheese.

Risotto with Tomatoes and Mozzarella

- 1 Tbsp butter
- 20 mL (1 Tbsp) oil from sun-dried tomatoes
- ½ cup onion, finely minced
- 1½ cups arborio rice
- 875 mL (3½ cups) vegetable stock or bouillon

- ⅓ cup sun-dried tomatoes, oil-packed, drained and chopped (reserve oil)
- 1 cup packed grated smoked mozzarella cheese
- salt to taste

Pressure Cooker

4–6 L (4–6 quart)

Serves 6 as an entree, 4 as a main course

Heat the butter and oil in pressure cooker. Sauté the onion until soft but not brown, about 2 minutes. Stir in the rice, making sure to coat it thoroughly with the fat. Stir in the stock or bouillon (watch for sputtering oil).

Lock the lid in place. Over high heat bring to high pressure. Adjust heat to maintain high pressure and cook for 6 minutes. Let the pressure drop using the quick-release method. Remove the lid, tilting it away from you to allow any excess steam to escape.

Taste the rice. If it's not sufficiently cooked, add a bit more stock as you stir. Cook over medium heat until the additional liquid has been absorbed and the rice is desired consistency, about 1 to 2 minutes. When the rice is ready, stir in the sun-dried tomatoes and mozzarella cheese, and add salt to taste. Serve immediately.

Vegetables

Azuki Bean and Pumpkin Stew

- 1 cup dried azuki beans (see Tips and Techniques)
- 750 mL (3 cups) water or vegetable stock (broth)
- 20 mL (1 Tbsp) oil
- 1 tsp ground ginger
- ½ tsp ground cinnamon
- 1 kg (2 lb) butternut pumpkin (squash), peeled and cut in 4 cm (1½ in) chunks
- 250 g (½ lb) parsnips, peeled and cut in 1.25 cm (½ in) pieces
- 1–2 Tbsp butter
- salt to taste

Pressure Cooker
4 L (4 quart)

Serves 4

Place the beans, water and oil in pressure cooker.

Lock the lid in place. Over high heat bring to high pressure. Adjust heat to maintain high pressure and cook for 14 minutes. Let the pressure drop using the quick-release method. Remove the lid, tilting it away from you to allow any excess steam to escape.

Stir in the ginger to taste, cinnamon, pumpkin (squash) and parsnips.

Lock the lid in place. Over high heat return to high pressure. Adjust heat to maintain high pressure and cook for an additional 4 minutes. Let the pressure drop using the quick-release method. Remove the lid, tilting it away from you to allow any excess steam to escape.

Stir in butter and salt to taste.

Tips and Techniques
Azuki beans can be easily obtained at any Chinese grocery store and in the Chinese section of many supermarkets. They are also used as the basis for red bean paste.

Antipasto

- 1 cup carrots, diced
- 1 cup green capsicum (pepper), chopped
- 1½ cups cauliflower florets, cut in small pieces
- 1 cup mushrooms, quartered
- ½ cup gherkins (dill pickles), chopped
- 1 cup celery, chopped
- 2 medium tomatoes, chopped and seeded
- 1 cup black olives, sliced
- ½ cup small onions, pickled and chopped
- 1 small jar artichoke hearts, drained and chopped
- 250 mL (1 cup) Napoletana sauce
- 250 mL (1 cup) tomato sauce (ketchup)
- 60 mL (3 tsp) olive oil

Pressure Cooker
4–6 L (4–6 quart)

Serves 4–6

Put everything in pot – carrots, capsicum (pepper), cauliflower, mushrooms, gherkins (dill pickles), celery, tomatoes, black olives, onions, artichoke hearts, Napoletana sauce, tomato sauce and olive oil.

Lock the lid in place. Over high heat bring to high pressure. Adjust heat to maintain high pressure and cook for 15 minutes. Let the pressure drop using the quick-release method. Remove the lid, tilting it away from you to allow any excess steam to escape.

Serve either in a large bowl for buffet-style service or in small bowls for individual serves.

Tips and Techniques
If you like, add a small can of good quality white tuna to this dish. Drain and add to vegetables, and let it simmer without the lid for another 3 to 4 minutes.

This dish keeps for a week in the fridge and freezes well.

Artichokes with Lemon Pepper Oil

- **4 medium to large artichokes**
- **250 mL (1 cup) water**

- **40 mL (2 Tbsp) lemon pepper oil**

Pressure Cooker

6–8 L (6–8 quart)

Serves 4

Trim the stems off the artichokes. Snip the sharp points off the ends of the leaves with kitchen scissors and wash carefully between the leaves. Place rack on the bottom of pressure cooker and add water. Place the artichokes inside cooker, flowering-side up and drizzle 10 mL (¹/₂ Tbsp) of lemon pepper oil over each artichoke.

Lock the lid in place. Over high heat bring to medium pressure. Adjust heat to maintain medium pressure and cook for 10 to 12 minutes. Let the pressure drop naturally. Remove the lid, tilting it away from you to allow any excess steam to escape.

Artichokes may be served either warm or cold.

Boston Baked Beans

- 2 cups dried navy beans
- 60 mL (3 Tbsp) cooking oil
- 1 Tbsp salt
- water to cover beans
- 250 g (½ lb) salt pork, diced, or bacon, sliced
- 4 Tbsp brown sugar
- 3 Tbsp molasses (black treacle)
- 1 tsp prepared mustard
- 1 medium onion, diced
- 80 mL (4 Tbsp) tomato sauce (ketchup)
- water

Pressure Cooker
4–6 L (4–6 quart)

Serves 4

Place the beans in pressure cooker. Add oil, salt and water to cover beans well. Soak overnight or for about 8 hours.

Sear or brown salt pork or bacon and drain. Add remaining ingredients and enough water to cover beans with about 2.5 cm (1 in) of water above the beans. Stir.

Lock the lid in place. Over high heat bring to medium pressure. Adjust heat to maintain medium pressure and cook for 45 minutes. Let the pressure drop naturally. Remove the lid, tilting it away from you to allow any excess steam to escape.

This is a very versatile dish. Serve it by itself, in warmed bowls or as an accompaniment to egg dishes and grills, on toast or even in sandwiches.

Caribbean Black Beans and Orzo Picadillo

- 1½ cups dry black beans
- 840 g (28 oz) undrained canned tomatoes, diced
- 1½ cups onions, coarsely chopped
- ½ cup raisins
- 3 cloves garlic, minced
- 1–2 jalapeño peppers, seeded and finely chopped
- 1 tsp ground cinnamon
- ½ tsp salt
- ¼ tsp ground cloves
- 20 mL (1 Tbsp) cooking oil
- 500 mL (2 cups) water
- ⅔ cup orzo, rosa marina or soup pasta
- ⅓ cup sliced pimiento-stuffed green olives
- ⅓ cup slivered almonds, toasted
- 12 flour tortillas

Pressure Cooker

6 L (6 quart)

Serves 6

Presoak beans for 4 hours. Drain and rinse the beans.

In pressure cooker combine the beans, undrained tomatoes, onions, raisins, garlic, jalapeño peppers, cinnamon, salt, cloves, oil and pasta. Add enough water to cover by 5 cm (2 in).

Lock the lid in place. Over high heat bring to medium pressure. Adjust heat to maintain medium pressure and cook for 6 minutes. Let the pressure drop naturally. Remove the lid, tilting it away from you to allow any excess steam to escape.

Stir in olives. Cover loosely (do not lock lid) and let stand for 5 minutes. Stir in almonds. Meanwhile wrap flour tortillas in foil and heat in a 180°C (350°F) oven for 10 minutes. Serve the picadillo with the warm tortillas.

Caribbean Stew

- 1 large onion, chopped
- ½ tsp salt
- 40 mL (2 tsp) vegetable oil
- ½ tsp dried thyme
- ½ tsp ground allspice
- 1 fresh chilli, minced
- 1 large sweet potato, cut in 4 cm (1 ½ in) chunks
- 375 mL (1 ½ cups) vegetable stock (broth)
- 2 small zucchinis (courgettes), cut in 2.5 cm (1 in) chunks
- 4 cups kale, shredded and loosely packed
- 1 ½ cups undrained canned tomatoes, chopped
- 20 mL (1 Tbsp) lemon or lime juice
- 2 Tbsp fresh coriander (cilantro), finely chopped
- salt to taste

Pressure Cooker

4 L (4 quart)

Serves 4

Sprinkle onions with the salt. In pressure cooker sauté onions in oil until softened, stirring occasionally. Add the thyme, allspice and chilli, and continue to cook for another 1 to 2 minutes. Stir in the sweet potato and stock and bring to the boil. Add the zucchini (courgette) and kale and pour tomatoes over the top. Do not stir.

Lock the lid in place. Over high heat bring to high pressure. Adjust heat to maintain high pressure and cook for 8 minutes. Let the pressure drop using the quick-release method. Remove the lid, tilting it away from you to allow any excess steam to escape.

Stir in the citrus juice, coriander (cilantro) and salt to taste.

Caribbean Rice and Beans

- 20 mL (1 Tbsp) olive oil or annatto oil (see Tips and Techniques)
- 2 tsp garlic, minced
- 1 cup onion, coarsely chopped
- 1 hot red chilli pepper, seeded and chopped, or 1 pinch crushed red chilli pepper flakes (generous)
- 1 cup red capsicum (pepper), diced
- 1 cup Roma tomatoes, coarsely chopped
- 500 mL (2 cups) boiling water; jiggle tops use 560 mL (2¼ cups)
- 1½ cups long grain brown rice, rinsed and drained
- ½ cup dried, grated, unsweetened coconut
- ½ tsp dried thyme or dried oregano
- 1 tsp salt or to taste
- 1 cup firmly cooked black-eyed peas
- ¼ cup fresh coriander (cilantro), finely minced, optional
- 2 ripe plantains, peeled, cut on the diagonal into thin slices and fried in a heavy frying pan lightly brushed with oil

Pressure Cooker

4–6 L (4–6 quart)

Serves 4–6

Heat the oil in pressure cooker. Cook the garlic, onions and chilli pepper over medium-high heat, stirring frequently, for 1 minute. Add the red capsicum (pepper), tomatoes, water (stand back to avoid sputtering oil), rice, coconut, thyme and salt.

Lock the lid in place. Over high heat bring to high pressure. Adjust heat to maintain high pressure and cook for 25 minutes. Let the pressure drop naturally for 10 minutes. Quick release any remaining pressure. Remove the lid, tilting it away from you to allow any excess steam to escape.

As you add the black-eyed peas and the (optional) coriander (cilantro), stir well to distribute the coconut. Serve in mounds, topped with fried plantains.

Tips and Techniques
The infused annatto oil, used in Latin American cooking, has a golden colour and a subtle taste. It is available at Hispanic markets but is easy to prepare at home (you can buy annatto seeds at specialist herb stores and in some delicatessens). Heat 1 Tbsp of annatto seeds in 1/4 cup (60 mL) of olive or canola oil and simmer over low heat for 5 minutes. Cool, then pour through a fine-meshed strainer. Discard seeds. Refrigerate oil until needed.

For a magnificent finish to this dish, fry up the ripe plantains and set them decoratively on top. A steamed green vegetable and a green salad will complete the meal. Plantains look like large green bananas until they are fully ripened, at which time they turn completely black and are at their sweetest. To peel plantains, cut shallow incisions down the length at about 4 cm (1 1/2 in) intervals and remove the skin. (Plantains resist peeling more than bananas do.)

Eggplant Caponata

- 60 mL (¼ cup) olive oil
- 60 mL (¼ cup) dry white wine
- 40 mL (2 Tbsp) balsamic vinegar
- 1 tsp ground cinnamon
- 1 large eggplant (aubergine), peeled and cut in 1.25 cm (½ in) cubes
- 1 medium onion, coarsely chopped
- 1 medium green capsicum (pepper), stemmed, cored and diced
- 1 medium red capsicum (pepper), stemmed, cored and diced

- 2 cloves garlic, peeled and finely chopped
- 420 g (14 oz) can diced tomatoes, drained
- 3 stalks celery, coarsely chopped
- ½ cup nicoise olives, pitted and chopped
- ½ cup sultanas (golden raisins)
- 2 Tbsp capers

Pressure Cooker
4–6 L (4–6 quart)

Makes 8 side dish servings or 12 hors d'oeuvres servings

In pressure cooker heat olive oil, white wine, balsamic vinegar and cinnamon over medium-high heat. Add eggplant, onion, capsicums (peppers), garlic, tomatoes, celery, olives, raisins and capers, and stir to mix well.

Lock the lid in place. Over high heat bring to medium pressure. Adjust heat to maintain medium pressure and cook for 8 minutes. Let the pressure drop naturally. Remove the lid, tilting it away from you to allow any excess steam to escape.

Serve hot, cold or room temperature.

Tips and Techniques
When used as a filling, it is best to drain off or reduce excess liquid.

This Mediterranean favourite makes great use of all the vegetables from your summer garden. Making it a day in advance enhances the complex blend of flavours.

Carrot Tsimmes

- 500 g (1 lb) carrots, cut on the diagonal in 4 cm (½ in) slices
- 250 g (½ lb) butternut pumpkin (squash), seeded and cut in 2.5 cm (1 in) chunks (peeling optional)
- 2 large sweet potatoes, peeled, halved lengthwise and cut in 1.25 cm (½ in) slices
- ½ tsp salt or to taste
- ½ tsp ground cinnamon
- ¼ tsp ground allspice
- 1 lemon, scrubbed, quartered and pitted
- 1 cup pitted prunes, halved
- 250 mL (1 cup) boiling water
- freshly squeezed lemon juice, optional

Pressure Cooker
4–6 L (4–6 quart)

Serves 6

Place all the ingredients except the optional lemon juice in pressure cooker.

Lock the lid in place. Over high heat bring to high pressure. Adjust heat to maintain high pressure and cook for 4 minutes. Let the pressure drop using the quick-release method. Remove the lid, tilting it away from you to allow any excess steam to escape.

Remove the lemon quarters and stir well. Season with lemon juice if desired. Have an extra lemon on hand to perk up the flavours, if desired.

Tips and Techniques
Substitute ½ cup apricots for half of the pitted prunes.

For a sweeter version, use ½ cup apple or orange juice instead of an equivalent amount of water.

Try parsnips, peeled and cut in 1.25 cm (½ in) slices, instead of butternut pumpkin (squash).

Chickpeas with Sweet Onions

- 1½ cups dried chickpeas (garbanzos), picked over and rinsed, soaked overnight in ample water to cover
- 20 mL (1 Tbsp) safflower oil or canola oil
- 2 tsp cumin seeds
- 500 mL (2 cups) vegetable stock (broth)
- 1 Tbsp ground coriander seeds
- 2 tsp sweet paprika
- ¼ tsp saffron threads
- 1 pinch crushed red chilli pepper flakes (generous)
- 1 tsp ground cinnamon
- 1 kg (2 lb) onions (use Spanish or white onions), peeled and thinly sliced
- 1 cup plum tomatoes, finely chopped
- salt to taste

Pressure Cooker

4–6 L (4–6 quart)

Serves 4–6

Drain and rinse the chickpeas (garbanzos). Set aside.

Heat the oil in pressure cooker. Sizzle the cumin seeds over medium-high heat just until they begin to pop, about 5 to 10 seconds. Add the stock (broth) (stand back to avoid sputtering oil), coriander, paprika, saffron threads, red chilli pepper flakes, cinnamon and reserved chickpeas (garbanzos). Set the onions on top followed by the tomatoes. (Do not stir at this point).

230

Lock the lid in place. Over high heat bring to high pressure. Adjust heat to maintain high pressure and cook for 18 minutes. Let the pressure drop naturally. Remove the lid, tilting it away from you to allow any excess steam to escape.

If the chickpeas (garbanzos) are not fairly tender (they should hold their shape but be quite soft), return to high pressure for a few more minutes or replace (but do not lock) the lid and simmer until they are done. With a slotted spoon, transfer a cup of the chickpeas (garbanzos) and onions to a food processor or blender and puree. Stir the puree back into the stew to create a thick sauce. Add salt before serving.

Tips and Techniques
This stew is delicious served in bowls on its own or over parsley or spinach fettuccine.

Do not be concerned if the onions and tomatoes come to the top of the cooker. They will shrink as the cooker comes up to pressure.

If using canned tomatoes, do not include the juice as it will interfere with the cooking of the chickpeas (garbanzos).

An alternative to pureeing the chickpeas (garbanzos) is to mash some against the side of the pot.

Creamy Mashed Potatoes

- **250 mL (1 cup) water**
- **1.5 kg (3 lb) russet potatoes, peeled and cut in 2.5 cm (1 in) chunks**
- **1 tsp salt plus more to taste**
- **4 Tbsp butter**
- **170 mL (⅔ cup) heavy cream or unthickened cream (half-and-half)**
- **freshly ground pepper, optional**

Pressure Cooker

4 L (4 quart)

Serves 4–6

Pour the water into pressure cooker. Add the potatoes and sprinkle with salt.

Lock the lid in place. Over high heat bring to high pressure. Adjust heat to maintain high pressure and cook for 8 minutes. Turn off the heat. Let the pressure drop using the quick-release method. Remove the lid, tilting it away from you to allow any excess steam to escape.

If the potatoes are not fork-tender, replace the cover and steam for a few more minutes over high heat. Drain the potatoes in a large colander. Set the cooker over low heat. Melt the butter and stir in the cream. Pass the potatoes through a ricer or the medium blade of a food mill directly into the butter-cream mixture. Using a whisk or slotted spoon, stir briskly to achieve a light, creamy texture. Add more cream to thin and more butter for added richness, if desired. Season to taste with salt and pepper (if using). Serve immediately.

For the variations on page 233, follow the main basic recipe above except where noted.

Tips and Techniques
Instead of cream, use potato cooking liquid, low-fat milk (2 percent milk) or buttermilk. (The latter will give potatoes a slightly tangy taste.)

Mustard Mashed Potatoes
Blend 1 1/2 Tbsp Dijon mustard (preferably wholegrain) and 40 mL (2 Tbsp) sour cream into 80 mL (1/3 cup) milk. Stir into melted butter before adding riced potatoes.

Garlic Mashed Potatoes
Cook 5 to 10 peeled cloves of garlic with potatoes. Pass garlic through food mill or ricer along with potatoes.

Cheesy Mashed Potatoes
Reduce butter to 2 Tbsp, and use milk instead of cream. After adding riced potatoes to milk, stir in 1 cup grated sharp cheddar (American), mild cheddar (Monterey Jack) or fontina cheese.

Sour Cream and Chives Mashed Potatoes
Substitute 1/2 cup sour cream for heavy cream. Use cooking liquid, as needed, to thin. Stir 3 Tbsp snipped chives into mashed potatoes.

Creole Okra

- **40 mL (2 tsp) olive oil**
- **2 tsp minced garlic**
- **2 cups onions, coarsely chopped, or white and light green parts of leeks, thinly sliced**
- **500 g (1 lb) okra, cut in 1.25 cm (½ in) slices**
- **2 cups Roma tomatoes, fresh or canned (drained), coarsely chopped**
- **250 mL (1 cup) water or substitute juice from drained tomatoes, plus water to equal 250 mL (1 cup)**
- **20 mL (1 Tbsp) apple cider vinegar**
- **2 stalks celery, cut in 1.25 cm (½ in) slices**
- **1 large red capsicum (pepper), seeded and diced**
- **1 tsp dried oregano leaves**
- **½ tsp dried thyme leaves**
- **1 large bay leaf**
- **1 pinch crushed red chilli pepper flakes**
- **1 tsp salt or to taste**

Pressure Cooker

4–6 L (4–6 quart)

Serves 4

Heat the oil in pressure cooker. Cook the garlic over medium-high heat, stirring constantly, until browned. Immediately add the onions and continue cooking, stirring frequently, for 1 minute. Add the okra, tomatoes, water (stand back to avoid sputtering oil), apple cider vinegar, celery, red capsicum (pepper), oregano, thyme, bay leaf, red chilli pepper flakes and salt.

Lock the lid in place. Set cooker on a heated flame tamer. Over high heat bring to high pressure. Adjust heat to maintain high pressure and cook for 1 minute (young, small okra) to 3 minutes (older, large pods). Let the pressure drop using the quick-release method. Remove the lid tilting it away from you to allow any excess steam to escape.

Stir well and add a bit more cider vinegar, if desired, to sharpen the flavours.

Tips and Techniques
Serve as a side dish in a small bowl. Alternatively, use the stew as a delicious topping for rice or pasta. And don't forget to pass the Tabasco sauce.

If you'd like to replicate the flavour of bacon or smoked ham so often used in Creole recipes, after cooking, stir in some liquid smoke flavouring, readily available in supermarkets.

Fresh Greens with Beetroot, Haricots Verts and Mustard

- **4 medium beetroots (beets), gently washed and trimmed**
- **250 g (½ lb) French or Blue Lake beans, trimmed**
- **125 mL (½ cup) water**
- **60 mL (3 Tbsp) balsamic vinegar**

- **1 tsp Dijon mustard**
- **40 mL (2 Tbsp) walnut oil**
- **6 serves of mixed salad greens**
- **¼ cup shelled walnuts in halves or pieces to garnish**

Pressure Cooker

4–6 L (4–6 quart)

Serves 6

In a larger pressure cooker place whole beetroots (beets) on the steaming rack with water in the bottom of the cooker.

Lock the lid in place. Over high heat bring to high pressure. Adjust heat just to maintain high pressure and cook for 10 to 14 minutes. Let the pressure drop naturally. Remove the lid, tilting it away from you to allow any excess steam to escape.

While the beetroots (beets) cook, prepare the beans. In a large frying pan, boil enough water to cover the beans. When the water is boiling, blanch the beans for 1 minute. Immediately remove the beans and refresh them in a large bowl of ice water. Drain and pat dry with towels. Cool beetroots (beets), slip off their skins and julienne.

Mix balsamic vinegar and mustard together. Slowly add the walnut oil while whisking to make a vinaigrette. Arrange greens on each plate. Toss the beetroots (beets) and beans in the vinaigrette to coat them and place on top of the greens. Just before serving, garnish with walnut pieces.

Fresh Peas and Carrots with Lettuce

- 1 Tbsp butter
- 5 cups peas, shelled
- 9 small carrots, cut in 6 mm (¼ in) slices
- 20 tiny white onions, peeled
- 1¼ cups lettuce, coarsely shredded

- 1½ tsp dried basil
- 1½ tsp dried rosemary, crushed
- ½ tsp salt
- ⅛ tsp pepper
- ½ cup water

Pressure Cooker

4 L (4 quart)

Serves 4

Melt the butter in pressure cooker. Add remaining ingredients and stir.

Lock the lid in place. Over high heat bring to high pressure. Adjust heat to maintain high pressure and cook for 1 minute. Let the pressure drop using the quick-release method. Remove the lid tilting it away from you to allow any excess steam to escape.

Serve hot.

Tips and Techniques

To cook smaller quantities, reduce all ingredients proportionately. Maintain a minimum 60 mL (¼ cup) water.

Garden Medley with Ham

- 1 kg (2 lb) fresh green beans, trimmed
- 2 onions, coarsely chopped
- 1 large red capsicum (pepper), coarsely chopped
- 3 yellow summer (crookneck) squash, sliced 2.5 cm (1 in) thick
- 4 red potatoes, scrubbed and sliced 1.25 cm (½ in) thick
- 2 cups (or more) cubed ham
- 125 mL (½ cup) chicken stock (broth)
- 2 Tbsp butter or margarine
- 1 Tbsp cornflour (cornstarch), to thicken sauce if desired
- 80 mL (⅓ cup) cold water, to thicken sauce if desired

Pressure Cooker
4–6 L (4–6 quart)

Serves 4–6

Place the rack in pressure cooker and add all ingredients.

Lock the lid in place. Over high heat bring to medium pressure. Adjust heat just to maintain medium pressure and cook for 3 minutes. Let the pressure drop using the quick-release method. Remove the lid, tilting it away from you to allow any excess steam to escape.

Drain, reserving liquid. Thicken sauce, if required, by adding cornflour (cornstarch) mixed in cold water, stirring over gentle heat and pouring over vegetable mixture. Serve immediately.

German Potato Salad

- 2½ Tbsp sugar
- 1 tsp salt
- ⅛ tsp pepper
- 1 tsp dry mustard
- 80 mL (⅓ cup) white vinegar
- 40 mL (2 Tbsp) water

- 2 Tbsp dried parsley flakes or 4 Tbsp fresh parsley, chopped
- 6 rashers bacon, diced
- 4 large potatoes, peeled and cubed
- 1 medium yellow-brown onion, thinly sliced

Pressure Cooker
4–6 L (4–6 quart)

Serves 4–6

Combine sugar, salt, pepper, mustard, vinegar, water and parsley; blend well to dissolve sugar.

Fry diced bacon in pressure cooker until crisp; remove with slotted spoon. Pour drippings into heatproof measure; return 60 mL (3 Tbsp) of the drippings to cooker. Add potatoes, diced cooked bacon and onion; toss to coat.

Lock the lid in place. Over high heat bring to medium pressure. Adjust heat just to maintain medium pressure and cook for 5 minutes. Let the pressure drop using the quick-release method. Remove the lid, tilting it away from you to allow any excess steam to escape.

Allow to cool and serve with salads or grilled meat dishes.

Green Beans with Tomatoes and Basil

- 6 Tbsp butter
- 5 cloves garlic. minced
- 1 kg (2½ lb) green beans, cut diagonally in 4 cm (1½ in) pieces
- 4 small tomatoes, peeled and cut in eighths

- 2½ Tbsp dried basil
- 1½ tsp salt
- ¼ tsp pepper

Pressure Cooker

4–6 L (4–6 quart)

Serves 4–6

Melt the butter in pressure cooker. Add garlic and stir for a few seconds. Away from heat add remaining ingredients and mix.

Lock the lid in place. Over high heat bring to high pressure. Adjust heat just to maintain high pressure and cook for 2 minutes. Let the pressure drop using the quick-release method. Remove the lid, tilting it away from you to allow any excess steam to escape.

Serve hot.

Tips and Techniques

To cook smaller quantities, reduce all ingredients proportionately but not below one-third of original amount.

Japanese Dashi Turnips

- **250 mL (1 cup) water**
- **40 mL (2 Tbsp) tamari (soy sauce)**
- **10 mL (2 tsp) mirin (Japanese rice wine), optional**
- **5 cm (2 in) strip kombu sea vegetable, rinsed, optional**
- **5 large dried shiitake mushrooms**
- **1 tsp sugar, optional**
- **750 g (1½ lb) medium turnips, peeled and cut in 2.5 cm (1 in) chunks**

Pressure Cooker

4–6 L (4–6 quart)

Serves 4–6

Bring the water and tamari to the boil in pressure cooker. Add the remaining ingredients.

Lock the lid in place. Over high heat bring to high pressure. Adjust heat just to maintain high pressure and cook for 1 minute. Let the pressure drop using the quick-release method. Remove the lid, tilting it away from you to allow any excess steam to escape.

If the turnips are not quite done – they should be crisp-tender – replace (but do not lock) the lid and let them continue to cook for a few more minutes in the residual heat.

When the turnips are done, remove the shiitake mushrooms. Slice off and discard the stems. Cut the caps into thin slivers. Finely chop the kombu (if using). Lift the turnips out of any remaining cooking liquid with a slotted spoon. Transfer to individual plates or to a serving bowl. Sprinkle the shiitake and kombu over the turnips and serve warm or at room temperature. Refrigerate any leftovers in a tightly covered glass container.

Tips and Techniques

This is a wonderful quick way to prepare a lightly salted turnip that works beautifully as a condiment but is mild enough to double as a vegetable side dish. The turnips develop an earthy brown tone from being cooked in the tamari; the shiitake mushrooms add a luscious density of flavour.

Dashi turnips last a week to 10 days in the refrigerator.

For a variation, substitute peeled swedes (rutabagas) cut in 1.25 cm (½ in) cubes for all or part of the turnips in this recipe.

Mediterranean Stuffed Capsicums

- 4 medium capsicums (peppers; red, green, orange and/or yellow)
- 385 g (12.3 oz) extra-firm low-fat silken tofu
- 420 g (14 oz) can Napoletana sauce
- 1 Tbsp chopped fresh oregano, or 1½ tsp dried oregano
- 1 tsp chopped fresh mint or ½ tsp dried mint
- 1 Tbsp chopped fresh chives or green onion (shallot, scallion)
- ¼ tsp ground cinnamon
- 20 mL (1 Tbsp) fresh lemon juice
- 1 cup dry couscous
- ⅓ cup pitted kalamata olives, thinly sliced
- 120 g (4 oz) low-fat feta cheese, crumbled
- 250 mL (1 cup) water
- 800 g (24 oz) jar tomato-based pasta sauce
- sprigs of fresh mint, for garnish

Pressure Cooker
4–6 L (4–6 quart)

Serves 4–6

To make the filling, using a paring knife, carefully cut a circle around the stem of the capsicums (peppers) and then pull out the stem. The hole at the top of each needs to be big enough to accommodate a large soup spoon. Remove the seeds and membranes and reserve the tops.

Chop tofu into small, bite-size pieces. In a large bowl, mix the tofu with all remaining ingredients except capsicum (pepper) bottoms and pasta sauce. Set aside.

Divide the filling evenly among the four capsicums (peppers), stuffing them carefully with a soup spoon. Put water in the bottom of pressure cooker and put the rack in place. Stand the capsicums (peppers) on the rack.

Lock the lid in place. Over high heat bring to high pressure. Adjust heat just to maintain high pressure and cook for 4 minutes. Let the pressure drop using the quick-release method. Remove the lid, tilting it away from you to allow any excess steam to escape.

While the capsicums (peppers) are cooking, warm pasta sauce in a 2 L (2 quart) pan over medium heat. When capsicums are ready to serve, spoon ½ cup of the pasta sauce on the bottom of four dinner plates or shallow pasta bowls. Place one cooked capsicum (pepper) in the middle of each plate and top with the reserved stem. Garnish with a sprig of fresh mint and some crumbled feta, then serve immediately.

Mixed Bean and Sausage Chilli

- 2 cups dried mixed beans (garbanzo, navy and pinto)
- 500 g (1 lb) sweet or hot Italian sausage, cut in 2.5 cm (1 in) pieces (remove the casings from the sausage, if desired)
- 1 ½ cups onions, chopped
- 2 cloves garlic, minced
- 2 Tbsp chilli powder
- 2 tsp dried oregano leaves, crushed
- 1 tsp ground cumin
- 1 tsp crushed red chilli pepper, optional

- 2 × 435 g (14 oz) cans stewed tomatoes, undrained
- 375 mL (12 oz) bottle beer or 375 mL (1 ½ cups) water
- 125 mL (½ cup) water
- 2 Tbsp tomato paste
- 125 mL (½ cup) water
- ¼ cup fresh coriander (cilantro), snipped, optional
- ½ cup coarsely grated cheddar (American) or tasty cheese

Pressure Cooker

4–6 L (4–6 quart)

Serves 6

Rinse beans. In a large saucepan combine beans and enough water to cover them. Bring to boiling, then reduce heat. Simmer for 2 minutes. Remove from heat. Cover and let stand 1 hour. Or omit boiling and soak beans overnight.

In pressure cooker cook sausage, half at a time, until brown. Remove sausages and set aside. Drain off fat. Drain and rinse the beans. Add beans, onion, garlic, chilli powder, oregano, cumin, crushed red chilli pepper (if desired), undrained tomatoes, beer or water, water and tomato paste.

Lock the lid in place. Over high heat bring to high pressure. Adjust heat to maintain high pressure and for pressure regulator to rock gently; cook for 18 minutes. Let the pressure drop using the quick-release method. Remove the lid, tilting it away from you to allow any excess steam to escape.

If mixture is too thin, cook, uncovered, over low heat until chilli is the desired consistency. Stir in coriander (cilantro), if desired. Sprinkle servings with cheese, if desired.

Potato and Ham Scallop Supreme

- **20 mL (1 Tbsp) cooking oil**
- **500 g (1 lb) cooked ham cut in 2.5 cm (1 in) cubes**
- **4 cups potatoes, sliced**
- **1 onion, chopped**
- **420 g (14 oz) can condensed cream of celery soup**
- **310 mL (1¼ cups) milk**
- **2 tsp salt**
- **⅛ tsp pepper**
- **12–18 hot asparagus spears, if desired**

Pressure Cooker

4–6 L (4–6 quart)

Serves 4–6

Heat pressure cooker. Add oil and brown ham. Remove from heat. Stir in potatoes and onion. Combine soup, milk, salt and pepper, and pour over potatoes.

Lock the lid in place. Over high heat bring to high pressure. Adjust heat just to maintain high pressure and cook for 3 minutes. Let the pressure drop using the quick-release method. Remove the lid, tilting it away from you to allow any excess steam to escape. Close lid securely. Place regulator on vent pipe.

If desired garnish with hot asparagus spears.

Potatoes Paprikash

- 20 mL (1 Tbsp) safflower oil or canola oil
- 1 cup shallots (green onions, scallions) or onions or leeks (use white and light green parts of leeks), finely chopped
- 125 mL (½ cup) water or vegetable stock (broth)
- 1 Tbsp sweet paprika
- 1 cup Roma tomatoes (use fresh or canned; drained), pureed
- 1 kg (2 lb) thin-skinned potatoes, scrubbed, halved and cut in 6 mm (¼ in) slices
- 1 tsp salt or to taste
- freshly ground pepper to taste
- 60–80 mL (3–4 Tbsp) plain low-fat yoghurt, or up to 80 mL (4 Tbsp) of sour cream

Pressure Cooker
4–6 L (4–6 quart)

Serves 4–6

Heat the oil in pressure cooker. Cook the shallots (green onions, scallions) over medium-high heat, stirring frequently, for 1 minute. Add the water or stock (broth) (stand back to avoid sputtering oil) and scrape up any bits that might be sticking to the bottom of the pot. Stir in the paprika and pureed tomatoes and bring to the boil. Add the potatoes, salt and pepper.

Lock the lid in place. Set the cooker on a heated flame tamer. Over high heat bring to high pressure. Adjust heat to maintain high pressure and cook for 3 minutes. Let the pressure drop using the quick-release method. Remove the lid, tilting it away from you to allow any excess steam to escape.

If the potatoes are not quite tender, replace (but do not lock) the lid and let them steam for a few minutes in the residual heat. Stir in the yoghurt or sour cream and adjust the seasonings before serving.

Tips and Techniques
These potatoes seem at home on an eastern European menu, accompanied by kasha and steamed Brussels sprouts.

To create an instant sauce, finely mince one of the raw potatoes. These small bits will virtually dissolve under pressure and thicken the water when you stir the cooked dish.

The yoghurt may be soy or dairy.

Potato Pie

- **butter**
- **750 g (1½ lb) potatoes, peeled and thinly sliced**
- **2 medium onions, chopped**
- **nutmeg, freshly grated**
- **salt and pepper**
- **170 mL (⅔ cup) vegetable stock (broth)**
- **310 mL (1¼ cups) water**
- **½ cup grated cheese**

Pressure Cooker
6–8 L (6–8 quart)

Serves 4

Butter an ovenproof dish that will fit into the pressure cooker. Layer the potatoes and onions in the dish. Sprinkle each layer with a little grated nutmeg and season well with salt and pepper. Pour the vegetable stock (broth) over the potatoes.

Pour water into cooker and place the rack into position. Stand the dish on the rack. Lock the lid in place. Over high heat bring to high pressure. Adjust heat to maintain high pressure and cook for 13 minutes. Let the pressure drop using the quick-release method. Remove the lid, tilting it away from you to allow any excess steam to escape.

Sprinkle the cheese over the potatoes and brown them under the griller (broiler) before serving.

Tips and Techniques
New potatoes might need slightly longer cooking times than those given here.

This dish is delicious also made with garlic (omitting the nutmeg) and using canned tomatoes instead of vegetable stock (broth).

Roasted Potatoes with Herbs

- **40 mL (2 Tbsp) olive oil**
- **1 medium onion, diced**
- **8 medium red potatoes, cleaned and quartered**

- **60 mL (¼ cup) water**
- **1 tsp Italian herbs**

Pressure Cooker

4–6 L (4–6 quart)

Serves 4

In pressure cooker heat oil over medium heat. Add onion and cook until softened. Add potatoes and brown, turning to brown all sides evenly. Stir well. Add water and Italian herbs and bring to the boil.

Lock the lid in place. Over high heat bring to high pressure. Adjust heat just to maintain high pressure and cook for 5 minutes. Let the pressure drop naturally. Remove the lid, tilting it away from you to allow any excess steam to escape.

Remove potatoes to a serving dish and ladle the onion herb sauce over them.

Tips and Techniques
This recipe gives the potatoes the golden browned look of oven-roasted potatoes and infuses the herb flavouring into the onion sauce.

Punjabi Buttery Black Lentils

- 1½ cups whole urad dal (black lentils)
- 1.25 L (5 cups) water
- 2 tsp cumin seeds
- 2 tsp coriander seeds
- 1 medium brown onion, quartered and finely sliced
- 1 large ripe tomato (about 250 g (8 oz)), cored and coarsely chopped
- 1 generous Tbsp tomato paste
- 2 fresh green chillies (serrano or jalapeño), minced (seeded if desired)
- 4 large cloves garlic, smashed and coarsely chopped
- 1 Tbsp ginger root, peeled and grated
- 1 tsp cayenne pepper
- ½ cinnamon stick
- 4 Tbsp butter
- 1 tsp salt plus more to taste
- 60 mL (¼ cup) heavy cream or unthickened cream
- juice of half a lemon
- 2 Tbsp chopped fresh coriander (cilantro) leaves

Pressure Cooker

6–8 L (6–8 quart)

Serves 8

Spread the lentils on a large tray and carefully pick over, discarding any tiny stones or bits of grit. Place in a colander and swish under running water with your fingers and rinse several times. Place lentils in pressure cooker and add water.

Toast the cumin and coriander seeds together in a small pan and grind with a mortar and pestle or in a coffee grinder. Add to lentils. Stir in the onion, tomato, tomato paste, chillies, garlic, ginger root, cayenne pepper, cinnamon stick and butter.

Lock the lid in place. Over high heat bring to medium pressure. Adjust heat to maintain medium pressure and cook for 30 minutes. Let the pressure drop naturally. Remove the lid, tilting it away from you to allow any excess steam to escape.

Add salt and cream. Stir well and add lemon juice. Garnish with coriander (cilantro).

Tips and Techniques

Makhani means anything made with cream or butter. This recipe uses both. Traditionally it is baked in the tandoor oven overnight to make use of the dying embers, but you get a similar result in the pressure cooker in 30 minutes.

You can find urad dal (black lentils) at any Asian or Indian market and often in the Asian section of larger supermarkets. They produce a reddish-orange, creamy base and an appealing pebbly texture. If you use smaller or split lentils, you'll end up with a very nice soup.

This dish is very spicy and rich. Don't hesitate to substitute sweet paprika for the cayenne pepper or reduce the amount of hot green chillies if you're heat sensitive.

Southwest Vegetable Casserole

- 20 mL (1 Tbsp) safflower oil or canola oil
- ¾ tsp cumin seeds
- 2 tsp garlic, finely minced
- 1 cup onion, coarsely chopped
- 1 medium red capsicum (pepper), diced
- 1–2 jalapeño peppers, seeded and diced, or 1 dried chipotle (smoked jalapeño) pepper, seeded and snipped into bits, or generous pinch crushed red chilli pepper flakes
- 250 mL (1 cup) water
- 2 Tbsp tomato paste
- 750 g (1½ lb) butternut or Japanese pumpkin (squash), peeled and cut in 2.5 cm (1 in) pieces
- 2 cups fresh or frozen corn kernels
- salt to taste
- 2 cups frozen baby lima beans, thawed
- ¼ cup fresh coriander (cilantro), minced

Pressure Cooker

4–6 L (4–6 quart)

Serves 6

Heat the oil in pressure cooker. Add cumin seeds and sizzle for 5 seconds. Add garlic and cook over medium-high heat, stirring frequently, until garlic turns light brown. Add onions, capsicum (pepper) and jalapeño peppers. Continue cooking, stirring frequently, for 1 minute. Add water, tomato paste, pumpkin (squash), corn and salt.

Lock the lid in place. Over high heat bring to high pressure. Adjust heat just to maintain high pressure and cook for 2 minutes. Let the pressure drop using the quick-release method. Remove the lid, tilting it away from you to allow any excess steam to escape.

If pumpkin (squash) is not quite tender, replace but do not lock lid; allow to steam a few more minutes in residual heat. Stir in lima beans and simmer, covered, until tender, about 2 to 3 minutes. Stir in coriander (cilantro) just before serving.

Spanish-style Pinto Beans

- 1½ cups dried pinto beans
- 1 large onion, chopped
- 2 stalks celery, sliced
- 750 mL (3 cups) water
- 40 mL (2 Tbsp) olive oil or vegetable oil
- 1 large green capsicum (pepper), chopped
- 2 tsp chilli powder
- ¼ tsp dry mustard
- ¼–½ tsp crushed red chilli pepper
- ¼ tsp salt
- 450 g (4.5 oz) can tomatoes, undrained and cut up
- 300 g (8 oz) can Napoletana sauce
- sour cream, optional
- ripe olives, sliced, optional
- cheddar cheese, shredded, optional

Pressure Cooker
4–6 L (4–6 quart)

Serves 6

Rinse beans. In a large saucepan combine beans and enough water to cover them. Bring to boiling, then reduce heat. Simmer for 2 minutes. Remove from heat. Cover and let stand for 1 hour. Or, omit boiling and soak beans overnight.

Drain and rinse the beans. In pressure cooker combine the beans, onion, celery, water and oil.

Lock lid in place. Over high heat bring to high pressure. Adjust heat to maintain high pressure and for pressure regulator to rock gently; cook for 8 minutes. Let the pressure drop using the quick-release method. Remove the lid, tilting it away from you to allow any excess steam to escape.

Drain beans. Return the beans to cooker. Stir in the capsicum (pepper), chilli powder, dry mustard, crushed red chilli pepper, salt, undrained tomatoes and Napoletana sauce. Bring to boil. Simmer, uncovered, for about 10 minutes. If desired, serve with sour cream, sliced ripe olives and cheese.

Stuffed Head of Cabbage

Cabbage

- 1 kg (2¼ lb) head green cabbage
- 60 mL (¼ cup) olive oil or butter
- 2 large onions, diced
- 2 cloves garlic, crushed
- ⅓ cup fresh parsley, minced
- 1 medium carrot, diced
- 2 stalks celery, chopped
- 500 g (1 lb) minced (ground) beef, lamb or turkey
- 1 cup long grain white rice
- ⅔ cup canned chopped tomatoes, undrained
- 1 tsp salt
- ½ tsp pepper
- 2 Tbsp dried dill
- 1 tsp dried thyme
- 1 tsp sugar
- 500 mL (2 cups) beef or chicken stock (broth)

Napoletana Sauce

- 60 mL (¼ cup) olive oil
- 1 medium onion, sliced
- 2 cloves garlic, crushed
- ½ green capsicum (pepper), diced
- 500 mL (2 cups) beef or chicken stock (broth)
- 1 cup canned chopped tomatoes, undrained
- 1 Tbsp brown sugar
- 1 tsp salt
- ½ tsp pepper
- 2 tsp dried oregano

Pressure Cooker

6–8 L (6–8 quart)

Serves 6–8

252

Cabbage

With a grapefruit or paring knife, hollow out your head of cabbage by taking out the centre core and removing the leaves as they are loosened until the wall of the cabbage forms a 5 cm (2 in) shell.

In pressure cooker heat the oil and then add onions, garlic, parsley, carrot and celery. Sauté for about 3 minutes. Add beef, lamb or turkey to the mixture and stir well. Add rice, tomatoes, salt, pepper, dill, thyme, sugar and stock (broth). Stir.

Lock the lid in place. Over high heat bring to high pressure. Adjust heat just to maintain high pressure and cook for 6 minutes. Let the pressure drop using the quick-release method. Remove the lid, tilting it away from you to allow any excess steam to escape.

Thoroughly stir the mixture and place it into your hollowed head of cabbage, mounding it at the top. Wrap a 60 cm (24 in) length of cheesecloth around the cabbage, overlapping it at the top. Set aside. Rinse out your container and wipe dry.

Napoletana Sauce

Heat oil for your Napoletana sauce and then add onion, garlic and capsicum (pepper). Sauté for 2 minutes. Add stock (broth), tomatoes, brown sugar, salt, pepper and oregano, stirring to blend together. Place a steamer basket over the sauce in your cooker. Place the cheesecloth covered cabbage in the steamer.

Lock the lid in place. Over high heat bring to high pressure. Adjust heat just to maintain high pressure and cook for 10 minutes. Let the pressure drop using the quick-release method. Remove the lid, tilting it away from you to allow any excess steam to escape.

Final Assembly

Transfer the cabbage to a platter. Carefully remove the cheesecloth. Ladle the Napoletana sauce over the top of the cabbage and around the platter. When serving, cut in 6 to 8 wedges.

Warm White Bean Vinaigrette

- 2 cups dried navy beans (pea beans or haricot beans) or great northern beans or cannellini beans
- 40 mL (2 Tbsp) olive oil
- 1 cup leeks (white and green parts), thinly sliced, or onions, coarsely chopped
- 2 tsp garlic, finely minced

- 2 tsp dried basil leaves
- 750 mL (3 cups) boiling water
- 1½ cups red cabbage, finely chopped
- 2–3 Tbsp drained capers
- 20–40 mL (1–2 Tbsp) balsamic vinegar or freshly squeezed lemon juice
- salt to taste

Pressure Cooker

4–6 L (4–6 quart)

Serves 5–6

Pick over and rinse beans, and soak overnight in ample water to cover. Drain and rinse the beans. Set aside.

Heat 20 mL (1 Tbsp) of the oil in pressure cooker. Cook the leeks and garlic over medium-high heat, stirring frequently, for 1 minute. Add the basil, water (stand back to avoid sputtering oil) and reserved beans.

Lock the lid in place. Over high heat bring to high pressure. Adjust heat to maintain high pressure and cook for 3 minutes (navy and great northern) or 5 minutes (cannellini). Let the pressure drop naturally for 10 minutes. Quick release any remaining pressure. Remove the lid, tilting it away from you to allow any excess steam to escape.

If the beans are not tender, replace (but do not lock) the lid and simmer until they are done. If time permits, allow the beans to sit in the cooker at room temperature with the lid slightly ajar for about 2 hours, during which time they will absorb most of the excess liquid.

If serving immediately, lift the beans with a slotted spoon or drain off most of the cooking liquid (save it for stock or for cooking grains) and transfer to a serving bowl. Stir in the chopped red cabbage and capers. Season the beans with the additional tablespoon of olive oil, balsamic vinegar to taste and salt.

Tips and Techniques

This is an elegant warm bean salad, nice for a luncheon meal any time of year. For an especially dramatic presentation, set individual servings in large radicchio or red cabbage cups. Garnish with cornichons, cherry tomatoes and nicoise olives. Steamed green beans and a hearty peasant loaf make good accompaniments. Leftovers are delicious at room temperature, refreshed with a drizzle of lemon juice.

Variations include chopped watercress leaves instead of chopped red cabbage, or you could add ¼ cup finely chopped red onion with the red cabbage and capers.

Olive Oil Braised Green Beans

- 1 kg (2 lb) French beans, trimmed and bisected lengthwise
- 1 medium white onion, chopped
- 3 cloves garlic, slivered
- 5–6 small Roma tomatoes, peeled and chopped
- 2 Tbsp tomato paste
- 1 heaped tsp Turkish hot pepper paste
- 375 mL (1½ cups) water, divided
- 1 tsp salt
- 1 tsp white (granulated) sugar
- 125 mL (½ cup) olive oil

Pressure Cooker
6–8 L (6–8 quart)

Serves 10

Place the beans, onion, garlic and tomatoes in pressure cooker. Dilute the tomato and pepper pastes in 125 mL (¼ cup) water and pour over the beans. Add the remaining water, salt, sugar and oil.

Lock the lid in place. Over high heat bring to medium pressure. Adjust heat to maintain medium pressure and cook for 18 minutes. Let the pressure drop using the quick-release method. Remove the lid, tilting it away from you to allow any excess steam to escape.

Serve chilled.

Tips and Techniques
Olive oil braising is a popular technique in Turkey, where people like their vegetables well cooked and full of flavour. These beans are typically served cold as part of a meze assortment. Turkish hot pepper paste is available at most Middle Eastern markets, though you can substitute a spoonful of hot paprika.

Desserts,
Cakes
and
Breads

Apple Granola Jumble

- **750 g (1½ lb) granny smith apples, peeled and coarsely chopped**
- **⅓ cup raisins**
- **¼ cup chopped walnuts (omit if granola contains nuts)**
- **60 mL (3 Tbsp) freshly squeezed lemon juice**
- **1½ tsp ground cinnamon (omit if granola contains cinnamon)**

- **1½ cups granola (maple walnut preferred)**
- **125 mL (½ cup) apple juice**
- **2 cups boiling water**
- **maple syrup, optional**
- **ice cream or sorbet**

Pressure Cooker
6–8 L (6–8 quart)

Serves 4

In a 1.25 L (1½ quart) heatproof casserole dish, toss the apples with the raisins, walnuts (if using), lemon juice and cinnamon (if using). Stir in the granola and apple juice. Place the rack and boiling water in pressure cooker. Lower the uncovered casserole dish onto the rack with the aid of a foil strip handle.

Lock the lid in place. Over high heat bring to high pressure. Adjust heat to maintain high pressure and cook for 12 minutes. Let the pressure drop naturally for 10 minutes. Quick release any remaining pressure. Remove the lid, tilting it away from you to allow any excess steam to escape.

If the apples are not sufficiently soft, return to high pressure for a few more minutes or replace (but do not lock) the lid and let them continue to steam in the residual heat. Remove casserole dish from the cooker with the aid of the foil strip. Stir well before serving. (The mixture is likely to be crumbly.) Add maple syrup to taste, if desired, and top each portion with a scoop of ice cream or sorbet.

Apple Topping

- **8 medium granny smith apples, peeled, cored and sliced**
- **250 g (8 oz) dried apricots, chopped**
- **250 mL (1 cup) orange juice**
- **½ cup sugar**
- **60 mL (¼ cup) lemon juice**
- **2 cinnamon sticks**
- **125 mL (½ cup) rum, optional**

Pressure Cooker

6 L (6 quart)

Serves 6–8

In pressure cooker add all ingredients. Allow liquid to begin simmering.

Lock the lid in place. Over high heat bring to high pressure. Adjust heat to maintain high pressure and cook for 1 minute. Let the pressure drop naturally. Remove the lid, tilting it away from you to allow any excess steam to escape.

Remove cinnamon sticks and serve over ice cream or as a filling for crepes.

Apple Wholemeal Bread Pudding

- **4 cups stale wholemeal (whole wheat) bread, cubed**
- **⅓ cup sultanas (golden raisins)**
- **310 mL (1¼ cups) milk**
- **½ cup apple butter**
- **2 eggs, beaten**
- **2 Tbsp sugar**

- **5 mL (1 tsp) vanilla**
- **½ tsp salt**
- **½ tsp ground cinnamon**
- **¼ tsp ground nutmeg**
- **500 mL (2 cups) water**
- **vanilla ice cream or frozen yoghurt**

Pressure Cooker
4–6 L (4–6 quart)

Serves 8

Combine bread and raisins. Mix remaining ingredients except water and ice cream. Pour over bread mixture. Toss and let stand for 20 minutes.

Spoon into greased 1 L (1 quart) soufflé dish or bowl. Cover dish securely with greased aluminium foil. Place cooking rack and 2 cups of water in pressure cooker. Place soufflé dish on rack.

Lock the lid in place. Over high heat bring to high pressure. Adjust heat to maintain high pressure and cook for 25 minutes. Let the pressure drop using the quick-release method. Remove the lid, tilting it away from you to allow any excess steam to escape.

Serve warm with ice cream.

Apricot Chocolate Bread Pudding

- 10 slices day-old French bread
- ½ cup raspberry preserve
- ½ cup dried apricots, chopped
- ½ cup bittersweet chocolate, chopped
- ½ cup finely chopped hazelnuts
- 3 eggs

- 1 L (4 cups) milk
- 1 vanilla bean
- ¼ cup sugar
- 1 pinch salt
- 1 Tbsp grated lemon rind
- 250 mL (1 cup) water

Pressure Cooker

6–8 L (6–8 quart)

Serves 4

Spread bread with raspberry preserve, tear into chunks and layer in a soufflé dish with dried apricots, chocolate and hazelnuts. Beat eggs with milk. Split vanilla bean lengthwise and scrape seeds into egg mixture. Mix sugar, salt and lemon rind. Add to milk mixture. Pour evenly over bread in the soufflé dish and cover dish with foil.

Cut a piece of foil 60 cm × 30 cm (2 ft × 1 ft) and double it twice lengthwise to create a strip for moving the dish to and from pressure cooker. In pressure cooker add water and insert rack. Lower soufflé dish in place with foil strip.

Lock the lid in place. Over high heat bring to high pressure. Adjust heat to maintain high pressure and cook for 15 minutes. Let the pressure drop naturally. Remove the lid, tilting it away from you to allow any excess steam to escape.

Serve warm or chilled.

Autumn Bread Dressing with Cranberries

- **5 cups bread cubes, lightly toasted**
- **⅓ cup dried chopped cranberries**
- **4 Tbsp unsalted butter**
- **1 cup onion, chopped**
- **1 cup celery with some leaves, chopped**
- **1 cup fresh Italian (flat-leaf) parsley, chopped**
- **250 mL (1 cup) chicken stock (broth)**
- **1 extra-large egg, well beaten**
- **1 tsp poultry seasoning**
- **1 tsp freshly ground black pepper**
- **1 tsp sea salt (Kosher salt)**

Pressure Cooker
5–7 L (5–7 quart)

Serves 4–6

In a large bowl combine the bread cubes and cranberries. In a 30 cm (12 in) frying pan melt the butter and sauté the onion and celery. Add the parsley towards the end. When almost cooked, splash with about 60 mL (¼ cup) of the stock (broth) and lower the heat so the celery loses some of its crunch.

Add the vegetables and the remaining stock (broth) to the bread and cranberry mixture. Blend in the beaten egg, poultry seasoning, pepper and salt. Butter the inside bottom and sides of a 1 L (1 quart) soufflé bowl. Fill with the bread mixture.

Cut a piece of foil to tent the top of the dish. Cover the surface loosely and hold in place with an elastic band if you wish. Place the dish on a foil strip and transfer to the rack of the pressure cooker. Add 250 mL (1 cup) water.

Lock the lid in place. Over high heat bring to high pressure. Adjust heat to maintain high pressure and cook for 15 minutes. Let the pressure drop naturally. Remove the lid, tilting it away from you to allow any excess steam to escape.

Remove the dish with the sling to a rack to cool a bit. Remove the foil top. It is optional to butter the top lightly and place under the griller (broiler) for a minute to crisp.

Tips and Techniques
This recipe yields a 1 L (1 quart) load for the 5–7 L (5–7 quart) pressure cooker. If using the 8–12 L (8–12 quart) size, you can use a larger soufflé dish 2–3 L (2–3 quart) size. (Double the amount of ingredients for the larger bowl.)

Banana Pudding Cake

- **butter and flour for preparing 1 L (6 cup/1 quart) bundt pan**
- **¾ cup wholemeal (whole wheat) pastry flour**
- **¾ cup unbleached white flour**
- **1 Tbsp bicarbonate of soda (baking soda)**
- **1 Tbsp baking powder**
- **⅛ Tbsp salt**
- **½ cup raisins**
- **2 large ripe bananas, cut in 1.25 cm (½ in) slices**
- **125 mL (½ cup) apple juice**
- **125 mL (½ cup) maple syrup**
- **40 mL (2 Tbsp) vanilla extract**
- **750 mL (3 cups) water**

Pressure Cooker

6–8 L (6–8 quart)

Serves 6

Butter and flour a 1 L (6 cup/1 quart) bundt pan. Mix dry ingredients in a bowl, add bananas, ensuring that they are coated with flour on both sides. Combine liquids, add to flour, mixing evenly.

Pour into bundt pan and cover tightly with foil. Using rack in pressure cooker, bring 3 cups of water to the boil. Lower bundt pan into cooker.

Lock the lid in place. Over high heat bring to high pressure. Adjust heat to maintain high pressure and cook for 35 minutes. Let the pressure drop using the quick-release method. Remove the lid, tilting it away from you to allow any excess steam to escape.

Remove bundt pan and place on wire rack to cool. Unmould and serve.

Caramelised Bagel Butter Pudding

- butter for greasing large soufflé dish
- 125 g (4 oz) unsalted butter
- 4 cinnamon and raisin bagels, cut in 8 mm (⅓ in) slices
- 6 egg yolks
- 60 g (2 oz) caster (superfine) sugar
- 1 vanilla pod
- 250 mL (½ pint) double cream
- 250 mL (½ pint) milk
- 60 g (2 oz) soft brown sugar (light or dark)

Pressure Cooker

6–8 L (6–8 quart)

Serves 6

Grease the largest soufflé dish that is able to sit in your pressure cooker with butter. Spread rest of butter over bagel slices.

Whisk together egg yolks and caster (superfine) sugar in a bowl until pale and creamy. Open the vanilla pod, scrape out the seeds and put both into a saucepan with the double cream and milk. Bring to the boil and then remove the pan from the heat. Pour two-thirds of this into the egg yolk sugar mixture and whisk well. Add the leftover third from the pan. Stir until it makes a sort of custard that coats the back of a wooden spoon slightly.

Arrange some of the bagel slices to cover the bottom of the soufflé dish. Pour 'custard' mixture over the bagels and let it soak in. Repeat with layers of bagels then custard, finishing with a bagel layer on top. Sprinkle half of the brown sugar on top.

Cover soufflé dish with cling wrap. Pierce with holes on the top. Leave to stand for 30 minutes.

Place rack in cooker with 250 mL (½ pint) of boiling water. Place soufflé dish into cooker, bring to high pressure and cook for 20 minutes. Let the pressure drop using the quick-release method. Lift soufflé out and remove cling wrap.

Sprinkle remaining leftover brown sugar and place under a hot griller (broiler) or use a blow torch to caramelise the sugar. Serve immediately, with ice cream or custard, or plain.

Caramelised Rice Pudding with Raspberries

- 1 vanilla pod, split
- 500 mL (1 pint) milk
- 75 g (2.5 oz) caster (superfine) sugar
- 60 g (2 oz) rice pudding
- 112 mL (4 fl oz) double cream
- icing (powdered) sugar for dusting

- 4 Tbsp raspberry jam (jelly)
- 60 g (2 oz) fresh raspberries to garnish
- chocolate leaves for decoration
- whipped cream for serving

Pressure Cooker

4–6 L (4–6 quart)

Serves 4

Place the vanilla pod, milk and caster (superfine) sugar in pressure cooker and bring to the boil. Stir the rice and return to the boil.

Put the lid on and bring to high pressure. Adjust heat to maintain high pressure and cook for 20 minutes. Let the pressure drop using the quick release method. Remove lid and give the rice a good stir to prevent anything sticking to the bottom of the pan. Cook gently for about another 2 minutes, until the rice has become thick and sticky. Remove from the heat and leave to cool.

Whip the cream in a bowl until it forms soft peaks, and fold into the cooked rice. Use a 6 cm (2.5 in) deep scone (biscuit) cutter and pour rice into this on a non-stick baking tray (sheet) (lightly greased). Repeat three times (makes four individual serves). Dust heavily with icing (powdered) sugar. Caramelise the sugar on top with a blow torch, or put on baking tray (sheet) under a very hot griller (broiler), until the sugar is bubbling and goes golden brown. Set aside to cool slightly.

To serve, using a fish slice, transfer all four rice puddings into the centre of a shallow bowl or onto individual plates. Serve with a good helping of raspberry jam (jelly), and garnish with fresh raspberries and chocolate leaves. For extra indulgence, add whipped cream.

Chocolate Kahlua Bread Pudding

- butter to grease a 1.25 L (5 cup) soufflé dish
- 2–3 Tbsp butter
- 12 × 1.25 cm (½ in) thick bread slices (use wholegrain, white, Italian or French bread, left out to dry for 12 to 24 hours)
- 320 mL (1⅓ cups) milk
- 125 mL (½ cup) Kahlua
- 4 large eggs, lightly beaten
- 2 × 85 g (3 oz) bars quality dark chocolate, coarsely chopped

Pressure Cooker
6–8 L (6–8 quart)

Serves 6

Generously butter a 1.25 L (5 cup) soufflé dish or suitable alternative. Set aside.

Cut a piece of aluminium foil 60 cm × 30 cm (2 ft × 1 ft) and double it twice lengthwise to create a strip for moving the pudding dish to and from pressure cooker. Set aside.

Butter the bread and cut each slice into 2 to 3 pieces. Arrange one-third of the bread on the bottom of the soufflé dish. In a food processor or with a whisk, combine the milk, Kahlua and eggs, and pour one-third of this mixture over the bread, turning the bread pieces over so that they thoroughly absorb the liquid. Distribute one-third of the chocolate on top of the bread-milk mixture. Repeat layering the bread, liquid and chocolate in this manner twice more, or until the dish is seven-eighths full. (Be sure to finish with a chocolate layer.)

Cover with aluminium foil so that the foil fits tightly around the sides and tucks under the bottom but allows some room on top for the pudding to expand. Set the pudding aside for 10 minutes to allow the bread to further soak up liquid.

Set a rack on the bottom of the cooker. Centre the soufflé dish on the aluminium foil strip and carefully lower it into the cooker. Fold the ends of the strip over the top of the pudding. Pour in enough water to reach one-third up the sides of the pudding dish.

Lock the lid in place. Over high heat bring to high pressure. Adjust heat to maintain high pressure and cook for 15 minutes. Let the pressure drop naturally. Remove the lid, tilting it away from you to allow any excess steam to escape.

Let the pudding cool slightly before lifting it from the cooker with the aid of the foil strip. If you are not serving the pudding immediately, cut open the foil top and let the pudding remain warm in the cooker, placing the lid ajar, for up to an hour. While the pudding is still warm, gently spread the top layer of chocolate with a knife to create icing (frosting). To serve, scoop out the pudding with a large spoon.

Christmas Pudding

- butter to grease pudding bowl
- 500 g (1 lb) raisins
- 500 g (1 lb) currants
- 500 g (1 lb) sultanas (golden raisins)
- 500 g (1 lb) breadcrumbs
- 500 g (1 lb) brown sugar
- 250 g (8 oz) suet
- 125 g (4 oz) mixed peel
- 125 g (4 oz) glace cherries, chopped
- 125 g (4 oz) almonds, chopped
- zest of 1 lemon
- zest of 1 orange
- 1 carrot, grated
- 1 apple, grated
- 1 Tbsp plain (all-purpose) flour
- 1 tsp mixed spice
- pinch salt
- 6–8 eggs, lightly beaten
- 300 mL (10 fl oz) stout or dark beer (Guinness is good) or 150 mL (5 fl oz) each brandy and milk
- hot custard, cream or brandy sauce for serving

Pressure Cooker

6–8 L (6–8 quart)

Serves 10–12

Mix dry ingredients first then mix with lightly beaten eggs and liquid. Grease the bottom of a bowl large enough to hold pudding and press mixture into it. Place wax paper over the top and then foil over that, crimping it around the edges to keep firm.

Lock the lid in place. Over high heat bring to medium pressure. Adjust heat to maintain medium pressure and cook for 120 minutes. Let the pressure drop naturally. Remove the lid, tilting it away from you to allow any excess steam to escape.

Store well wrapped for as long as possible for better flavour. Some people make Christmas puddings one year before eating. Serve with hot custard, cream or brandy sauce.

Creamy Honey Rice Pudding

- **1 cup long grain rice**
- **2 mL (½ tsp) olive oil**
- **560 mL (2¼ cups) water**
- **⅓ cup honey**
- **½ cup sugar**
- **190 mL (¾ cup) evaporated milk (low fat can be used)**

- **60 mL (¼ cup) low-fat or skim milk**
- **3 egg yolks**
- **⅓ cup raisins, optional**
- **5 mL (1 tsp) vanilla extract**
- **ground cinnamon to taste**

Pressure Cooker

4 L (4 quart)

Serves 4

In pressure cooker combine rice, olive oil and water.

Lock the lid in place. Over high heat bring to high pressure. Adjust heat to maintain high pressure and cook for 8 minutes. Let the pressure drop using the quick-release method. Remove the lid, tilting it away from you to allow any excess steam to escape.

Add honey and sugar to rice mixture. Stir in evaporated milk, milk and egg yolks. Cook over medium heat for 3 minutes or until mixture thickens. Stir constantly. Add raisins and vanilla extract. Spoon into dishes and sprinkle with cinnamon. Serve hot or cold.

Chocolate Cheesecake

- butter for greasing 18 cm (7 in) spring form pan
- ¼ cup chocolate biscuit (cookie) crumbs
- 500 g (16 oz) cream cheese
- ½ cup sugar
- 2 Tbsp plain (all-purpose) flour
- 4 large eggs
- ¼ cup sour cream or plain yoghurt
- 2 × 85 g (3 oz) bars quality dark chocolate, melted and cooled to room temperature
- 625 mL (2½ cups) water
- strawberries for garnish

Pressure Cooker

6–8 L (6–8 quart)

Serves 6–8

Cut a piece of aluminium foil 60 cm × 30 cm (2 ft × 1 ft) and double it twice lengthwise to create a strip for moving the pan to and from pressure cooker. Set aside.

Cover the exterior bottom and sides of an 18 cm (7 in) spring form pan with a large sheet of aluminium foil so that no water can seep in. Liberally butter the pan and distribute the biscuit (cookie) crumbs, tilting and shaking the pan to coat the bottom and sides. Set aside.

In a food processor, blend the cream cheese, sugar and flour until smooth, for about 15 seconds. Add the eggs, sour cream or yoghurt and melted chocolate, and process for 5 seconds. Scrape down the bowl and process for another 5 seconds. Pour into the prepared pan.

Cover with buttered aluminium foil so that the foil fits tightly around the sides, but allows some room on top for the cheesecake to expand. Set a rack on the bottom of the cooker. Pour in 625 mL (2½ cups) of water. Centre the pan on the foil strip and gently lower it into the cooker. Loosely fold the ends of the foil strip over the top of the dish.

Lock the lid in place. Over high heat bring to high pressure. Adjust heat to maintain high pressure and cook for 20 minutes. Let the pressure drop naturally for 10 minutes. Ensure all steam is released. Remove the lid, tilting it away from you to allow any excess steam to escape.

Let the cheesecake cool for a few minutes before removing it from the cooker with the aid of the foil strip. Set on a cooling rack, remove the foil and let it cook to room temperature. Refrigerate overnight. Before serving, release and remove the sides of the spring form pan. Serve from the base of the spring form pan, garnished as desired.

Tips and Techniques
This version improves in taste and texture after overnight chilling.

Use an 18 cm (7 in) spring form pan, or a 20 cm (8 in) pan that fits comfortably into your pressure cooker with about 2.5 cm (1 in) to spare between the pan and the sides of the cooker. Ensure the ingredients are at room temperature before you begin.

The cheesecake can be stored in the refrigerator for up to 3 days and in the freezer for 3 months. It does beautifully either way. Add toppings just before serving.

When you remove the aluminium foil cover after steaming, there may be a small puddle of water on the top of the cheesecake. Just sop it up gently with a paper towel. If the cake is not quite set in the centre, it will firm upon cooling.

For serving, top with plump, ripe strawberries for an elegant presentation and an irresistible flavour contrast.

Eggnog Cheesecake

- 3 × 250 g (8 oz) packets cream cheese, at room temperature
- ¾ cup sugar
- 80 mL (⅓ cup) eggnog
- 3 large eggs
- 30 mL (1½ Tbsp) brandy

- 3 Tbsp plain (all-purpose) flour
- 500 mL (2 cups) water
- 125 mL (½ cup) sour cream
- 1 Tbsp sugar
- 5 mL (¼ tsp) brandy
- ¼ tsp ground nutmeg

Pressure Cooker

6–8 L (6–8 quart)

Serves 6–8

Put the cream cheese in a large bowl. Beat with an electric mixer on high until softened, 30 to 45 seconds. Mix in the sugar. Beat in the eggnog, then the eggs, one at a time. Reduce the speed to low and beat in the brandy and flour.

Scrape the mixture into a greased 18 cm (7 in) spring form pan and wrap the pan tightly in foil. Place a rack in pressure cooker, along with the water. Position the spring form pan on the rack. Cover and lock the lid in place. Over high heat bring to high pressure. Adjust heat to maintain high pressure and cook for 40 minutes. Let the pressure drop naturally. Remove the lid, tilting it away from you to allow any excess steam to escape. Gently remove the pan from the cooker and unwrap the cheesecake. Cool to room temperature.

Meanwhile make the topping. Combine the sour cream, sugar, brandy and nutmeg in a small bowl. Mix until blended. Spread the topping over the cheesecake and chill for at least 2 hours in the refrigerator before serving.

Fudge

- **420 g (14 oz) can sweetened condensed milk**
- **180 g (6 oz) chocolate chips**

- **500 mL (2 cups) water**
- **1 cup chopped walnuts**
- **20 mL (1 Tbsp) vanilla, optional**

Pressure Cooker

4–6 L (4–6 quart)

Serves 6–8

Combine condensed milk and chocolate chips in a bowl that will fit loosely in pressure cooker. Cover bowl with aluminium foil. Place water, cooking rack and bowl in cooker.

Lock the lid in place. Over high heat bring to high pressure. Adjust heat to maintain high pressure and cook for 5 minutes. Let the pressure drop using the quick-release method. Remove the lid, tilting it away from you to allow any excess steam to escape.

Remove bowl. Stir mixture until evenly blended. Do not beat. Add walnuts and vanilla. Blend until smooth. Drop teaspoonfuls onto waxed paper. Allow to cool.

Gingered Apple Pudding

- butter to grease a 1.25 L (5 cup) soufflé dish
- 2 Tbsp butter or margarine, room temperature
- 1 cup coarse wholemeal (whole wheat) breadcrumbs, slightly, but not bone dry
- 500 g (1 lb) apples, peeled, cored and grated
- 250 mL (1 cup) milk
- 3 large eggs
- 2 Tbsp molasses (black treacle)
- ⅓ cup brown sugar, firmly packed
- 60 mL (¼ cup) sour cream
- ½ tsp ground ginger
- 1 tsp ground cinnamon
- 1 pinch salt
- ½ cup walnuts, coarsely chopped, optional
- whipped cream, for garnish
- 2–3 Tbsp crystallised ginger, chopped, for garnish, optional

Pressure Cooker
6–8 L (6–8 quart)

Serves 6–8

Generously butter a 1.25 L (5 cup) soufflé dish or suitable alternative. Set aside.

Cut a piece of aluminium foil 60 cm × 30 cm (2 ft × 1 ft) and double it twice lengthwise to create a strip for moving the pudding dish to and from pressure cooker. Set aside.

In a food processor, combine the softened butter and breadcrumbs. Transfer to the soufflé dish and stir in the grated apples. Set aside.

In the food processor, blend together the milk, eggs, molasses, brown sugar, sour cream, ground ginger, cinnamon and salt. Pour the liquid and walnuts (if using) over the breadcrumbs and apples, and gently stir to blend.

Cover the soufflé dish with aluminium foil so that the foil fits tightly around the sides, leaving some room on top for the pudding to expand. Set a rack in the bottom of the cooker. Centre the pudding on the foil strip and lower it into the cooker. Pour in enough water to reach one-third up the sides of the pudding dish.

Lock the lid in place. Over high heat bring to high pressure. Adjust heat to maintain high pressure and cook for 15 minutes. Let the pressure drop naturally. Remove the lid, tilting it away from you to allow any excess steam to escape.

Let the pudding cool for a few minutes before removing it from the cooker with the aid of the foil strip. If not serving the pudding immediately, cut a few slits in the foil top and let it remain warm in the cooker, placing the lid on, but not locking, for up to 1 hour.

To serve, scoop out the pudding with a large spoon. Dress with a generous blob of the whipped cream and garnish with chopped ginger.

Lemon Cheesecake

- **butter to grease a spring form pan**
- **½ cup chocolate wafer or shredded wheatmeal biscuit (graham cracker) crumbs**
- **500 g (16 oz) cream cheese at room temperature**
- **½ cup sugar**
- **2 large eggs**
- **20 mL (1 Tbsp) fresh lemon juice**
- **1–2 tsp lemon zest**
- **2 mL (½ tsp) vanilla extract**
- **500 mL (2 cups) water**
- **4 cups fresh fruit, chopped for serving**

Pressure Cooker
6–8 L (6–8 quart)

Serves 8

Grease bottom and sides of an 18 cm (7 in) spring form pan with butter. Coat the sides of pan with wafer or biscuit crumbs and distribute the remaining crumbs on the bottom of pan.

Using an electric mixer or food processor, blend the cream cheese and sugar until smooth. Add the eggs, lemon juice and zest, and vanilla. Pour the batter into the prepared pan.

Pour water into pressure cooker. Set a rack on the bottom of the cooker to raise the cheesecake above the water. Centre the uncovered pan on a foil strip made from twice doubling a 45 cm (1½ ft) long piece of standard-width aluminium foil. Lower it onto the rack. Fold down the ends of the strip so they don't interfere with closing the cooker.

Lock the lid in place. Over high heat bring to high pressure. Adjust heat to maintain high pressure and cook for 15 minutes. Turn off the heat. Let the pressure drop naturally. Remove the lid, tilting it away from you to allow steam to escape.

Let the steam subside before lifting the pan from the cooker with the aid of the foil strip. Set on a wire rack to cool. If there is a small pool of condensed water in the middle of the cake, blot it up with a paper towel. Serve warm, or cool to room temperature, cover and refrigerate for at least 4 hours or overnight. Release and remove the rim of the spring form pan. Serve plain or with fresh fruit on top.

Orange Cheesecake with Orange Sauce

- **340 g (11 oz) can mandarin sections, well drained, juice reserved**
- **250 g (8 oz) cream cheese**
- **½ cup sugar**
- **2 eggs**
- **½ cup toasted wholemeal (whole wheat) breadcrumbs**

- **500 mL (2 cups) water**
- **¼ cup sugar**
- **2 tsp cornflour (cornstarch)**
- **125 mL (½ cup) reserved mandarin juice**
- **2 mL (½ tsp) orange extract**

Pressure Cooker

6 L (6 quart)

Serves 8

Line soufflé dish or 15 cm (6 in) spring form pan with aluminium foil. Decoratively arrange mandarin sections in bottom of dish.

Beat cream cheese until smooth. Beat in ¹/₂ cup sugar. Beat in eggs, one at a time. Pour mixture over mandarin sections. Sprinkle with breadcrumbs. Cover dish securely with aluminium foil.

Place cooking rack and water in pressure cooker. Place dish on rack. Lock the lid in place. Over high heat bring to high pressure. Adjust heat to maintain high pressure and cook for 20 minutes. Let the pressure drop using the quick-release method. Remove the lid, tilting it away from you to allow any excess steam to escape.

Remove cheesecake and cool in soufflé dish on wire rack. Loosen edges and unmould. Refrigerate until chilled.

Meanwhile mix sugar and cornflour (cornstarch) in small saucepan. Stir in 125 mL (¹/₂ cup) of reserved mandarin juice. Cook and stir until sauce boils and thickens. Stir in orange extract. Let cool and spoon sauce over cheesecake.

Pineapple Upside Down Cheesecake

Pineapple Cheesecake

- butter to grease a spring form pan
- 600 g (20 oz) can pineapple chunks in unsweetened pineapple juice
- 1 Tbsp butter
- 1 Tbsp sugar
- 3 extra large eggs at room temperature
- 2 Tbsp cornflour (cornstarch)
- ¾ cup sugar
- 5 mL (1 tsp) pure lemon extract
- 500 g (1 lb) cream cheese, softened
- 125 mL (½ cup) sour cream
- ¾ cup well-drained crushed pineapple, juice reserved

Pineapple Curd

- 375 mL (1½ cups) reserved pineapple juice
- 1 Tbsp sugar
- 1 Tbsp cornflour (cornstarch) mixed with 20 mL (1 Tbsp) water
- 2 Tbsp crystallised ginger, chopped

Pressure Cooker

6–8 L (6–8 quart)

Serves 6

Pineapple Cheesecake

Cut a piece of aluminium foil 60 cm × 30 cm (2 ft × 1 ft) and double it twice lengthwise to create a strip for moving the pudding dish to and from pressure cooker. Set aside.

Butter the sides and bottom of an 18 cm (7 in) spring form pan. Cut a piece of parchment paper to fit inside the bottom of the pan. Cover the exterior bottom and sides of the pan with a large sheet of aluminium foil so that no water can seep in. Set aside.

Drain the pineapple chunks well. Reserve the juice for making the curd. Place on paper towels and blot all the excess liquid off the chunks.

In a heavy frying pan (cast-iron is best), melt the butter. Add the pineapple single file over the surface. Sauté, turning to brown evenly. Add the sugar towards the end to obtain a nice charred brown look. When coloured well, remove from the frying pan and cool.

When cooled carefully place each piece of pineapple on the parchment lined bottom of the pan. Start on the outside rim and work around in circles. Leave the centre circle clear.

In a food processor, blend the eggs, cornflour (cornstarch), sugar and lemon extract. Add the softened cream cheese and sour cream and process until smooth. Open the bowl, scrape down the sides. Add the crushed pineapple and blend with on and off strokes until well mixed. Pour the mixture carefully over the arranged pineapple chunks. Cover with buttered foil so that the foil fits tightly around the sides but allows some room on top for the cheesecake to expand.

Set a rack on the bottom of pressure cooker. Pour in 625 mL (2¹/₂ cups) of water. Centre the pan on the foil strip and gently lower it into the cooker. Loosely fold the ends of the foil strip over the top of the pan.

Lock the lid in place. Over high heat bring to high pressure. Adjust heat to maintain pressure and cook for 25 minutes. Let the pressure drop naturally. Remove the lid, tilting it away from you to allow any excess steam to escape. Remove the foil lid, blot up any excess water from the top of the cheesecake with a paper towel. Cool completely and then chill.

Pineapple Curd
In a small heavy pot, place all of the reserved pineapple juice you have. Add the sugar and boil the volume down to about 250 mL (1 cup). Mix the cornflour (cornstarch) and water together and add to the hot syrup. Stir well to incorporate. Cook until the sauce thickens and is shiny and clear. Add the crystallised ginger, chopped very fine. Cool the mixture at room temperature. The pineapple curd will be used to finish off the cheesecake after you follow the next steps.

Final Assembly
Remove the cooled cheesecake from the pan by running a sharp knife along the sides. Release the spring. Place a serving plate on the surface of the cake. Reverse the cake. With the tip of a small sharp knife, remove the bottom of the pan from the surface. Peel off the parchment paper. Use the pineapple curd to lightly glaze the pineapple pieces without masking them. Place the remaining curd in the centre of the cake.

Scottish Clootie Dumpling

- 225 g (8 oz) plain (all-purpose) flour plus 60 g (2 oz) for sprinkling
- 1 tsp bicarbonate of soda (baking soda)
- 1 tsp mixed spice powder
- 1 tsp ground cinnamon
- 1 tsp ground ginger
- 175 g (6 oz) caster (superfine) sugar plus 1 Tbsp for sprinkling
- 100 g (4 oz) sultanas (gold raisins)
- 1¼ tsp sea salt (fine)
- 85 g (3 oz) stoned date, chopped
- 100 g (4 oz) vegetable suet, shredded
- 50 g (2 oz) raisins
- 1 medium apple or carrot, grated
- 1 Tbsp molasses (black treacle)
- 150 mL (¼ pint) buttermilk
- 1 large egg
- 250 mL (8 fl oz) whipped double cream flavoured with 40 mL (2 Tbsp) of whisky to serve, or use a freshly made custard sauce

Pressure Cooker

6–8 L (6–8 quart)

Serves 6

Scottish Clootie Dumpling

Sift all dry ingredients together, with sea salt. Stir in the vegetable suet, dried fruits and the apple or carrot. Add the molasses (black treacle), egg and buttermilk, then mix together. When finished the mixture should have a cake-like dropping consistency.

Using an old pillowcase, large piece of muslin or tea towel, put into boiling water, squeezing out excess water using gloves, as it will be very hot. Lay wet cloth on a clean surface and sprinkle a 30 cm (12 in) circle in the centre with the extra flour and caster (superfine) sugar. Spoon the dumpling mixture on top of the floured surface, then bring corners up on top and tie with string, not too tight, as the dumpling will expand.

Use the rack in the pressure cooker and put water to just below the rack as the dumpling will have to cook for 90 minutes on high pressure. Lock the lid in place. Over high heat bring to high pressure. Adjust heat to maintain pressure and cook for 90 minutes. Let the pressure drop naturally. Remove the lid, tilting it away from you to allow any excess steam to escape.

Meanwhile preheat oven to 180°C (350°F). Remove dumpling from the cooker and undo cloth. Place in the oven and cook for 15 minutes, until the outside of the dumpling has dried off. Serve in chunky wedges, with the flavoured whisky cream or a freshly made custard sauce.

Tips and Techniques
The dumpling should have a shiny coating and a moist flavoursome interior. Any leftovers can be microwaved, or as the Scots like, fried with bacon, egg and sausage, with tomatoes and mushrooms, for a great cooked breakfast!

Spiced Apple Crunch

- **butter to grease a baking dish**
- **1 cup dry breadcrumbs**
- **¼ cup sugar**
- **½ tsp ground cinnamon**
- **1 lemon (juice and rind)**

- **3 apples, sliced**
- **¼ cup butter, melted**
- **500 mL (2 cups) water**
- **whipped cream for serving**

Pressure Cooker

4 L (4 quart)

Serves 4

Butter a 16 cm (6 in) baking dish.

Combine breadcrumbs, sugar, cinnamon and juice and rind of lemon. Place alternate layers of apples and breadcrumb mixture in baking dish. Pour melted butter over ingredients and cover bowl firmly with aluminium foil.

Place water, cooking rack and bowl in pressure cooker. Lock the lid in place. Over high heat bring to high pressure. Adjust heat to maintain pressure and cook for 15 minutes. Let the pressure drop using the quick-release method. Remove the lid and the rack with baking dish. Loosen the foil and cool. If you wish to add more colour and crunch, run the dish quickly under the griller (broiler). (Watch carefully to prevent burning).

Serve this warm with whipped cream or a la mode.

Tips and Techniques
Instead of apples you might prefer to try peaches for this dish.

Steamed Chocolate Pudding Cake

- ⅔ cup sugar
- 3 Tbsp butter, softened
- 1 whole egg, beaten
- 125 mL (½ cup) buttermilk
- 2 mL (½ tsp) vanilla
- ¾ cup plain (all-purpose) flour
- ¼ cup unsweetened cocoa
- 2 tsp baking powder
- ½ tsp bicarbonate of soda (baking soda)
- ¼ tsp salt
- 1 L (4 cups) water
- icing (powdered) sugar

Pressure Cooker

4–6 L (4–6 quart)

Serves 6

In a large bowl mix sugar and butter. Stir in egg, buttermilk and vanilla. Mix flour, cocoa, baking powder, bicarbonate of soda and salt. Stir into egg mixture. Pour into a greased 1 L (1 quart) bowl or soufflé dish. Cover bowl securely with greased aluminium foil.

Place cooking rack and water in pressure cooker. Place bowl on rack. Lock the lid in place. DO NOT place pressure regulator on vent pipe. Heat until steam gently flows through vent pipe. Cook for 60 minutes. Remove cake and let cool in bowl on wire rack for 5 minutes. Transfer from bowl and let cool on a wire rack. Sprinkle with icing (powdered) sugar.

Wholemeal Cinnamon Raisin Bread Pudding

- **butter to grease a soufflé dish**
- **4 beaten eggs**
- **2 cups milk**
- **¼ cup sugar**
- **¼ cup brown sugar**

- **1 tsp vanilla**
- **½ tsp ground cinnamon**
- **3 cups wholemeal (whole wheat) bread cubes**
- **⅓ cup raisins**

Pressure Cooker
4–6 L (4–6 quart)

Serves 6

Grease a 1.25 L (1½ quart) soufflé dish. Tear off two 50 cm × 5 cm (20 in × 2 in) pieces of heavy aluminium foil. Crisscross the strips and place dish in the centre.

In a mixing bowl beat together the eggs, milk, white sugar, brown sugar, vanilla and cinnamon using a wire whisk or rotary beater. Add bread cubes and raisins. Let stand for 5 minutes.

Place rack in pressure cooker and add water to just below rack. Pour bread mixture into prepared soufflé dish and cover with foil. Bringing up the foil strips, lift the ends of the strips and transfer dish into the cooker. Fold ends of foil strips over the top of the dish.

Lock the lid in place. Over high heat bring to high pressure. Adjust heat to maintain high pressure and cook for 20 minutes. Let the pressure drop naturally. Remove the lid, tilting it away from you to allow any excess steam to escape.

Using foil strips, carefully lift the bread pudding out of the cooker. Remove foil. Place on a wire rack and cool for 15 minutes. Serve warm or cover and chill.

Index

A

Almond Cod with Peas................. 193
Amarillo Chicken Soup Served Over Mexican Rice.......................... 58
Anchor Bar Chicken Wings 160
Antipasto.. 221
Apple Granola Jumble.................. 258
Apple Topping 259
Apple Wholemeal Bread Pudding.. 260
Apricot Chocolate Bread Pudding.. 261
Arroz con Pollo 156
Artichokes with Lemon Pepper Oil.. 222
Autumn Bread Dressing with Cranberries...................................... 262
Azuki Bean and Pumpkin Stew 220

B

Banana Pudding Cake.................. 263
Barbecue Beef Short Ribs 85
'Barbecued' Pork with Sweet Potatoes... 134
'Barbecued' Spareribs................... 132
Barley Risotto Primavera 200
Basmati Salad with Corn and Roasted Red Capsicums 201
Bean and Barley Soup with Mushrooms 32
Beauy Chicken 158
Beef and Bean Chilli with Roasted Red Capsicum 86
Beef in Beer with Dijon Gravy.......... 91
Beef Roast with Amber Ale 83
Beef Roast with Vegetables 113
Beef Stock.. 71

Beef Stroganoff 93
Beef with Tomatoes and Chipotle Peppers............................. 92
Black Beans and Sausage (Jeijoada) 135
Black-eyed Pea and Sausage Soup.. 37
Blanquette de Veau........................ 96
Blue Cheese Dipping Sauce......... 160
Boeuf Bourgegnone....................... 90
Bolognese Sauce.............................. 81
Borscht... 39
Boston Baked Beans...................... 223
Boston Clambake........................... 195
Bowtie, Beef Tips and Mushrooms....94
Braised Turkey Breast 159
Brown Rice and Lentil Stew 202
Brown Rice and Vegetables 203
Brunswick Beef 130
Butternut Pumpkin Bisque............... 40

C

Cabbage Sweet and Sour Soup with Caraway.................................... 41
Cajun Black Bean and Sausage Gumbo.. 42
Calabacita: Spanish Steak............. 98
Caramelised Bagel Butter Pudding.. 264
Caramelised Rice Pudding with Raspberries 265
Caribbean Black Beans and Orzo Picadillo 224
Caribbean Rice and Beans 226
Caribbean Stew 225
Caribbean-style Rice and Beans ...204
Carolina Barbecue Pork 138
Carrot Tsimmes................................ 229

285

Chana Dal Pilaf............................... 205
Cheesy Mashed Potatoes 233
Chicago Steak Rollups................... 100
Chicken and Dumpling
Casserole.. 161
Chicken and Rice with Gravy....... 163
Chicken and Vegetable Chilli 164
Chicken Biryani 206
Chicken Cacciatore 165
Chicken Curry 166
Chicken Noodle Soup 50
Chicken Soup with Rice................... 51
Chicken with Cracked Pepper..... 168
Chicken with Lentils and Spinach ... 169
Chicken, Vegetable and
Saffron Soup 68
Chickpeas with Sweet Onions 230
Chinese Beef, Rice and Baby
Meatballs 101
Chocolate Cheesecake 270
Chocolate Kahlua Bread
Pudding... 266
Chop Suey 139
Christmas Pudding.......................... 268
Chucky's Carrot Soup..................... 46
Coq au Vin 170
Corned Beef with Vegetables 103
Costa Azzura Osso Buco................. 99
Country-style Steak and Kidney
Pudding... 95
Creamy Honey Rice Pudding....... 269
Creamy Mashed Potatoes............ 232
Creamy Potato Soup with Onions
and Cheddar...................................... 67
Creamy Rice with Vegetables...... 210
Creole Okra...................................... 234
Crispy Pork with Avocado and
Tomato Salsa 136
Cuban Black Bean Soup 52
Curried Rice with Chicken,
Peas and Currants........................... 208
Curry Spice Mix 166
Cypriot Chicken............................... 171

D

Dill Pickle Beef Roast...................... 111

E

East Indian Chicken........................ 172
Eggnog Cheesecake 272
Eggplant and Mushroom Pasta
Sauce 80
Eggplant Caponata 228

F

Far East Pepper Steak 104
Fennel and Scallop Bisque.............. 53
Five Bean Soup 54
French Country Beef 105
Fresh Greens with Beetroot,
Haricots Verts and Mustard 236
Fresh Peas and Carrots with
Lettuce 237
Fruity Rock Chicken....................... 182
Fudge 273

G

Garam Masala Spice Mix.............. 166
Garden Medley with Ham 238
Garlic Cheese Croutons 45
Garlic Mashed Potatoes 233
German Potato Salad 239
Gingered Apple Pudding............. 274
Gramma's Beefy Vegetable
Soup 35
Greek Beef... 107
Green Bean and Ham Soup 57
Green Beans with Tomatoes
and Basil.. 240

H

Ham and Pineapple Slice 140
Hungarian Beef Goulash Soup 33
Hungarian Goulash 108

I

Irish Lamb Stew 190
Irish Potato Soup 66
Italian Chicken Pockets 173

J

Jambalaya with a Difference 154
Jambalaya 162
Japanese Dashi Turnips 241
JB's Chicken and Mushroom
Casserole 174

K

Kylie Jayne's Texas Barbecue Beef
Roast 125

L

Lamb Biryani 207
Lamb Hot Pot 191
Leek, Potato and Butternut
Pumpkin Soup 31
Lemon Cheesecake 276
Lemon Herbed Chicken 175
Les Halles Five Onion Soup 44

M

Macaroni with Steak 211
Mediterranean Stuffed
Capsicums 242
Mexican-style Pork 141
Milwaukee-style Spareribs 119
Minestrone 62
Mixed Bean and Sausage Chilli 243
Mongolian Pork Roast 142
Munchen Beef and Cabbage
Rolls 87
Mustard Mashed Potatoes 233

N

Napoletana Sauce 252
New England Fish Chowder 64

New Mexico Tomato Brisket 118
Noodle Goulash 213

O

Olive Oil Braised Green Beans 256
One Dish Pasta with Meat Sauce ... 212
Orange Cheesecake with
Orange Sauce 277

P

Pasta e Fagioli 214
Pineapple Upside Down
Cheesecake 278
Pinto Bean and Pepper Soup 65
Porcupine Meatballs 117
Pork in Beer and Onions 143
Pork Ragù 144
Pork Roast 146
Pork Vindaloo with Spinach
and Potatoes 152
Potato and Ham Scallop
Supreme 244
Potato Leek Soup 73
Potato Pie 246
Potatoes Paprikash 245
Poulet Cocotte Grandmaman 176
Poultry Stock 72
Punjabi Buttery Black Lentils 248

Q

Quick 'n' Easy Chicken Soup 47

R

Raspberry Chicken 180
Risotto Alfredo with Chicken
and Peas 215
Risotto with Gruyere and
Parmesan 216
Risotto with Mushrooms
Piédmontese 217
Risotto with Tomatoes and
Mozzarella 218

Roast Chicken 178
Roasted Potatoes with Herbs 247
Rosemary and Orange Beef 110

S

Sauerbraten 114
Savoury Meatball Soup 61
Scandinavian Beef Roast 124
Scottish Clootie Dumpling 280
Shanghai Black Bean Soup 36
Short Ribs in Coconut Milk 115
Shredded Beef Tacos 116
Simply Pork Chops 147
Smoked Sausage Supper 148
Sour Cream and Chives
Mashed Potatoes 233
Southern Chicken and
Sausage Gumbo 48
Southwest Vegetable Casserole 250
Soy Chicken 181
Spanish-style Pinto Beans 251
Spareribs and Sauerkraut 149
Spiced Apple Crunch 282
Split Pea with Ham Soup 70
St Patrick's Day Corned Beef
Dinner 121
Steak and Onions 120
Steamed Chocolate Pudding
Cake 283
Stuffed Chicken Breasts 186
Stuffed Head of Cabbage 252
Stuffed Pork Chops 150
Stuffed Snapper 197
Sunday Beef and Dumplings 88
Sweet 'n' Sour Chicken 184
Sweet and Sour Pork
Spareribs 151
Sweet and Sour Prawns 196
Sydney Cove Beef Dinner 102

T

Tangy Gingered Pumpkin and
Apple Soup 56
Thai Chicken Soup 74
Tomato and Roasted Capsicum
Soup 60
Traditional Beef Stew 122
Traditional French Beef 106
Traditional Scotch Broth 69
Turkey and Vegetable Hot Pot 187
Turkey Vegetable Soup 75
Tuscan Beef Roast 109

V

Veal and Mushroom Cream 126
Veal Paprika 127
Veal with Dumplings 128
Vegetable and Pasta Soup 76
Vegetable Biryani 207
Vegetarian Broccoli Corn
Chowder 38
Vichyssoise 77

W

Warm Chicken Salad 188
Warm White Bean Vinaigrette 254
Watusi Peanut Soup 30
Whiting in Creole Sauce 198
Wholemeal Cinnamon Raisin
Bread Pudding 284
Winton Beef Soup 34

Y

'Ye Olde' Beef Roast 112

Z

Zucchini Bisque with Tomatoes and
Fresh Basil 78